Divesting Business Units

Divesting Business Units

Making the Decision and
Making It Work

Marilyn L. Taylor
University of Kansas

Lexington Books
D.C. Heath and Company/Lexington, Massachusetts/Toronto

Library of Congress Cataloging-in-Publication Data

Taylor, Marilyn L.
    Divesting business units.

    Bibliography: p.
    Includes index.
    1. Corporate divestiture. I. Title.
HD2746.6.T38   1988   658.1'6   86-45765
ISBN 0-669-14294-8 (alk. paper)

Published simultaneously in Canada
Printed in the United States of America
International Standard Book Number: 0-669-14294-8
Library of Congress Catalog Card Number: 86-45765

The paper used in this publication meets the minimum requirements of American National Standard for Information Sciences—Permanence of Paper for Printed Library Materials, ANSI Z39.48-1984. ∞™

88 89 90 91 92 8 7 6 5 4 3 2 1

Contents

Figures

Tables

Foreword

The decade of the 1980s has witnessed an intense period of change in the ownership of corporate America. Conglomerates that were built in the 1960s became more focused by selling peripheral operating units. More and more large acquisitions by "corporate raiders" were followed by divestiture of the various pieces to the highest bidders. Leveraged Buy-out (LBO) groups, fueled by pools of venture capital for equity and "junk" bonds for debt, acquired some of America's largest firms; then by divesting some of the pieces (called "slicing and dicing"), the acquirers could repay significant portions of debt while retaining the "jewels" that constituted the most desirable (for them) parts of the acquired company. The process could be described as one of acquiring at "wholesale" and selling components at "retail" to the highest bidder.

The process as a whole has added significant financial value to those with the knowledge and the courage to play the game, whether acquiring or divesting. Fortunes have been made especially during this period by those who, with entrepreneurial spirit, have been active on both sides, effectively creating value by developing a portfolio of productive assets by selective acquisitions and divestitures.

Virtually every business is composed of discrete elements, and invariably a few of the elements (roughly 20%) account for the majority of the value (about 80%) of the total business. A product line is composed of several or many individual products. A division is typically composed of several product lines. Most manufacturing businesses have more than one channel of distribution. Distributors typically divide their markets into geographic territories. Retailers have several to hundreds or even thousands of store locations. One of the fastest and most effective ways to increase profits, cash flow, and value is to phase out, withdraw from, or divest of the segments or elements that are the weakest, and to then focus the resources on the areas of greatest strength. While most seasoned managers are aware of this strategic principle as applied to products, product lines, channels of distribution, geographic territories, and retailing locations, many are not familiar with the process when it comes to the phasing out or divestiture of entire operating units.

Marilyn Taylor has written this book to take some of the mystery out of the operating unit divestiture process. It is an amazingly practical book for one written by a person who is principally academic; the author writes in the lingo that most business practitioners use. The book is not a theoretical treatise; it is oriented for use by corporate executives and business unit managers. For example, chapter 3 describes specific ways to inform the management of the divestiture unit that the unit is going to be sold; chapter 4 suggests ways to retain the loyalty and maintain productivity during the divestiture process. Chapter 5 shows specific ways (by example) to establish and approximate value using approaches that are both quantitative and qualitative and using the perspectives of both the buyer and the seller. Five methods are described for finding the most qualified buyers. Chapter 6 may provide inspiration and confidence to any operating unit management team thinking of acquiring their unit from the parent corporation. Chapter summaries tell readers what they should have gotten out of the chapter. Finally, negotiating is almost completely nonacademic and totally pragmatic. This is where money, potentially very big money, is won or lost on a transaction. Marilyn Taylor describes in chapter 7 solutions to resolve stalemates, ways to avoid pitfalls, and tips that can be used in negotiations in a variety of settings.

Divesting takes courage because it is a delicate process involving complex issues of employees, customers, competitors, suppliers, intermediaries, and usually a lot of money. For companies that have not done it before, divestiture can be intimidating because there are so many ways to do it and so many judgments to make that could significantly affect the outcome. When should you tell the management? How do you keep their loyalty during the process? When and how much detail do you disclose to an interested competitor who may be willing to pay the most for the business unit? When should you use an intermediary? Should you openly advertise that you want to sell the unit or discreetly approach a few potential buyers who you think might be interested? Should you offer it to the management; if so, when and how?

Marilyn Taylor's book deals with these and the multitude of other serious questions involving divestitures in an immanently readable style. And for those who have the time and interest, there are lots of supporting and referring notes at the end of each chapter.

Anyone managing a business that has more than one operating unit should be knowledgeable about divestitures. This book provides the kind of background on the process that should help make easier the decision to divest, and it will help ensure a successful execution of the decision.

—*J.B. Fuqua*
Chairman, Fuqua Industries Inc.

Preface and Acknowledgments

R esearch streams are begun for one of two reasons: the author's personal needs or interests or company concerns. The research on which this book is based started with both.

The beginnings of the research were opportunistic. Mike Herman, senior vice-president and chief financial officer of Marion Laboratories, and I were both members of another board. Because of our acquaintance and discussions Mike visited the University of Kansas School of Business, where I teach. That visit led to further discussions, and they led to a case, Marion Laboratories, which has become a classic—a tribute primarily to Mike's understanding of what was needed in a classroom case and the skills of graduate student Ken Beck. Because of the Marion Labs case, I developed an interest in how companies manage divestiture of business units, and that led to a series of cases that focused on the Marion subsidiaries—Kalo and American Stairglide, as well as a partially completed case on a third subsidiary, Optico.

The Marion case series led to a set of preliminary questions about divestiture: What circumstances lead to divestiture? How do companies handle the people in the unit to be divested? How is the strategy of the unit revamped? How is the selling process conducted? What are the critical issues in transferring the unit to the new owner? The next four years led to a series of interviews with thirty companies (acknowledged in appendix A) and several case studies, including Fuqua Industries, Inc., Martin Theatres, Carmike Cinemas, and Toastmaster. In addition, a number of students, singly or in teams, wrote cases for classroom presentation.

In 1984 United Telecommunications and the Field Studies Program at the University of Kansas cosponsored an executive roundtable, attended by a dozen executives who met over a day and a half to talk about the issues confronting their companies as they undertook divestiture of business units. The candor of the individuals who participated and their continuing contributions to our understanding of divestiture have been invaluable.

Over the 1985–1986 academic year, the University of Kansas and another source of income sponsored my sabbatical year, part of which I spent in interviewing executives from various companies. With the research essentially complete, I began this book.

The investigation underlying this project is primarily of a clinical nature. It continues the work of earlier researchers. The list of those who have contributed to our understanding of divestiture is short. The earliest investigations were carried out by Stuart Gilmour and Wes Marple, both of whom documented the shock of the organizations that early undertook divestiture activity. Later work took place in the 1970s. The reasons for divestiture have been investigated in the work of Irene Duhaime. The role of the divisional executive was a focus for Danielle Nees. Others have contributed by writing for the practitioner audience, although their conclusions are not as systematically grounded in data as the work of Duhaime, Nees, Gilmour, and Marple. In the mid-1970s, Bob Hayes foresaw that divestiture would become one more legitimate and usual activity in the set of strategic activities undertaken by companies. I applaud his foresight.

I have attempted in this book to chronicle what I have learned through the generosity of the more than thirty firms that participated in this project. Also largely unrecognized are the efforts of many of my students who wrote cases on companies that had undertaken divestitures. In all, they shared the experiences of more than sixty firms. In a few instances, students conducted executive interviews, which augmented our understanding.

This project was not solely my brainchild. Especially in the early stages, the investigation was shaped through discussion after discussion with my Field Studies Program colleagues. In particular I note here V.K. Narayanan. Another close colleague, John Garland, kept current with the project and continually combed his sources for references to divestiture activity, especially in the United Kingdom and Europe. At all phases, the continuing encouragement of Dean John Tollefson was invaluable. C.R. Christensen and Doug Anderson of Harvard University, as well as Gordon Fitch and Dave Shulenburger at the University of Kansas, have played key roles in the support system that led to this book. Doctoral student Danny Kinker was involved in a spectrum of the research and lent considerable insight at early phases. I delight to acknowledge the support of these close colleagues, whose continuing affection and encouragement cannot be fully valued.

Finally, as always, families bear the brunt. My husband, Bob, and our young son, Chris, forewent many hours of my time. My now-grown daughter, Theresa, worked as my secretary–research assistant at various times. Like all other families during a long research program, they have alternately contributed as well as detracted with the needed diversions—a mite's hockey game, church, long-distance telephone calls to Theresa in college. In all these I am blessed, give thanks, and express my deepest love and gratitude.

Introduction

A mong the most difficult decisions that senior executives undertake is divestiture. An early project with Marion Laboratories, Inc. with the help of Michael Herman, now senior vice-president and chief financial officer, underscored the problems. The work with Marion gave impetus to this project, which has focused on how companies manage the process of divesting business units. The research underlying the book has been ongoing since 1982. During that time, I have crisscrossed the United States visiting major cities, mostly east of the Rockies, to talk with executives in almost fifty companies. With few exceptions, the names of the companies and executives used in this book are disguised. The executives in the companies were primarily the vice-president of business development or strategic planning, the chief executive officer, and, in some instances, also the head of the divested divisions. Talking with the executives has never been boring. Most have been willing to share their experiences in divesting business units.

Divestiture is a process; it has distinct stages. Companies were aware of the required sequencing and also aware that the process is often poorly managed. I undertook this project with the idea that divestiture, an often difficult task, could be improved if I delved into various firms to ask how they did it and how they could do it better. This book concentrates more on the how; it is primarily descriptive. But it also contains useful recommendations that arose from the experiences of these firms. The book follows generally the sequence of events expected in a divestiture. At the conclusion of each chapter are two sections of recommendations: one addressed to corporate executives and the other to division management.

The process of divestiture can be divided into several stages. In this book, I have used the following stages: decision, managing personnel, marketing the unit, and negotiations. Marketing has a subset I refer to as management buyouts, which is of sufficient interest to warrant a chapter to itself. In addition, I have focused briefly on ethical concerns in the last chapter, although these issues are implicit in each stage.

The Decision

The circumstances that prompted the firms in this study to divest one or more business units were widely varied. They included financial-economic reasons as well as political-social reasons. In addition, the circumstances can be categorized as corporate level and unit level. Seldom, if ever, did a firm divest for only one reason. Let me give you a few examples. Medical Industry Supply, Inc. (MISI) divested one of its divisions because the unit was not performing at the level of other units (financial-economic reasons at the unit level). The buyer approached the company and was well-liked and respected by MISI. Thus, there were also political-social reasons at the corporate level.

In a similar vein, the chairman of Financial Services Company had continual run-ins with the head of one of his divisions. At management meetings, the chairman would give instructions to the head of the division, whom he then expected would carry out the directives. But he never did. The unit was not doing well, and the chairman finally sold the unit and informed the division manager only after the fact. This situation was clearly a financial-economic set of circumstances at the unit level, but it also illustrates political-social difficulties between the unit and corporate.

Industrial Products (IPI) undertook a diversification program that involved a high debt requirement. In order to pare down the debt, IPI decided to sell off the consumer products divisions, which had not been performing up to the expected level. Clearly the situation included both a corporate-level as well as a unit-level financial-economic set of circumstances.

Probably the most celebrated divestiture I studied was the paired divestitures of Vickers and Swift by Esmark. It is clear that to solve the problems in the Swift divisions (financial-economic problems at the unit level), chairman Don Kelly chose to sell the winner, Vickers, and take the extraordinary gain to cover the losses that would be incurred with Swift. In essence Vickers was sold for corporate financial-economic purposes.

In short, there are no clean reasons for divestiture. In fact, usually several circumstances came together to give impetus to a divestiture decision. (To understand the full flavor of various circumstances that sparked divestiture, refer to figure 2–2.) Further, contrary to a strongly held notion, corporate did not have to have a new chief executive to allow a divestiture to happen. Indeed in many of these firms, the set of senior corporate executives remained relatively stable before and after the divestiture. In addition, it is clear that executives can also even let go of the unit that first gave impetus to their career. There is no clearer example than Don Kelly's cleaning up Esmark by selling Vickers (a performer) and Swift (a difficult unit). Kelly had spent nearly his entire career at Esmark, the adopted name for Swift after considerable diversification.

It is clear that firms often divest too late. In this study, the unit had usually slid in performance before the company reluctantly let it go. There were exceptions, however (for example, with the Vickers divestment). And sometimes—perhaps more frequently than recognized—a buyer approached the company. It is clear that firms should consider divestiture a possibility for every unit. Earlier divestiture consideration can often increase the value of the unit to all parties.

Consideration of divestiture should be part of the normal planning process. Through divestiture contingency planning, a firm can be more creative and thorough in the selling process. For example, if it is known that divestiture contingency planning is a regular part of the strategic planning process, the list of potential buyers is likely to be longer when the decision is actually made. Further, contingency plans can be made outlining what would need to be done if a firm decided to divest: should the unit be encouraged to grow, remain as is, or be trimmed in preparation for divestiture? Finally, divestiture would not be as much of a shock to the division personnel if such contingency planning were explicit.

Talk about divestiture can make division unit management nervous but not if it is a regular part of the planning process. One firm I talked to insisted that it has a planning culture in which it encourages division management to propose divestiture of their own unit. This firm rewards unit management variously—some on the basis of growth and others on the basis of cash generation. Divestiture is a form of cash generation, and thus a division manager could be rewarded for proposing and helping to execute divestiture of his or her own unit.

Managing Division Personnel

Once corporate has decided to divest, much needs to be done. A priority issue is to do all possible to maintain the integrity of the unit to be divested. Clearly companies are concerned about the possible effect of a divestiture announcement on the productivity and morale of a unit. Some have found ways to handle the divestiture process with regard to personnel not just in a humane manner but in a manner that promotes the productivity and morale in the unit in spite of the uncertain circumstances. How do they do it?

One of the big decisions is whether to tell those affected. In this study, firms ranged all the way from not telling any unit personnel until after the deal was completed to firms that announced the impending divestiture to all division employees before they had talked to any buyers. The continuum of possibilities is wide. The biggest fear on the part of corporate if unit management is informed early about the impending divestiture is that unit personnel will leave. The experiences of the firms in this study, however, suggest that this fear may be grossly exaggerated. What is the best way? Should unit personnel always be informed shortly after the decision? It all depends. Let me explain.

One factor that has to be considered is the amount of time that is expected to elapse before a buyer is found. If corporate expects a long time before a buyer is found, it should tell the unit, or at least the unit management, because the longer the rumor mill has to do its work, the more negative will be the potential impact.

It is difficult to determine how long a sale will take. But if corporate has decided not to tell unit management and the first few potential buyers do not work out, corporate should reverse its decision and make the situation known to division mangement. Otherwise corporate runs the risk of having the unit management learn about the divestiture from a potential buyer, with all the attendant feelings of betrayal.

Another reason to tell unit mangement is that corporate will find them to be potentially valuable allies. For example, corporate executives may have scant knowledge of the unit's industry; unit management may be able to identify potential buyers to whom that unit is worth more. Further, unit management should be best able to ascertain when and how to tell the rest of unit personnel about impending divestiture.

If the unit is not sold promptly, corporate will no doubt have to revamp the goals and perhaps operations of the unit, and it probably will not be able to do so without raising some suspicion on the part of unit personnel. In addition, division management no doubt can think of ways to manage that unit more adeptly given impending divestiture than corporate can.

Corporate management may decide to make it worthwhile to unit management to be cooperative. For example, bonuses can be modified to reflect changed goals, strategy, and operational needs. In addition, special bonuses can be designed. In this study, most firms preferred to keep the special bonuses dependent on qualitative judgment—that is, whether in the judgment of corporate division mangement was cooperative and helpful in the divestiture. One firm used what I call a commission bonus: the more that corporate got for the unit, the more division management got. In this instance, it was a sliding bonus. If corporate received 50 percent more for the unit than it had originally planned, division management was given 30 percent of the extra 50 percent. If corporate received only what it had originally planned, division management might get only 5 percent of the price over a certain base. Some firms essentially paid a commission but kept the evaluation basis subjective.

Bonuses, which can go quite far down in the organization in order to retain key personnel, were typically paid half at the time of divestiture and half in six to twelve months, depending how long the buyer might need such key personnel. Such bonuses were a way of maintaining the value of the unit for the buyer obstensibly at the seller's expense. Such bonus arrangements made sense. A potential buyer could recognize that the seller had the value of the unit in mind when the bonuses went into place.

One cardinal rule regarding bonuses needs to be noted: they should be firmly in place before the announcement is made of the impending divestiture.

Money, however, goes only so far. Clearly for many division managers, learning of a divestiture is a harsh blow. The situation may require considerable personal support, including assurances that corporate will seek a good buyer, that a job will be available in the parent company if the eventual buyer does not have one for the individual, that outplacement help will be effected if all else fails, and that the personal presence and assurance of appropriate corporate executives will be available. How much personal presence and assurance occurred depended on the relationship between corporate and the division and the kind of culture and expectations corporate wanted to inculcate in the broader organization.

In large conglomerates, personal support from corporate for division management may be at odds with the culture. One firm ran fairly lean at corporate; it had assigned only one person and his small staff to take care of selling fifty units within about eighteen months. That corporate executive could not provide close support to the division managers in each unit.

There is a balance, to be sure. But a lot can be gained from designing both monetary and personal support systems at the time of divestiture. The benefits can appear in the quality of the buyers, the buyers' assessment of the worth of the unit, the morale and productivity of the unit, and the messages to the broader organization.

Marketing the Unit

Selling a unit is analogous to marketing any specialty good; the steps are the same: target appropriate buyers, define what is to be sold (the product), set an appropriate price, design an appropriate promotion and advertising program, and choose the best channel through which to sell the unit. These are the proverbial four Ps: product, price, promotion, and place.

Target Buyers

Where does corporate find buyers? If the divestiture is a sudden decision, the list of buyers may be very short. If it is a normal part of the contingency planning process, the list may be quite lengthy. For the purpose of this book, I divided buyers into three categories: inside the firm, outside the firm but inside the industry, and outside the industry. Inside the firm can include management buy-outs. Since I speak of management buy-outs at length below, I will defer comments regarding unit management here. However, other executives within the broader firm may be considered as potential buyers. For example, Conglomerate, Inc. sold a unit to the then current vice-chairman.

Inside the industry usually makes best sense. If the unit is small, competitors are one set of possibilities. One fascinating competitor purchase occurred when

Consumer Products, Inc. sold its unit that produced the "Cadillac" product line to the firm that made the "Chevrolet" of the industry. The question to ask is which firm would most benefit from the unit to be divested. One or more of several aspects, including product line, facilities, people, or R&D capabilities, might interest a potential buyer. What a selling firm is looking for is potential buyers with whom the unit has synergy. For example, it was clear that Regen, Inc. purchased a unit from Medical Supplies, Inc. in part because of the strength of the management. A consultant to Regen, Inc. had firmly told them that to expand their own in-house unit, they would have to improve management. In another instance, corporate approached a potential buyer to consider the distribution system the unit had in place.

If the unit is large, the Federal Trade Commission (FTC) may disallow other large competitors as potential buyers. Although the FTC has become more amenable to such horizontal combinations, corporate will have to confront the risk that the FTC may prohibit a deal that has almost been completed. It might be better to think about suppliers and customers who might be interested in forward or backward integration strategies. There were more horizontal combinations among the firms in this study than sales to suppliers and customers, but they should be considered.

Outside the industry, the limit is set only by one's contacts. Companies that are forming units in the same or related industries are possibilities. Companies that have stated that they are interested in diversifying and investor groups, such as merchant bankers or private investor groups, are also possibilities. Depending on the circumstances, non-U.S. buyers might be considered.

Product

With regard to the product, it is necessary to consider what is to be sold. This is a step in the process where division mangement can be helpful. Perhaps it would be better to sell the unit without some of the real estate, or it might be advantageous to sell some of the product lines separately. Ascertaining both on-the-balance-sheet assets as well as off-the-balance-sheet assets is critical. If the value of the division is dependent on its personnel, they must be managed carefully with regard to rewards and personal support.

Price

Setting an appropriate price dovetails with defining the product. Firms do use net present value approaches. It is also clear that with time and experience, corporate becomes more adept at estimating the price of a unit, relying less on actual figures.

There are other considerations too. For example, the value depends on what is being sold. Firms became creative sometimes about the assets included with a division if the buyer was a good buyer but had difficulty coming up with the needed cash. In addition, corporate might structure the payment of the price creatively. For example, Conglomerate, Inc. sold a unit for cash plus a royalty charge on each unit of product sold for the next five years. Conglomerate, Inc. said there was more money forthcoming from the royalty payments during that five years than in the ten years the unit had been with the company. In other instances, corporate might retain possession of facilities but insist on long-term leases with the buyer. Such an arrangement may decrease the price sufficiently to help a worthy buyer effect the purchase and to retain a positive financial statement effect from the deal.

It may put division management in a conflictual situation to be involved in actually setting price; however, they can be helpful in identifying hidden assets, including real estate, recent R&D discoveries that may have value, planned introduction of product lines, and so forth. The potential impact of division management's participation in this process argues strongly for informing them earlier than is often done.

Channels

A critical decision is whether to use an investment banker or a broker. There seemed to be biases against brokers, although occasionally firms did use them. Investment bankers can be helpful in various ways. If corporate has had experience with divestitures, executives are unlikely to need an investment banker unless the deal is quite large and complicated. Smaller units can probably be handled in house. The decision of whether to use an investment banker heavily depends on how comfortable the corporate executive charged with executing the divestiture feels about working alone. Investment bankers can be used for various purposes—from taking care of the total divestiture to simply approaching a buyer anonymously or providing an outside assessment of the value of the unit.

Investment bankers can also be a nuisance. One of the gripes of firms that had used investment bankers was that the investment banking firm often had to gear up with regard to their knowledge of the industry and the unit. To size up the unit, the investment banking firm might send in its junior consultants. That kind of interference from a swarm of drones who are increasing their knowledge at the firm's expense might not feel comfortable, and it definitely cannot be done if corporate has decided not to inform division management about the impending divestiture. For smaller companies that are undertaking divestiture, their CPA firm or lawyer might be sufficiently helpful.

Finally, firms have to think about how public they want to be with regard to advertising that a unit is for sale. The gamut in this study went all the way from Beatrice, which advertised that fifty or more units were for sale, to Consumer Products, Inc., which approached only one potential buyer in a distant city in a private club.

Another consideration is whether corporate should approach multiple buyers simultaneously or single buyers sequentially. Again, it all depends. If corporate believes there are a number of buyers, a public bid system might work, although several issues may be raised in the process. Certainly division management has to be told early. Corporate has to be ready to disseminate a lot of information fairly broadly about the unit to all comers. Corporate may feel uncomfortable about such an open bidding process. For example, it might put the unit at an extreme competitive disadvantage to have proprietary information known widely. A sequential approach to buyers may be useful instead. In this case, it may be useful to use an investment banker or broker to make the initial approach to firms that may have an interest, keeping private the identity of the unit and parent company.

Signaling

Approaching buyers and advertising the unit is part of a larger activity I call signaling. Signaling refers to letting a number of constituencies know what the firm is up to and why. Constituencies in the case of divestiture include potential buyers, the investment community, investors, other employees, the unit personnel, suppliers, and buyers. Each of these entities must be considered in the process. It is clear that firms think through the messages they send, including the timing, content, and media. For example, with regard to the investment community, firms generally signal a change in strategy as a justification for the divestiture.

To suppliers, buyers, and unit personnel, the message usually attempts to allay concerns about the unit's being an ongoing business. Some firms set up careful and elaborate systems for keeping personnel, suppliers, and buyers informed about the divestiture activities. It is one of the costs of doing an open divestiture. If a firm decides to conduct a closed divestiture and lets all constituencies know only after the deal is consummated, the risk is that constituent members may find out in the interim and react negatively, to the detriment of the unit. What to do depends to some degree on the kinds of risks corporate wants to run.

Management Buy-outs

Management buy-outs, the sale of the unit to the unit's senior management or perhaps the entire employee body, have definitely increased since 1980. This phenomenon has spread to Great Britain and Europe and now seems to be occurring in Australia as well.

A number of factors appear to have contributed to the increased activity. That more units are available has certainly helped. The increase in entrepreneurialism has had an impact. In a similar vein, there is some indication that many middle managers have felt thwarted in the climb up the corporate ladder and find the challenge of their own firm a welcome opportunity. Further, there have been few failures. Most of the management buy-outs, of course, have been heavily leveraged. Those undertaken early in the 1980s were especially at risk since the cash flow had to support both heavy interest charges and repayment of the debt. At the worst, most of these debt packages have been renegotiated. The drop in interest rates alleviated the cash flow drain somewhat, and the bull market experienced through fall 1987 made it relatively easy to replace debt capital with equity in shorter and shorter periods of time. Indeed the situation became so favorable that some firms stopped thinking of unit management as the last-resort buyer and began to consider unit management much earlier in the buyer consideration process, sometimes as the first potential buyer on a list.

Units that are appropriate for management buy-outs have defined characteristics. There must be an asset base. Thus service companies are not appropriate candidates. Usually the units are in slow-growing industries that are not highly cyclical. Thus the cash flows are fairly steady and can be dependended upon to service the interest charges and the debt repayment. The management of the unit must have sufficient strength and depth to carry the unit forward as a freestanding business.

The funds to support managment buy-outs have come from a variety of sources. Usually the management team puts up a minimum of equity money, perhaps as little as 10 percent or less of the purchase price. Investors like to be sure that the amount of investment by management is a significant portion of each management investor's personal wealth base, however. In many instances, unit managers have put second mortgages on their homes and asked for family help to come up with the capital. Other sources of funding include local or regional banks. Venture capitalists have found that the payoffs are reasonable and pose much less risk than a new venture. And merchant bankers and other private investor groups have also contributed capital to the management buy-outs.

Negotiations

Negotiations vary with regard to who carries them out. Who is in charge with the divestiture activity often changes over time. The set of decision makers may be different from the individual who conducts the actual negotiations. It depends on the size of the firm, who has expertise at corporate, and how easily the deal with the buyer falls into place.

Negotiations include a number of issues. Price is the most important but not the only one used to qualify buyers. From a financial viewpoint, corporate considers the ability of the individual to consummate the deal. Finding such information, especially in the case of private buyers, may be difficult and in some instances better relegated to an investment banker.

But nonfinancial issues are also important. The next most critical issue is the integrity of the buyer. The executives I talked to preferred to do business with potential buyers whose integrity they could count on. Selling firms may back away when potential buyers begin to handle negotiations in less than an open manner. However, money does talk, and if the selling firm is under pressure, even a buyer who has raised the ire of a seller can sometimes consummate a deal.

Sellers, however, do look for other aspects of integrity. Among the issues the firms in this study considered were how the buyer would treat unit employees, whether the unit was to be treated as one to grow or exploit, how well respected the reputation of the buyer was in the marketplace as a means of protecting the name and reputation of the unit to be sold, and whether the seller would feel comfortable dealing with the buyer during postdivestiture transactions (for example, with regard to product liability, warranty, and accounts receivable claims). The issue of financial versus nonfinancial issues in qualifying a buyer depends, of course. Sellers have preferences based on their value systems and cultures. But there are also issues of ultimate worth and carrying out implicit or explicit promises made to unit personnel, suppliers, and customers.

A number of issues can cause a deal to break off. Foremost is price. Others are asset versus stock transaction, employee pension plans, product liability claims, warranty claims, and merchandise credits.

Ethics and Other Issues

The divestiture process is replete with ethical issues at each stage. I recognized them in the decision process in such issues as, "Should we divest, given that we just finished a strategic plan for the unit that indicated we intended to grow it?" In this instance, there was an explicit promise to unit management as well as shareholders. Ethical issues came up repeatedly with regard to how unit personnel are treated in a divestiture. What role is unit management expected to play? How are they rewarded? What personal support systems are given to them in a usually stressful time period? Ethical issues also came up in how buyers were approached, how the unit was represented to buyers, and how negotiations were carried out.

In management buy-outs, division management could be in potentially difficult ethical dilemmas. One such set of circumstances surrounds getting the unit ready for sale. The actions needed to maximize the unit's value for corporate may not be in line with minimizing the price for the potential buyer.

In addition, if corporate decides to seek additional potential buyers, unit management often must play host when such buyers conduct on site visits. On-site buyer visits are fraught with internal conflict for unit management especially when unit management wants to be recognized as a potential buyer.

Conclusion

While the study reflected in this book has been far-reaching, it is by no means exhaustive; a number of other issues need attention. I have attempted to sketch some of these in the hope that other companies will be encouraged to share their experiences and resources with other researchers, who might fruitfully investigate the issues. Divestiture is a fascinating process. It needs much additional attention in order to improve the value of the process to the seller and the buyer, as well as unit personnel. The insights and recommendations presented in this book may well challenge firms to develop their ability at carrying out the process more adeptly.

1
Historical and Conceptual Perspectives

merican business faces a rapidly changing environment: globaliza-
tion of markets, industrial restructuring, new government-business
relations, and a number of demographic and social problems. In the
midst of the evolving milieu stands the American business organization, which
itself is undergoing continual evolution.[1] After World War II, industrial
restructuring in the United States first took the form of related (intraindustry)
domestic and international growth followed by conglomerization (growth
through unrelated diversification). More recently it has been suggested that
the United States is in a process of deconglomerization, as William Simon,
former secretary of the treasury, observed in 1983.[2] The consulting community has also noted the deconglomerization movement.[3] Deconglomerization has meant that divestiture has become frequent occurrence; nevertheless,
it has been neglected by both researchers[4] and corporate America.[5] The frequency of divestiture and the extent of financial and human resources involved
require attention.

Early in the 1970s, one keen observer of American industry predicted "If
the 1960's were qualified as the Age of Acquisition, then the 1970's promise
to be the Decade of Divestiture."[6] This writer clearly expected that divestiture
would become a common strategic phenomenon. There has indeed been
evidence that divestiture is becoming an accepted alternative among other
strategic choices. As we entered the 1980s, my colleagues and I noted that
divestiture had become just another part of the strategic plank of American
firms.[7] Yet in the late 1980s, after more than a decade of active divestiture experience, firms still encounter difficulty with the process. For many firms, it
remains a traumatic event.

The purpose of this investigation was to identify the phases and understand the process of divestiture and various issues that confront managers in
each of these phases. Of special concern was the various ways with which executives manage these issues.

Historical Background

The diversification of American firms has been well documented. Even casual observers will note that the larger American firms initially pursued strategies focused on one product, a set of products, or one industry and have evolved to a much more diversified base. Chandler first documented the evolutionary pattern of large American firms.[8] This noted business historian observed that large American firms first enlarged geographically as the communication and transportation systems of the country allowed such expansion. To meet the needs of increasingly complex organizations, executives in American firms developed administrative systems to control farflung operations.[9] Not until after World War II, however, did firms move aggressively to diversify beyond the industry in which the firms were founded. By the late 1950s, U.S. firms had experienced the first four of the categories of growth and diversification noted in figure 1–1, but little of the fifth category.

The diversification movement following World War II is clearly documented.[10] In 1949, about one-third of the Fortune 500 companies derived over 95 percent of their sales from a single business. Today less than 5 percent of the Fortune 500 can be classified as competing in a single business. Indeed the most distinctive feature of today's large industrial corporations is their diversity and their accompanying multiple layers of general management.[11]

Horizontal: The business activities involve one or more of the same or closely related products in the same geographic market—for example, a chain of retail women's wear buying another retail women's wear chain.

Vertical: The business activities had a potential buyer or seller relationship prior to being brought into one firm—for example, a candy manufacturer acquiring a sugar refinery.

Product extension: The business activities are functionally related in production and/or distribution but sell products that do not compete directly with one another—for example, a soap manufacturer acquiring a bleach manufacturer.

Market extension: The business activities manufacture the same products but sell them in different geographical markets—for example, a fluid milk processor in Washington acquiring a fluid milk processor in Chicago.

Unrelated: The consolidation of two essentially unrelated firms—for example, a shipbuilding company buying an ice cream manufacturer.

Source: Adapted from *Statistical Report on Mergers and Acquisitions* (Washington, D.C.: Federal Trade Commission, 1975).

Figure 1–1. Diversification Categories

Why have American firms diversified, and what have been the consequences? Most frequently cited has been the desire to reduce the firm's risk of dependency on one product, market, or industry. In addition, senior executives' drive for managerial control and power is cited as playing a major role.[12] Senior executives wield considerable power, indeed often virtual autonomy, in the decisionmaking for large U.S. firms. Other factors have also been influential. The growth patterns firms faced in their traditional markets have been a critical factor. Immediately after World War II, U.S. companies were in an enviable position. Of the developed nations, only Canada and the United States had economic systems and production capacities that were virtually undamaged during the war. Demand for goods was high in part because wartime shortages of consumer durables had created a seller's market. U.S. government policy encouraged factories to meet these demands at home and abroad, and as a result, U.S. capacity greatly expanded. At the same time, reconstruction programs enabled the industrialized nations, particularly Japan, Germany, and Great Britain, to regain their industrial capacity. Increasing international competition led to intense domestic competition. By the 1960s worldwide demand began to slow. The result was a buyer's market.

The drive to grow is deeply embedded in U.S. firms. Many executives equate growth with success, and most innately feel that not to grow is to die. In the 1960s, traditional markets were slowing in growth, yet many firms were experiencing high stock price multiples. Driven to growth but often thwarted by slowing growth or even saturation in their historical markets, firms diversified, and frequently through acquisitions rather than internal growth. Federal Trade Commission (FTC) actions often thwarted horizontal and vertical mergers, however. The combination of factors led to numerous unrelated acquisitions, many executed through stock purchases. The era of the conglomerate dawned in the 1950s with Royal Little's Textron.[13] Firms such as Fuqua Industries, Inc. came into being as the vogue swept the United States during the 1960s. The conglomerate game of driving up earnings per share by buying firms at a multiple lower than that of the parent firm was repeated over and over.

But for most firms, the game could be carried on only for so long. Firm after firm followed a classic three-stage pattern:

Stage 1: Diversifying through acquisition.

Stage 2: Running into funds constraints to meet the needs of all the acquisitions.

Stage 3: Divesting businesses whose acquisition only a few short years prior had been welcomed with such fanfare.

The conglomerate era of the 1960s led to considerable problems for many firms (figure 1–2). Problems occur for many reasons, as we shall see in chapter 2.

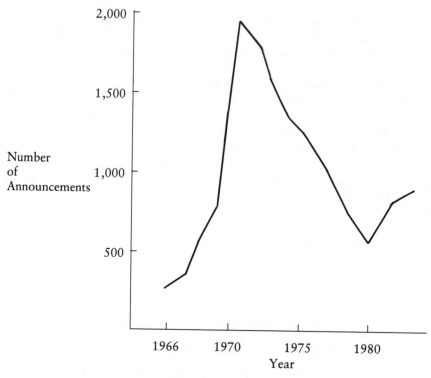

Source: W.T. Grimm, *Mergerstat Review*. (Chicago: W.T. Grimm, 1985).

Figure 1–2. Number of Divestitures in the United States, 1963–1984

Some who observed the divestiture phenomenon argued that the trend was grow-ing as a result of the unsuccessful mergers and acquisitions executed in the United States and Europe in the 1960s.[14] More recently another author came to a similar conclusion:

> Almost inevitably, then, those acquirers who still lacked in-depth understand-ing of and skill at running or managing these acquisitions five or ten years later found those unrelated mergers and acquisitions have been divested or put up for sale. Divestiture strategy has become a critical factor in strategic management practice today.[15]

Conglomerate diversification efforts have always been considered suspect from the point of view of value maximization to the shareholders; however, conglomerization makes sense from the perspective of senior executives.[16] It enlarges the control of senior executives in firms that chose the strategy of unrelated diversification. Scholars draw attention to the concerns of senior executives as a central factor in the decision to divest, in addition to such more general objectives as maximization of shareholder wealth.

Just as acquisition became increasingly frequent in the late 1960s and into the 1970s, so divestiture became common beginning in the 1970s. The aggregate number of divestitures varies from year to year, but since the late 1960s, it has remained a continuing phenomenon (see figure 1–2).

The process of acquiring business units has received considerable attention.[17] In spite of the frequency of occurrence, however, divestiture has received relatively little attention.[18] The neglect seems to arise from the assumption that divestment is simply the "other side of the coin." As one executive put it: "For everyone that gets divested, someone gets acquired. So we're always playing with acquisition. We're just playing with who's acquiring and who's divesting." The process of acquiring has been viewed as a positive move in the growth-oriented business climate. Divestiture has more often had negative connotations.

Divestiture

Some Definitions

Several definitions for divestment or divestiture exist. Vignola calls it "the dispossessing, ridding, or freeing of businesses, products, plants, distribution facilities owned by companies." To Gilmour, it is the counterpart of investment choice in the resource allocation process. And Duhaime sees it as "the disposal by a firm of some portion to itself."[19] Also a number of different forms and levels (or objects) of divestment can be identified (figure 1–3). The term *divestiture* can be used to cover a gamut of activities. Indeed divestitures may take various forms. Five—liquidation, selling off assets, selling product lines, selling ongoing entities, and spin-offs—are summarized in figure 1–4.

Senior executives make many difficult strategic decisions. Among the most difficult is often whether to divest. Once the decision is made, the divestiture must be implemented. Managing the implementation process is handled in various ways. Two examples will illustrate. In the first, the chairman of the board of a medium-sized company ($750 million) reported that he had been dissatisfied for some time with the performance of the unit. "I talked with Bill, the unit head, on at least three occasions," said the chairman. "Each time he said 'Yeh, yeh,' he'd do it. Finally I called him one day and said, 'Bill you're sold!' " Three months later the buyer had put the building up for lease and moved all the operations three states away. Just a couple of people went with the unit—not including Bill. The second example concerns telling unit management. "When we decide a unit is for sale," said the vice-president of strategic planning and rumored heir apparent of this $1.5 billion company, "We tell the senior management of the unit as soon as possible. We try to keep the

Forms
  Liquidation
  Selling off assets
  Selling product lines
  Selling as an ongoing business
  Spin-off
  Sale/leaseback

Level (or objects)
  Asset
  Product
  Strategic Business Unit
  Division
  Total firm

Reasons
  Obsolescence
  Liquidity pressures
  Inability to compete profitably
  Lack of balance in the corporate portfolio
  Forced (regulatory)

**Figure 1–3. Divestment Forms, Levels,
and Reasons**

employees of the whole unit informed. For example, we put out a periodic memo to all employees giving them the latest update. . . . We're going to buy and sell more units in this industry and we want to be known as people of integrity with which to deal."

These two scenarios represent widely disparate ways in which the divestiture process is managed. The experiences of the thirty firms that participated in this study covered a wide variety of choices for implementing divestiture.

Much of the current wisdom in the field of strategic management provides conflicting advice on the issues of acquisition and divestment. Popular authors Peters and Waterman, on the one hand, advise firms to "stick to their knitting" and refrain from conglomerate acquisition.[20] The portfolio models, on the other hand, prescribe divesting or acquiring in order to balance the portfolio. Which advice is taken is likely to depend on senior executive preference. Both conglomerate acquisitions as well as divestments have been on the rise. The continuing merger and acquisition activity in the United States suggests that the divestiture that invariably follows will remain significant for many years to come.

U.S. firms are in the process of continual strategic restructuring. Some are retaining their original identity; others are moving to entirely new identities. This book is about one aspect of that restructuring: the divestiture of business units.

Liquidation: Usually occurs as a case of last resort. If the parent is solvent, liquidation may occur if no buyers for the ongoing operation exist and the sunk costs of ceasing operations and selling the assets for whatever the market will bear is financially less costly than maintaining the ongoing entity.

Selling off assets: Selling plant, property, or equipment.

Selling product lines: Selling off product lines is a fairly regular occurrence in some industries and some companies. If the company, for example, regularly buys products or sets of products from others, it may frequently sell a product line or part of a line to a competitor.

Selling an ongoing entity: Occurs when the agreed-upon package includes the product line(s) and one or more functions. For example, the package might include the product line(s) and the entire marketing staff but not the manufacturing facilities or R&D. In many instances, the divestiture includes the subsidiary "lock, stock and barrel" with any pruning to be done later by the acquirer. Sometimes the divestment may consist only of the product line and the executive cadre.

Spin-off: A special form of selling an ongoing entity. This divestment form consists of legally and organizationally separating the entity so that it is an ongoing entity in its own right. Two possibilities then exist: the stock of the subsidiary may be distributed to the parent company shareholders or the entity may be sold to an outside buyer. A number of FTC rulings forcing divestiture take the form of spin-offs.

Figure 1–4. Forms of Divestiture

Analogy with Divorce

Divestiture of business units is not a new strategy; it began as early as the 1950s. Substantial divestiture activity, however, began in the late 1960s (see figure 1–2). Those who investigated it at that time found that firms were extremely reluctant to undertake "divorce" and experienced considerable trauma over both the divestiture decision and the process of managing it.[21] An early observer of divestiture noted that the decision to divest was highly sensitive; it was made only at the highest levels and required support of the board; and centralized companies were less likely to divest than divisionalized ones.[22]

Reactions to acquisition and divestiture are not too different from social reactions to marriage and divorce. Marriage is a happy event and the expectations are that the newly formed union will yield more to the participants than the sum of their individual inputs. So, too, acquisitions are often undertaken with the hope of synergy. Such is not always the case, of course; and divorce or divestiture often carries the connotation of an unhappy ending.

There is a popular misconception that acquisition and divestiture are two sides of the same coin, with divestiture simply being a reverse acquisition. A company can simply rotate the procedures it uses in making acquisitions and use them for making divestiture. It is true that acquisition and divestiture are two sides of the same coin, but they are opposite sides. And although they share certain characteristics, their differences are both numerous and crucial. They require different approaches, different kinds of information, different methods of analysis, and different management practices. Moreover, they are negotiated in a completely different psychological atmosphere.[23]

Executives too suggest that acquisition and divestiture are different. One author has made an eloquent argument that divestiture is different from acquisition for three reasons:

1. It hurts.
2. A divestiture is for keeps. The divestiture decision is one of the least reversible decisions that a man makes in his career. An acquirer can reverse without significant loss; a divestor cannot.
3. The risks and rewards in divestiture are different. An acquirer is giving up something relatively certain (e.g., cash) for something less certain (e.g., future streams). A divestor reduces his risk (assuming payment).[24]

The chairman of a widely diversified conglomerate put it more succinctly: "Selling a company takes more courage than buying one."[25]

It is small wonder that within companies, the process of divestiture—unlike the process of acquisition—receives little systematic attention. Some of the reasons for the neglect revolve around the negative connotations associated with divorcing a business unit. In explaining the lack of systematic attention, executives in this study said:

> The whole process of marriage [acquisition] relates to the whole process of divorce [divestment], and clearly what we are talking about here is divorce. One of the reasons we don't have a department for it is it's not nice to have a department for divorce. Divorces are not nice. They are not fun. They have great personal traumas.

> There is not much planning for divestiture but plenty for acquisition . . . because that's positive and fun. . . . And I could go a long way to argue that the way in which most companies divest is pretty poor. Why? Because most planning units have more "optimism for business," not as based in reality as it should be. We tend to always say, "Well, I know the thing is not doing well, but we're going to get better real soon." And what happens after a period of years is that we end up finding ourselves saying, "Well, now I know reality." . . . I think also part of it is [that] the timing [of when] we choose to divest

isn't really thought through carefully. . . . I would also argue [divestment] is such a muddy business and no one wants to father or be the shepherd of the divestiture process . . . and the ones who could probably shepherd it the best want to get as far away from the divestiture process as possible.

The analogies with divorce are warranted in some cases, especially where firms first encounter divestiture. Marriage or acquisition is accompanied by positive expectations, which are readily and joyfully announced publicly.[26] Divestment, or divorce, on the other hand, indicates that those expectations were not met. Today there is less sense of failure associated with divestiture than in the past. There is instead a more realistic realization that bad units do not necessarily connote bad management.

Practitioner-oriented guidance in the early 1970s was not systematically grounded but contained advice for neophyte divestors.[27] At least two authors who systematically investigated divestment during the late 1960s were sensitive to the trauma that accompanied it.[28] These early writers demonstrated the negative connotations associated with divestiture. Their investigations depicted early divestments as admittance of failure.

The failure syndrome was exacerbated at a personal level by the prevailing notion of the universality of management skills. This attitude clearly pervaded U.S. firms, as well as U.S. business schools, in the 1960s. The assumption was that if individuals can learn the skills of managing, they can transfer these skills readily from one industry to another. One executive in a firm that aggressively diversified during the 1970s put it this way: "Hell it's not [our product]. It's the management. With this team we could sell anything. . . . It's the sense of invincibility that has led to [our] success."[29]

When a unit had to be divested, executives often regarded the event as a personal indictment of their lack of management talent. One observer described divestment thus:

It would appear that routine divestment analysis should be part of the strategic planning process. . . . There is considerable evidence that it is not. This is because the divestment decision is one of the few decisions that forces the executive to say, 'I was wrong.' . . . The decision to divest and the implementation . . . is: (1) the single most unpalatable decision a company manager can make; (2) one of the most significant decisions in terms of short- and long-range profitability; (3) the one business move where emotion is more likely to prevail over judgment; and (4) a business maneuver usually made late and most often undertaken without adequate study.[30]

Analogies can readily be made between marriage or acquisition/merger on the one hand and divorce or divestiture on the other. The advent of acquisitions and mergers is usually accompanied by considerable positive briefings of the investment community, the public, and the firms involved. Divestment, on the other hand, indicates that the firm has run into difficulty. For example, divested units typically have been termed "dogs," following the portfolio nomenclature formulated by the Boston Consulting Group matrix.

Dealing with the process of divestiture exacts a toll from the (old) parent-seller, the entity itself, and the (new) parent-buyer. This project investigated how the process of divestiture is managed, primarily from the point of view of the seller. It was undertaken with the expectation that systematic study of the issues would yield observations leading to increased values for the seller and the buyer, with reduced negative outcomes that often ensue for the divested unit. There is much to be gained by systematically investigating divestment. Two senior executives from different companies explained:

> How do you get your board to recognize this business has got to go? . . . Not wait until it's on the auction block, that it's all scrap value? . . . I, looking back on my experience as an investment banker and as an operating guy [realize] . . . you could have done much better for your shareholders than [wait] to the point where it's salvage. . . . How do you get your company to bite the bullet [and] sell it while it does have good cash flow, while the earnings are there so someone who wants to invest in the business can build it into a viable piece at a price that you like? My experience is that everybody always sells out too late.

> And so you start finding yourself relegating this to some dark corner of the company and the real pressure . . . is to get the thing done by the end of the year rather than to think of all the critical steps that are really important to make the process positive for both the company shareholders as well as the entity being spun off.

Divestment mandates attention so that the divesting firm, the acquiring entity, and the divested entity can benefit and so that the social costs that typically attend divestment can be minimized.

Divestiture Effectiveness

Divestment effectiveness has been explored only implicitly and then usually in the normative practitioner literature.[31] Most of this work is now dated or was poorly grounded in systematic observation. The executives participating in this study suggested that divestment has both objective or financial components, as well as subjective or personal components. The examination of divestments by two firms illustrates.

In both firms, corporate executives established specific absolute dollar targets and expressed satisfaction that the financial targets were reached. In addition, the executives from the parent companies voiced satisfaction with the

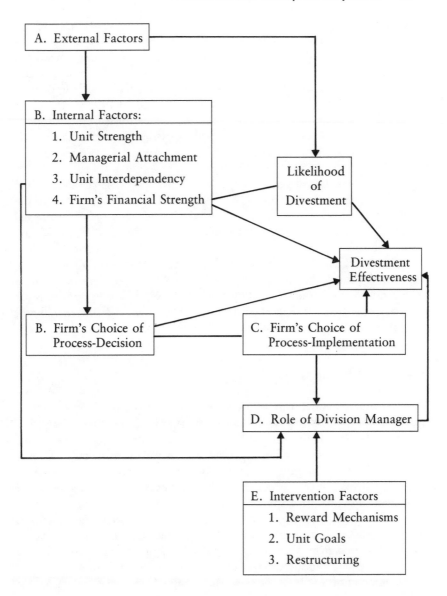

A. External Factors

B. Internal Factors:
   1. Unit Strength
   2. Managerial Attachment
   3. Unit Interdependency
   4. Firm's Financial Strength

Likelihood of Divestment

Divestment Effectiveness

B. Firm's Choice of Process-Decision

C. Firm's Choice of Process-Implementation

D. Role of Division Manager

E. Intervention Factors
   1. Reward Mechanisms
   2. Unit Goals
   3. Restructuring

PHASES:
↓ 1. Occurrence 2. Recognition 3. Decision 4. Implementation

Figure 1–5. General Model of Divestment Effectiveness

ongoing personal relationships with the executives of the divested unit. In one instance, the chief financial officer (CFO) who coordinated most of the divestment activity stated, "We are still friends," and "It [the divestment] has been a good deal for them [the managers of the divested units]." These perceptions were confirmed in interviews with managers in the divested units.[32] In the second company, the chairman and chief executive officer (CEO) maintains an ongoing personal relationship with the manager of the divested unit. He spoke with satisfaction that the divestment had allowed the division executive the freedom to try his own wings. The division executive, now an independent businessman, reiterated this satisfaction.

A number of factors appear to play a role in divestment effectiveness; some of them are portrayed in figure 1–5. Not much attention has been paid to the issue of managing divestment in either the management literature or in firms. Executives point out that they spend a great deal of time with acquisition activities. Divestments, however, are not "fun" and have "great personal traumas . . . [and are] very painful for both sides." As a result, practices for managing the divestiture process are often poor. However, it is clear that some of the firms participating in this project have found ways to help ease the transition for the parties involved and thus increase the value of the transaction to seller, buyer, and divested unit.

Divestiture of Business Units

This study focused on business units that were divested as ongoing businesses.[33] Figure 1–6 shows a typical structure for larger, diversified companies. In this book, I refer to the entity to be divested as a *unit* or a *business unit.* Organizationally it may have been a group, a division, or a collection of units previously associated with multiple groups or divisions. In the study, divestiture took several forms but was usually a sale to another organization, a leveraged management buy-out, or a spin-off.[34]

The term *business unit* (or, alternatively, *strategic business unit, division,* or *business*), usually indicates a part of the parent company that can stand alone as a focused firm; that is, it derives most or all of its revenue from a set of highly related products. The unit is usually in a single industry.[35] Further, the unit contains at least the basic rudiments of the functions needed for a stand-alone firm. For a manufacturing firm, these basic functions include production and marketing. The set of activities divested might also include R&D or developmental engineering, as well as some staff functions such as accounting, personnel, and, less likely, legal. In essence, most divestitures involve a firm that is functionally structured.

Service firms are not dissimilar since divestiture usually involves the sale of the facilities used for delivering the service, as well as the marketing activities

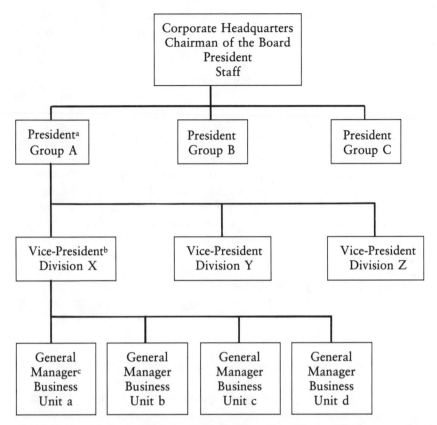

[a]An alternative title is executive vice-president. One author (Ohmae, 1982) suggests that the Strategic Group be referred to as the Strategic Sector.

[b]An alternative title is senior vice-president or president.

[c]An alternative title is president.

Figure 1–6. Typical Organizational Structure for a Diversified Firm

for these lines of service. In addition, the divestments reported in this book involved the transfer of the responsibility for the employees to the new owner. In essence, then, this book focuses on the divestiture of parts of a company that can become stand-alone firms. And, indeed, several did become stand-alone firms.

Discussion about the designation of parts of diversified firms as business units, or more particularly strategic business units, is in order here. The *strategic business unit* (SBU) was coined in a study that GE conducted internally in 1957. In 1969 GE's CEO brought in McKinsey & Company to study the company's planning system and activities. The main recommendation of the study was that GE reorganize into strategic business units, which were "reasonably self-sufficient businesses that did not meet head-on with other strategic business units."[36] Although in implementation GE modified the McKinsey recommendations regarding reorganization into SBUs, the basic underlying concept of SBUs and the companion tools of portfolio techniques became cornerstones for managing the company. The McKinsey matrix and other similar tools became critical to understanding and managing the increasingly diversified businesses in the American scene.

Designation of SBUs, however, is not as simple as it may appear.[37] Designation of a newly acquired business as an SBU normally poses no problems. The difficulties begin when a firm attempts to realize operational synergies among its business activities. Forming SBUs from ongoing parts of the parent firm may be far more difficult. Realignment into SBUs may involve delicate political issues regarding organizational status and appropriate hierarchical structure. Even greater problems may be encountered in a company that, although diversified, nonetheless operates in fairly related business activities. Designating the boundaries of SBUs in these instances may be tremendously tricky. One recent observer notes, "Most companies experience considerable difficulty in designating, interrelating, and aggregating SBUs, and they have to consider a range of technical, administrative, and resource allocation issues when making these choices. . . . The task of designating SBUs is no longer a straightforward one but requires considerable judgment as to which criteria provide the proper basis for planning for future competition."[38]

Variation also exists in aggregating business units. Usually firms aggregate business units into related business groupings. For example, although highly diversified, Fuqua groups its units into broadly related categories.[39] In contrast, Textron, except for its Aerospace Divisions, does not break its units into groupings with similar product areas.[40]

Impact of Portfolio Planning

The use of portfolio techniques to manage diversified firms began in the mid-1960s. Firms began to diversify beyond the ability of CEOs to understand the individual businesses fully. Some simplification was necessary. The increasing use of portfolio techniques and their impact on U.S. industry have been well documented.[41]

Prior to the development of portfolio techniques, the usual procedure was for the CEO to review major resource allocation decisions on a one-by-one basis. The portfolio techniques turned attention away from the individual requests and linked the proposals to the competitive performance of the divisions, their strategic plans, and the effect on both the portfolio and longer-term cash flows of the company. Portfolio approaches have had positive outcomes for firms, including clarifying expectations regarding divisions, legitimizing different sets of expectations for various divisions, fostering the development of clusters of businesses into SBUs and larger related groupings, and legitimizing divestiture.[42] But they have also had negative outcomes for firms, including the possibility of self-fulfilling prophecy (if a unit is designated a "dog", it may be treated like a dog, and thus perform like a dog) and the possibility that these approaches ignore the operating realities of a business and perhaps the expertise of those who operate the unit.[43]

Previous Investigation into Divestiture

Divestiture has received some attention by investigators. Early work demonstrated the potential triggers to divestment and the negative connotations associated with it.[44] Later work focused on industry-level factors and their linkages with firm-level strategies.[45] More recent work has systematically examined the triggers to divestment.[46] Insight into the divestiture process and specifically the role of the division manager in that process occurred in the late 1970s.[47] Yet is it clear that the literature on divestiture of business units remains sparse. As one astute senior vice-president of business development and former partner of a major consulting firm put it, "The divestiture process is one that's been overlooked by a lot of people. There's not a lot of good work out there." (A summary of the literature to date appears in appendix B.)

A broad review of the literature suggests that three groups of research efforts are visible in the area of divestment. The first approach focuses on industry-level factors and their linkage to the firm-level strategies. Specifically the argument goes that the divestiture decision, like other major decisions, should be anchored in corporate strategy, which in turn must be rooted in a thorough analysis of the structure of the industry.[48] A second stream of investigators look at the factors that lead to divestment and their implications for stock market performance. Central to these approaches is the belief that proactive and carefully integrated corporate actions leads to long-term returns.[49] A third group looks at the process of divestment; these provide firm-specific evidence on what triggers divestment and how it is carried out.[50]

The Divestment Investigation

I used a qualitative or clinical approach throughout this entire project. A qualitative research methodology is one that includes "ethnography, case studies, in depth interviews, and participant observation."[51] The pros and cons of qualitative approaches have been discussed elsewhere.[52] Included among the criticisms are the potentials for parochialism, lack of generalizability, validity, and reliability of findings. On the other hand, qualitative approaches provide opportunity for developing a holistic understanding of the phenomena under study.

Qualitative methods are highly appropriate for developing an understanding of dynamic processes and for phenomena that have received scant attention. These approaches are described as "subjective, close the data, [with] insider perspective, grounded, discovery-oriented, exploratory, expansionist, descriptive, inductive, and process-oriented."[53] Qualitative approaches are especially useful in the development of grounded theory, that is, discovering constructs from the data obtained from first-hand observation of the phenomenon or informants familiar with it.[54] Thus qualitative approaches are often referred to as phenomenological. Because this study was concerned with processes and little prior research had been conducted, a qualitative approach was appropriate.

The project was conducted in four phases (figure 1–7). The book reports descriptively on the findings and draws conclusions and recommendations from those findings for executives engaged in divestiture, specifically executives from the parent-selling company and the unit divested. The overall intent of the project was to enrich our understanding of organizations' processes and functioning as they pursue strategic courses.

The Companies

The thirty companies involved in this project ranged in 1985 sales from $194 million to $29.5 billion. By the conclusion of the project, three companies had been acquired or merged into other firms. For these companies, I report the last available year of operating revenues. These firms ranged in terms of diversity, from Fuqua operating in 1986 in lawnmower manufacturing, film processing,

Stage or Phase	Activity	Outcomes
I. Initial exploration	Case study	Developed initial set of open-ended questions to guide phase II
II. Continuing exploration (external and internal sources of data; $N = 20$ firms)	Interviews with senior executives	Developed preliminary issues and conceptualization of process
III. Validating the findings	Executive roundtable (10 firms)	Affirmed and expanded issues from phase II
IV. Establishing the conclusions (external and internal sources of data; $N = 10$ firms)	Series of case studies	Affirmed and expanded issues

Figure 1–7. Phases of This Investigation

and banking, to Marion Laboratories, which concentrated even at the height of its diversity primarily in health-care-related fields and today concentrates in pharmaceuticals. The data included publicly available material, annual reports, and internal documentation. They were supplemented by personal interviews with first- or second-tier corporate executives—that is, the CEO or corporate vice-president of strategic planning. In three companies, the researchers were able to interview executives from divested subsidiaries. (The characteristics of the firms are summarized in appendix A.)

Overview

The following seven chapters follow the process of divestiture experienced by these firms (figure 1–8). Figure 1–8 indicates the chapter(s) that focus on the particular stage, along with key issues integral to the stage. For the most part,

Chapter	Stage	Issues
2	Triggering Events	Economic Corporate Unit level
2	Decision	Actors involved Facilitating influences
3,4	Managing the Unit to be Divested	Informing division executives Changing unit goals Structural realignment Roles for division management Compensation
5,6	Marketing the Unit	Identifying the product Identifying buyers Qualifying buyer Management-leveraged buy-outs Characteristics Outcomes Dangers
7	Negotiations	First contact Price range testing Face-to-face negotiations
8	Outcomes	Financial Qualitative Ethical

Figure 1–8. Divestiture Process Stages and Issues: An Overview

the chapters are descriptive, although recommendations for corporate executives and division managers appear at the conclusion of each chapter. Chapter 2 focuses on the triggering events (the factors that contribute to a divestiture decision) and the process of the divestment decision. Chapter 3 examines issues of division personnel and especially the role of the division manager. Chapter 4 considers various ways of rewarding division executives and controversies that surround these choices. Chapter 5 covers the marketing activities involved in selling the selected unit. Chapter 6 discusses management-leveraged buy-outs, which have become a popular mode of divesting. Chapter 7 summarizes several of the critical negotiation issues, as well as the negotiation process. Chapter 8 captures the ethical dilemmas that the divestiture process poses for the various players. It also summarizes the findings from the project and identifies the gaps in our knowledge to date, thus setting the stage for future investigations.

Notes

1. Its history from the industrial revolution through World War II has been chronicled in Alfred D. Chandler, *Strategy and Structure: Chapters in the History of American Industrial Enterprise* (Cambridge: MIT Press, 1963).

2. "A Free Marketer Shows the Way," *Newsweek*, September 8, 1983. Simon is a founder of Wesray, a specialist firm in buy-outs, and was involved in the RCA–Gibson Greetings transaction.

3. John Patience, director, McKinsey Company, Chicago.

4. Irene M. Duhaime, "Influences on the Divestment Decision of Large Diversified Firms" (Ph.D. diss., University of Pittsburgh, 1981); Stuart C. Gilmour, "The Divestment Decision Process" (Ph.D. diss., Harvard University, 1973).

5. V.K. Narayanan, Marilyn L. Taylor, and D.G. Kinker, "Strategic Management of Divestment in the United States" (paper presented to the Strategic Management Society, Paris, 1983).

6. Robert Hayes, "New Emphasis on Divestment Opportunities," *Harvard Business Review* (July–August 1972): 55.

7. This observation is also made by Peter N. Walmsley, "Divestiture Planning," in James R. Gardner, Robert Rachlin, and H.W. Allen Sweeny, *Handbook of Strategic Planning* (New York: Wiley, 1986), pp. 1–13, 34.

8. Chandler, *Strategy*.

9. Alfred P. Sloan Company, *My Years with General Motors* (New York: Doubleday, 1969).

10. Richard P. Rumelt, *Strategy, Structure, and Economic Performance* (Boston: Division of Research, Graduate School of Business Administration, Harvard University, 1974).

11. Richard Hamermesh, *Making Strategy Work* (New York: Wiley, 1986), p. 19.

12. Often referred to as the managerial elite or the dominant coalition in a firm.

13. Royal Little is widely recognized as the Father of the Conglomerate Era. See his *How I Lost $100 Million, and Other Useful Advice* (Little, 1976) and "Textron in the Eighties" by Allan Conway and Norman Berg (Boston: HBS Case Services, 1983).

14. John Thackray, "Disinvestment: How to Shrink and Profit," *European Business* (Spring 1971): 50–57.

15. Robert Boyden Lamb, ed., *Competitive Strategic Management* (Englewood Cliffs, N.J.: Prentice-Hall, 1984).

16. Executives may be thought of as the managerial elite. Galbraith refers to the managerial elite as technocracy. Other scholars prefer the term *dominant coalition*, although this designation refers to the senior executives responsible for the major decisions in the firm and may thus constitute a somewhat smaller group than Galbraith's managerial elite. John Kenneth Galbraith, *The New Industrial State* (Boston: Houghton Mifflin, 1978).

17. Marilyn L. Taylor, Natalie T. Taylor, and Frederic Hooper, "Corporate-Level Factors—Their Impact on Incidence of Divestiture" (Boston: Strategic Management Society, 1987). See, for example, Malcolm E. Salter and W. Weinholdt, *Diversification through Acquisition* (New York: Free Press, 1979).

18. Gilmour, "Divestment Decision"; Duhaime, "Influences."

19. Gilmour, "Divestment Decision," p. 1; Duhaime, "Influences," p. 1; Leonard Vignola, *Strategic Divestment* (New York: American Management Association, 1974), p. 5.

20. T. Peters and R.H. Waterman, *In Search of Excellence* (New York: Harper & Row, 1982).

21. Gilmour, "Divestment Decision"; W. Marple, "Financial Aspects of Voluntary Divestitures in Large Industrial Companies" (Ph.D. diss., Harvard University, 1967).

22. Thackray, "Disinvestment."

23. Hayes, "New Emphasis," p. 56.

24. Ibid., pp. 55–56.

25. "Fuqua Industries" from Utyherhoeven, Ackerman, and Rosenbloom. In 1965, J.B. Fuqua acquired a controlling interest in the Natco Corporation. The company was later renamed Fuqua Industries Incorporated, and became the base for an aggressive series of acquisitions.

26. Indeed the August 1987 issue of *Euromoney* is entitled, "M&A: for Richer, for Poorer." The cover is an impressionist painting of a nineteenth-century wedding.

27. C.F. Vignola, *Strategic Divestment.*

28. Gilmour, "Divestment Decision"; Marple, "Financial Aspects."

29. Marilyn L. Taylor and Louis B. Barnes "Holbrook Tire Service" (Boston: Harvard Case Services, 1975), p. 2.

30. Peter Hilton, *Planning Corporate Growth and Diversification* (New York: McGraw-Hill, 1970), pp. 17, 112.

31. Vignola, *Strategic Disinvestment*; Gordon Bing, *Corporate Divestment* (Houston: Gulf Publishing Company, 1978).

32. Three of the four divestments the researchers investigated in this firm were management buy-outs.

33. Organizations can also sell assets (plant, property, or equipment) or product lines. In extreme instances, units are shut down and, usually, liquidated. These kinds of strategic decisions can also be critical and difficult to make and implement. Indeed some of the findings may be applicable to such situations.

34. Two of the companies described spin-offs. Spin-offs occur when a unit is separated organizationally and legally. Stock is issued for the new company and distributed to shareholders.

35. Certainly firms may sell multi-industry divisions, but these cases are not usual.

36. Hamermesh, *Making Strategy Work*, p. 187.

37. Kenichi Ohmae, *The Mind of the Strategist* (New York: Penguin Books, 1982).

38. Hamermesh, *Making Strategy Work*, pp. 85, 87.

39. Marilyn L. Taylor, "Fuqua," Field Studies Program, School of Business, University of Kansas, 1987.

40. Conway and Berg, "Textron."

41. Hamermesh, *Making Strategy Work*.

42. Ibid., pp. 102–104.

43. Ohmae, *Mind*.

44. Gilmour, "Divestment Decision."

45. Michael E. Porter, "Please Note the Location of Your Nearest Exit: Exit Barriers and Planning," *California Management Review* (Winter 1976): 21–23; Kathryn R. Harrigan, "Deterrents to Divestiture" *Academy of Management Journal* 24, no. 2 (1981): 306–323.

46. Duhaime, "Influences"; Taylor, "Fuqua."

47. Nees, "Increase your Divestment Effectiveness."

48. Porter, "Please Note"; Harrigan, "Deterrents."

49. Duhaime, "Influences."

50. Gilmour, "Divestment Decision"; "Increase."

51. C.S. Reichardt and T.D. Cook, *Qualitative and Quantitative Methods in Evaluation Research* (Beverly Hills: Sage Publication, 1979).

52. H.S. Becker, "Problems of Inference and Proof in Participant Observation," *American Sociological Review* 23 (December 1958) and *Sociological Work: Methods and Substance* (Chicago: Aldine, 1970); E. Webb, T. Donald, R. Campbell, I. Schwartz, and L. Sechrest, *Unobtrusive Measures: Nonreactive Research in the Social Sciences* (Chicago: Rand McNally, 1966); I. Mitroff, *The Subjective Side of Science* (Amsterdam: Elsevier, 1974); R. Merton, "Insiders and Outsiders: A Chapter in the Sociology of Knowledge," *Varieties of Political Expression in Sociology* (Chicago: University of Chicago Press, 1972).

53. Reichardt and Cook, *Qualitative and Quantitative Methods*.

54. B.G. Glaser and A.L. Strauss, "Discovery of Substantive Theory: A Basic Strategy Underlying Qualitative Research," *American Behavioral Scientist* 8 (February 1965): 5–12, and *The Discovery of Grounded Theory: Strategies for Qualitative Research* (Chicago: AVC, 1967).

2

Divestiture-Triggering Circumstances

D ivestiture has become recognized as a legitimate strategic option and is less often considered a sign of failure today than in the past. Firms nevertheless still take longer than might be necessary to come to the decision to divest. This chapter focuses on the circumstances that might trigger divestiture. A major purpose is to encourage corporate executives to consider potential divestiture circumstances during the normal planning cycle.

The divestiture decision is usually a complex process. Describing it requires delving into the triggering circumstances or reasons for the divestiture and examining the constellation of individuals participating in the decision. The divestiture decision is difficult to study. Many of the deliberations are cloaked in secrecy, and discussions often occur on an ad hoc basis, intermingled with other issues. Said one executive, "A number of us had casually discussed it [the possibility of divestiture] from time to time for several years. It was not a brilliant thought by one person." Hence, taking on the role of an observer of the decision process is difficult. Moreover, often little is documented.[1] Nonetheless, a sketch of the process is possible from the recollections of participants.

This chapter first focuses on the circumstances that trigger divestiture and the individuals involved in the decision. It then examines six aspects of the divestment decision that have not been pursued previously. It appears that (1) there are a number of roadblocks to divestiture that (2) lead to the divestment decision's often being made later than dictated by good business judgment. These roadblocks (and ensuing delays in decisions) can be overcome by (3) a holding (versus operating) company orientation, (4) an internal champion for the decision, (5) appropriate reward mechanisms, and (6) reorganization of the company (figure 2–1).

The Triggering Circumstances

Several aspects of divestiture-triggering circumstances are relevant. First, they may be internal or external to the firm. Indeed, in opportunistic situations,

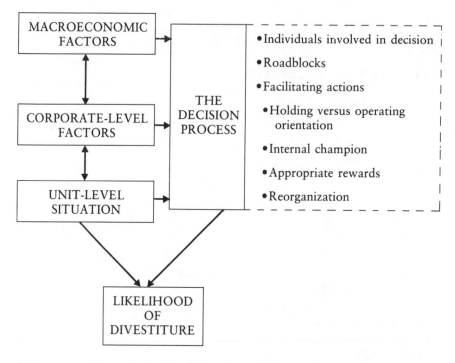

Figure 2–1. The Divestiture Process: Triggering Events

initiation may come from a potential buyer outside the firm prior to any consideration of divestiture by corporate or divisional executives. Second, these factors may
be categorized as primarily financial or organizationally based (figure 2–2). Third,
internal circumstances that trigger divestiture may occur at the business unit level or
at the corporate level or at both levels simultaneously or sequentially. Finally, firms
seldom divest for one reason only. These reasons for divestiture may be referred to
as *triggering circumstances*. Any particular triggering circumstance can usually be
traced back to previous developments and decisions.[2]

The triggering circumstances clearly vary. Some are rational-economic in basis;
others are sociopolitical or organizationally based. Some may have both kinds of
characteristics. Several may occur simultaneously or sequentially.

In few divestitures is there only one reason for the decision. Often a hierarchy
of factors is involved. There is not simply a reason that leads to divestiture but rather
a process with many interrelated factors. Although that process varies from firm to
firm and divestiture to divestiture, a pattern can be discerned. First, some event usually
suggests the possibility of divestiture. For example, heavy financial leverage may lead
to divestiture in order to generate funds to reduce the debt load. But events are not
usually isolated. The increased financial leverage has usually been preceded by an

investment decision requiring a heavy outlay of funds. In today's environment that investment decision is often a large acquisition. In the following discussion, we first examine unit-level triggering events, then those at the corporate level, and finally external triggering events.

Unit-Level Triggering Circumstances

Most frequent among the factors leading to divestiture is difficulty in the unit itself. The unit may be encountering financial difficulties for several reasons: the industry may be changing, perhaps because of technology advances; the market may be declining; the unit may be subject to a prolonged effect from an economic downturn; or the CEO or other senior executives may be at odds with the head of the unit.

The following discussion considers first the example of Esmark and two subsidiaries, Swift and Vickers. Swift, a meat-packing company, had been the original core of Esmark, the name taken after considerable diversification in the late 1960s and into the 1970s. Swift was founded in the last century by Gustavus Swift, and the tradition was a proud one.[3] However, industry changes led to severe financial difficulties at the Swift division over a prolonged period of time. Even the efforts and genius of chairman of the board (COB) and CEO Don Kelly could not turn the tide.

Finally after a decade of various "fix-it" strategies, Esmark sold its petroleum division, Vickers. Vickers was Esmark's star performer. The extraordinary gains from the sale of Vickers were used to cover the parent company's losses as it spun off SIPCO, the new name for the remaining Swift activities. The coupling of these twin divestitures was a radical transformation needed in order to shed the troublesome meat units at Swift.

It is clear that Esmark, the parent company, made many and prolonged attempts to mend the difficulties in Swift, the historical core of the company. The poignancy of the situation is heightened by the fact that Don Kelly had literally grown up in his career in Swift, no doubt augmenting his attachment to the unit. Indeed, Kelly at one time called his failure to turn Swift around and make it one of the top food companies in the world one of the "biggest regrets of my business career."[4]

In a second example, the unit head had ignored the CEO's advice on multiple occasions. Although the COB had tried to rectify the difficulty in the subsidiary, he finally had to decide to disinvest. The incident might be viewed as the COB's final discipline of a unit chief unheeding of the CEO's directives; however, the unit was encountering performance difficulties. The CEO's credentials in the industry were highly respected. Although known for running a tight ship, the CEO was not vengeful. Perhaps if the unit had been successful, rejection of the COB's suggestions might have been tolerated. The combination of poor performance and disregard for the CEO's advice was more than could

Source	Financial (or rational-economic)	Organizationally Based (or sociopolitical)

Internal to the company	Liquidity needs of parent company[a]
	
	Strategic fit (does not fit with direction parent company is pursuing)[a]
	
	Not meeting original expectations (e.g., growth, earnings, return)[a]
	
	Greater return on parent company's money can be obtained by reinvesting elsewhere[a]
	
	Top executives may want a unit whose performance is more predictable
	
	Desire to eliminate certain kinds of liabilities (e.g., pensions)
	
	Poorly performing unit (due to):[a]
	  Industry is in a downturn
	  Unit is not positioned properly
	  Substantial losses taking place in unit
	  Other financial indicators
	
	Stock price of parent is depressed and "the waters can be muddied" by combining operating and divestiture losses
	
	Technology leaps forward and company has difficulty catching up (the R&D requirements are beyond parent company resources)[a]
	
	Return on management time
		Strategic fit (does not fit with direction parent company is pursuing)[a]
		
		Corporate cultures do not mesh
		
		New set of top executives[a]
		
		Dissatisfaction with the business unit's management
		
		Management turnover at the unit level with no ready replacement
		
		Return on management time

External to the company	Negotiation with competitor to buy or sell (includes notion of distinctive competence and thus to what company the unit is worth more)	Commitment of president to security analysts must be carried through (public relations)
	Pressure from creditors	Change in laws (e.g., environmental liabilities)[a]
		FTC forced[a]
		Competition or other buyer approaches parent company
		"Poison pill" defense (to avoid takeover)

[a]Also identified by Irene M. Duhaime, "Influences on the Divestment Decision of Large Diversified Firms" (Ph.D. diss., University of Pittsburgh, 1981).

Figure 2–2. Triggering Events to Divestiture

be tolerated. Whether the CEO would have reacted differently had the unit been doing well is, of course, speculative. However, it is likely that he would have managed the divestiture quite differently if the unit had been doing exceedingly well.

Two aspects of these divestitures must be noted. First, in neither instance was the total firm dependent either financially or operationally on the unit that was divested. The first example, Esmark, by the late 1970s was a conglomerate, a highly diversified company of which the units in the meat-packing industry were by this time simply a part. The firm acted as a holding company—or to use another analogy, as an orphanage. Selling the meat-packing unit was analogous to adopting out a "problem child" in order to achieve "peace" for the remaining "household." In the second example, the divested unit had been a forward vertical integration move for the firm. However, the core of the firm was a sufficient critical mass within the industry. In addition, the core as well as the unit could operate as independent entities.

In neither instance were there significant barriers to exit.[5] There was a potentially significant barrier to exit present in the Esmark situation: management attachment. But this attachment had apparently been eroded in the long years in which Kelly and others had attempted to repair the situation.[6] In the second example, there was no barrier to exit in the form of managerial attachment. The unit had been acquired relatively recently and did not comprise a significant portion of the company. Moreover, the relationship between the COB-CEO and the unit chief had eroded any semblance of barrier to exit that might be derived from interpersonal attachment between individuals.

The pattern is clear. Initially some factor—in these instances difficulties in the unit—suggests some action. Generally the parent corporation will attempt to rectify the situation; however, when the efforts are not successful, the parent corporation will ultimately consider divestiture, even if the unit is the long-standing historical core of the company. Contrary to suggestions from other research, divestiture does not require a turnover in the executive suite.[7]

It is important to note the reaction of a corporation undertaking a divestiture program when a unit obviously does not fit in the strategic sense and yet is profitable. One conglomerate largely in the food industry had a small unit in the publishing field. Asked why the parent retained the unit, the executive in charge of the extensive divestiture program said, "Yes, I know it does not fit. But it is damn profitable." And as another executive put it regarding fit and profitability, "Profit makes a good-fitting shoe."

Usually the reasons for divestiture are multiple. As noted in the second example, both the negative performance of the unit and the controversy between the COB-CEO and the unit executive were factors in the decision.[8] There are, of course, numerous other reasons for divestiture. The interaction among many of the factors is both interesting and provocative. Many of the factors involve the corporate parent in conjunction with or in spite of the performance of the unit. For example, if the parent is doing well financially and the unit is small and the management of the unit is trusted, the unit's poor performance may continue for quite some time before divestiture is considered. Esmark is such an example, although confounded by the fact that the meat-packing unit was the historical core of the company.

Corporate-Level Triggering Circumstances

Triggering circumstances at the corporate level take a number of forms. This section examines two issues that are often linked together: less-than-desired financial performance and changing strategic thrust.

Among the difficulties encountered by the parent that lead to the divestiture of units, none is as painful, perhaps, as the shortage of funds from continuing financial difficulties in major parts of the corporation. Usually divestiture consideration will focus first on the units contributing to the "hemorrhage." Only later will other units be considered. The following example illustrates corporate factors leading to divestiture.

Esmark's simultaneous divestiture of Vickers, its petroleum subsidiary, and Swift, its meat-packing and foods subsidiary, took an unusual twist. Esmark had experienced difficulties with Swift for a number of years. The gestalt finally accepted by the board was to divest of the petroleum unit. The divestiture of Vickers led to significant extraordinary gains; closing and divesting some of the meat units incurred extraordinary losses. In addition, prepartion for the partial spin-off Swift Independent required a nearly $200 million infusion of funds for the pension fund and working capital. Esmark's deliberate matching of the gain from Vickers with the funds outflow from Swift was not an innovation. Indeed firms match gains and losses from divestitures regularly. But the magnitude of the transaction certainly made it the most visible such action taken by a company up to that time.

In other instances, the corporation may be redirecting its strategic thrust. Usually this change occurs because the senior executives are disappointed in the financial performance of the company. For example, Industrial Products, Inc. (IPI) had focused on consumer products for a number of years; however, the firm's financial performance, and especially its stock price, had languished. The decision was made to reorient the company toward industrial products, a marked departure from the previous strategy. The company undertook a major acquisition of an industrial products manufacturer to accomplish the strategic reorientation. The acquisition required taking on considerable debt, and ostensibly IPI divested in order to pare the debt obligation. In actuality, IPI executives were dissatisfied with the performance of a number of the consumer-oriented units, some it had held for a number of years.

IPI's situation is an example of the adage that a firm can feed only so many mouths at any one time. With the parent's mid-1970s major acquisition, which cost $737 million, IPI entered a difficult period, and eventually the consumer divisions were sold.

Conglomerate, Inc., with $750 million in revenues, had a similar experience in the late 1970s when it acquired a conglomerate worth $1 billion. The sale of three of the acquired company's subsidiaries over the eighteen months paid for the acquisition. The CEO and founder of Conglomerate Inc. coined the word "mergerectomy" to describe the company's actions.

Carving up a diversified acquisition in order to pay for the debt undertaken to make the acquisition is not unusual. Although many acquisitions tend to be of focused business units rather than conglomerates, the merger mania that swept the country in the early 1980s led to some celebrated examples of both merger and mergerectomy. When Allied acquired Bendix, that celebrated merger led to a flurry of divestment; some of the divested units came from Allied and some from Bendix.[9]

In the case of Consumer Products, Inc. the overall firm was financially robust. In 1976, however, the firm encountered its first downturn in sales and profit. The jolt was painful and occasioned by oversupplying the distribution channel with the company's major product line. The downturn provoked a reexamination of the firm's total strategy. A champion for returning to basics arose, and ultimately all but the central core of the company was divested. Rationally the decision was a good one, as figure 2–3 demonstrates. During 1980–1981, the firm divested everything that did not fit the revised mission of returning to basics.

Some observers have insisted that divestiture will not occur unless there has been a turnover in top management. The chairman of a large, regional

Sales		
Group A (core)	71.4%	72.2%
Group B	7.9	5.2
Other	20.3	22.5
Total	100.0%	100.0%
Operating profit, before corporate expenses		
Segment A (core)	93.8	93.5
Segment B	3.0	1.5
Other	3.1	5.0
Total	100.0%	100.0%
Operating profit/operating assets		
Segment A (core)	80.2	78.7
Segment B	4.1	4.3
Other	15.3	16.9
Total	100.0%	100.0%

Figure 2–3. Consumer Products, Inc.: Sales, Profits, and Identifiable Assets, by Group Segment

investment banking firm, whose firm was involved in more than a dozen divestitures in the early 1980s, adamantly held to this view: "There is only one reason why this takes place, and *that* is the triggering event to divestiture, and that is because senior management changed. They got a new president, and that's why it is all going to take place!" There are numerous examples of instances in which a change in top management occasioned significant divestitures. For example, Beatrice was involved in a long run of acquisitions during the 1950s and 1960s. Only with the move of James Dutt to the position of CEO in 1979 did divestiture activity start in earnest.

However, it is not necessary for a change in top management to have occurred in order for divestiture to take place. Indeed other investigators have found only a loose link between change in top management and divestiture activity,[10] and case after case suggests that the change is not a necessary precondition for divestiture. Consider the following situations:

> Don Kelly had been a significant executive in the core company before attaining the top executive post at Esmark. Kelly is regarded as the chief architect of the simultaneous divestitures of Vickers and Swift. Indeed, Kelly spent a decade attempting to attenuate the Swift situation and also was a chief architect of building Vickers, Esmark's integrated petroleum subsidiary. Thus Kelly had a greater ability to understand the potential of the simultaneous divestiture than perhaps a new executive would have.[11]

> Except for rearrangement of responsibilities, the set of senior executives at Consumer Products, Inc. remained essentially stable throughout the 1970s.

> The set of senior executives at IPI remained essentially stable during the time of the divestitures.

> At Conglomerate, Inc. the set of executives remained relatively stable until 1981. In the aftermath of a dispute revolving around the most appropriate means of taking the company private, two senior executives ultimately left the firm, and the company appointed a new CEO. The subsequent divestiture of the petroleum subsidiary was a major divestiture but was not connected with the dismissals.[12]

External Triggering Circumstances

The most common external triggering circumstance is approach by a potential buyer. Such initiatives are frequent, perhaps more so than is full recognized. There are certainly instances where such initiation sparked the parent firm's willingness to consider divestiture, as some examples will demonstrate.

Beatrice Companies sold Dannon to BSN, a private company with links to the original owners who had sold the unit to Beatrice. Dannon was the market leader in yogurt and a profitable unit. Beatrice had not considered selling the unit prior to the BSN approach.

A large firm in the communications field had committed to diversification. The directions that the diversification would ultimately take were uncertain. After about eight years of some small acquisitions, the firm turned over the diversified portion of the company to a group vice-president. His vision for his group was clear and was predicated on an acquisition the firm had made about a year prior. That unit had avant-garde technology in its field and significant growth potential. Indeed, the reasons that the owner-founders sold to the larger firm were classic: inability to generate enough funds to fuel the growth. The major portion of the new parent's revenues came from a "cash cow." In short, there promised to be sufficient funds to fuel the new subsidiary's growth for many years without posing any significant risk to the overall firm. However, a major company approached the parent's board and CEO with an offer that, according to the board, "could not be refused." The original purchase price for the subsidiary had been about $15 million. With the infusions from the parent corporation, the total investment was about $50 million. The offer was approximately $150 million, with some additional payments contingent on the performance of the unit under the new ownership. According to one account, the decision to divest was made while the group vice-president was out of town, and he was quite unprepared for the announcement upon his return. Analysts predicted that the firm would have difficulty finding a new focus for its diversification attempt, as indeed occurred. As might be expected, the group vice-president left the firm a few months after the divestiture.[13]

As a third example, a large food conglomerate had announced its intention to divest a number of units over ensuing months as part of a major restructuring program. The firm consisted of diverse units that had generally been purchased as ongoing firms and were run by the management in place at the time of purchase. In many instances, the owner-founders of the acquired firms had remained in place after acquisition. Following a change in top management, the new CEO committed to restructuring the firm through two means: reducing the number of units to a more manageable set and combining units that operated in similar markets in order to achieve operating economies or other synergies. One set of subsidiaries slated for combination were five companies that made similar products. Before the consolidation could be effected, however, a buyer approached the company with an offer to purchase all five. The units, which had not been slated for divestiture, were sold.

Firms experience pressure from other external parties to sell units. The following two examples illustrate supplier pressure and pressure from creditors. In the first, Specialty Building Materials, Inc. (SMBI) was the largest specialty distributor of its type in North America. The firm had diversified into surveying and drafting equipment. Its supplier was a Japanese firm that provided among the most advanced designs available for the market. After a number of years of a mutually beneficial association, the executives of the Japanese manufacturer approached SBMI. In essence, the Japanese firm either wanted to buy the distributor or establish their own distribution company. SMBI sold. In the second example, International Harvester went through the 1970s as a profitable company. In 1979 it had a record $370 million profit on sales of $8.4 billion. The next four years, however, resulted in losses of $2.9 billion. Creditor pressures led to massive restructuring. After divestiture of its construction and agricultural equipment businesses, the company was renamed Navistar International and concentrated on heavy and medium trucks and spare parts.[14]

Recently the incidence of management buy-out has surged. These instances are often a combination of internal and external initiation. (See chapter 6.)

The Divestiture Decision Process

Who makes the decision to divest? Most would answer the CEO; however, because the process is often complex, generally more than one person at corporate is involved in the decision-making process. The process consists of at least four stages:

1. Recognition of the divestiture possibility.
2. Discussion.
3. Decision.
4. Ratification by the board.

Who is involved varies with the stage as the following discussion suggests.

Stage 1: Recognition

The recognition of the divestiture possibility has been discussed; however, it needs to be reiterated that the CEO is not always first to suggest that a divestiture be undertaken. Indeed the initiation may come from at least five sources: the vice-president of strategic planning,[15] the chief financial officer, unit management, an outside investment banker, or an outsider buyer. An example of each is in order.

The vice-president of strategic planning in Company A reviewed all of the company's units as a regular part of the corporate planning process. Under his direction, careful attention had been given to policy development for both acquisition and divestiture. The reexamination of the unit came as a result of conversations between the group vice-president to whom most of the units reported and the vice-president of strategic planning.

The chief financial officer at Consumer Products, Inc. was a chief proponent of the divestiture program. Prior to working with CPI, he had been a partner in an investment banking concern in New York and in this activity had become used to buying and selling of companies. Thus he found it easier than others in the firm to propose selling units. When he told about the history of the divestiture program, he pointed out that the CEO had had to "get the gestalt" in order for the divestiture program to move forward.

Unit management may propose a buy-out of their own unit. One example occurred with a Midwest Products Inc. subsidiary. Foster Stewart, the head of the unit, wanted to own his own firm. One potential acquisition, he realized, was the unit he was running. He commissioned an investment banking concern to contact the chairman of his company without revealing the source of inquiry. When the matter was discussed, Stewart revealed that he was the individual leading the inquiry for purchase.

The situation posed a high risk for Stewart. If his proposal to buy the unit was not accepted, he might well jeopardize his relationship with Midwest's chairman. The buy-out proposal was first made to the executive committee, who knew Stewart was the proposed buyer, and they presented the offer to the COB without identifying the buyer. The COB studied the proposal and then said, "Well, let's ask Stewart what he thinks. He's running the unit." There was an uncomfortable silence until a number of the executive committee said, "Well, it's Stewart who wants to buy." The ensuing silence was broken when the COB threw back his head and laughed. The buy-out proposal was accepted, and the deal was consummated. (Not all such proposals for buy-outs turn out successfully for unit management.)

Investment banker initiation may occur infrequently. Only once in this research did initiation by an investment banking firm lead to divestiture. The investment banking concern had handled several leveraged buy-outs in the previous three years. Its chairman went to the head of the business unit and essentially asked, "Have you ever considered owning your own unit?" At first the answer was "no." After a few days of thought, however, the business unit head called the chairman and said, "Let's talk."[16] The proposal was accepted by the parent company, and the deal was consummated a few months later.

Outside buyer initiation may occur more frequently than is readily apparent. The earlier example of Dannon yogurt's sale to BSN is only one instance of several in this project.

A word of caution is needed here: it is not always clear who initiated the suggestion to divest. In one company, at least two individuals laid claim, and a third described himself as deeply involved. Although speculative, at least two explanations are possible. First, individuals form close relationships during their professional associations within companies. Professional colleagues may become close personal friends. In such relationships, it is quite possible to enter into discussion, with each person thinking that he or she made the initial suggestion. Second, and perhaps more likely, divestment as a strategic alternative is more widely understood and accepted today than in the past. The circumstances that ultimately trigger the divestiture are also usually discussed at length. Therefore, two individuals wrestling with the same set of circumstances might separately but simultaneously come up with divestiture as a solution. Since the solutions tend to surface in discussions, separate but overlapping sets of individuals may be discussing the matter at approximately the same time. Under such circumstances, there would be confusion over who first proposed the idea to divest.

Stage 2: The Discussions

In no instance was the decision to divest made after one discussion. Multiple people and multiple discussions were involved. The initiator or champion of the idea might be the CEO or someone else. However, an initiator other than the CEO placed himself at risk. The risk for unit management in proposing a buy-out were described in the Midwest incident. The risks are not less for other members of management who might propose and support a divestiture proposal that is ultimately turned down.

Those opposing a divestiture program that will be implemented also may run risks. In one firm, the individual most vocal about his opposition to the divestiture had been responsible for managing the group of units that were divestiture targets. Ultimately most of the units were removed from his set of responsibilities and grouped as discontinued businesses under the person who had championed the divestiture. Within a year, the individual who had argued against divestiture left the firm.[17]

Stage 3: The Decision

Ultimately the parent company must move forward. The specific point of when the decision is actually made is not fully clear. Actually three points may be involved: when the consensus occurs, when delegation to initiate action occurs, and when action is undertaken. Thus, one point may occur when the CEO has come to full acceptance that divestment must be undertaken or when the executive committee has a consensus that divestiture should be undertaken. An argument can be made that the decision occurs when the CEO says to a particular executive, "We have got to divest those businesses. You take over." Delegation thus occurs. Still another argument is that the decision is not actually made until action occurs; that is, corporate informs unit management a divestiture will occur and begins to seek a buyer. Some divestiture decisions are rescinded, usually if an appropriate buyer cannot be found for the unit.

Stage 4: Ratification by the Board

In only one case was it even suggested that a board member had initiated the possibility of divestiture.[18] In a number of instances, board members were not involved in the decision process, although they were notified as matter of routine.

In other instances, the board ratified the decision. Whether the board is involved in approving the decision depends on its size and the charter of the firm. The larger is the unit to be divested, the more likely it is that the board will at least provide routine approval of the decision. Board members may, however, be deeply involved in the discussion, frequently when the CEO must persuade them to vote in favor of the proposed divestiture. Certainly the board carried critical weight in the Esmark divestiture program. Kelly indicated that he spent considerable effort persuading the board, especially on the program involving simultaneous divestiture of Vickers and Swift.

The divestiture decision must ultimately have the support of the CEO. For example, in Consumer Products, Inc. the chief financial officer clearly indicated that the CEO had to get the "gestalt" before the idea of divestiture could be put forth to the chairman and then to the board. Moreover, the concurrence of several board members was potentially difficult because they had been with the company during the period of acquisition.

Characteristics of the Decision Process

There are several characteristics of the divestiture decision that must be understood in order to manage the various phases: the potential roadblocks, delay of decisions, holding versus operating orientation, the role of the champion, reward mechanisms, and restructuring to accomplish the divestiture.

Roadblocks

The decision to divest is often difficult to make. The roadblocks are frequently of a sociopolitical nature. One executive observed:

> I just want to say I have observed the phenomenon. . . . A lot of executives are close. The guy sitting next to you at the board meeting [may be] the guy that's running that dog. He doesn't recognize it [the need to divest], and you don't want to hurt him . . . [or] you don't want to offend the chairman who's in love with that acquisition. . . . We don't act rationally.

Another, a vice-president of strategic planning explaining why divestitures would not have taken place without a crisis atmosphere, indicated that roadblocks could be one level down in the organization: "It's very tough for a CEO to make a team come to the idea of taking that write-off as an ordinary course of doing business." As a third example,

> The chairman foresees no hope for it but doesn't want to offend or commend the president just because his view is that the thing should be sold, and there is a difference of opinion. [So they say:] "Let's bring in Consultant X and have him do an objective study of what to do." So the chairman engages the consultant.

Delayed Decisions

The roadblocks may be sociopolitical in nature, or they may be the result of not wanting to admit failure. One senior executive of strategic planning put the matter this way:

> I don't want to . . . overcriticize the role of the planning process, but I think part of what we do here . . . [is] not as based in reality as it should be, and we tend to always say, "Well, I know the thing is not doing well, but we're going to get better real soon." And what happens after a period of years is we end up finding ourselves saying, "Well, now I know reality." Reality *isn't* these plans. Reality is, this business just isn't doing that well at all, and we decide to divest . . . quite often at the wrong time when the business now [has] had twelve years of very low profitability.

Getting companies to consider divesting a unit earlier than usually occurs may be a critical element in value enhancement:

> How do you get your board to recognize this business has got to go? . . . Not wait until it's on the auction block, that it's all scrap value? . . . I, looking back on my experience as an investment banker and as an operating guy, . . . you could have done much better for your shareholders than wait to the point where it's salvage. . . . How do you get your company to bite the bullet [and] sell it while it does have good cash flow, while the earnings are there so someone who wants to invest in the business can build it into a viable piece at a price that you like? My experience is that everybody always sells out too late.

Holding versus Operating Orientation

Although divestiture is often a difficult decision to make, there are actions that companies can take that will facilitate the decision. The executives in the study differentiated between diversified or conglomerate holding companies on one hand and operating company environments on the other. Executives referred to the differences as cultural or personality. For example, one said,

> I think it's really cultural. I will maintain that in companies that are run as portfolios, it is easier to divest units than in operating companies. In an operating company, it's harder because there is an emotional investment in the industry, your whole lives, a lot of associations, psyche, personal relations.

One executive in particular noted the difficulties in the operating portion of the company. He described his situation as one where the president and chairman were "operating managers," but one group was managed as a portfolio. This portfolio group was about one-third of the company:

It was a very traditional type of business. It was performing in a traditional manner . . . and they wouldn't do a thing. They didn't act when the triggers were there . . . [so] you've got to go for an aspect of a portfolio manager and that kind of mind-set because where the indications were that something should have been done in the operating division atmosphere, very little was done. I think it's personality.

The executives articulated the characteristics of each of these kinds of companies. Some executives noted it was difficult to categorize their companies because most companies have characteristics of both. One said succinctly, "We are both." Another noted that in recent years, his company's management had become more "involved in playing the game with portfolio management" though it was still an operating company. Still another stated that his company was created as a holding company but concerned itself with strategy and thus had aspects of an operating company.

The executives made analogies between holding companies as orphanages that managed orphans for adoption and families that carefully planned marriages for their children. A similar analogy was made between the holding company with many mistresses and an operating company with fewer units, which were managed on a closer emotional basis, more like a wife. Regardless of the basis for the analogy—wife versus mistress or parent versus adopter—the executives pointed out that the culture of the company and the observed personality of the executives are different between the two kinds of companies. The decision to divest is facilitated in a holding company. In the operating companies, there are more emotional and operational ties, and divestiture is thus more difficult to decide upon and implement.

Role of the Champion

One way to get confrontation of the divestment decision is for a champion for the decision to arise. The champion may be internal (for example, a senior executive in either a staff or operating role) or external (for example, a consultant). An internal champion can be effective in getting the issues confronted and acting as a catalyst for the decision; however, this role is fraught with risks, as the executives explained:

We [are] talking about the personal risk of the person who is willing to make that decision [or] protest that decision. Once you stand up, you're taking substantial personal risk. . . . if you just sit on your duff and wait until the thing becomes a pile of junk, you aren't taking a risk. The guy that's running the division does.

You need a champion to recognize the stuff doesn't work. Certainly you're blessed [if] that guy [is] an operating executive saying, "Hey, guys, this isn't working. We should get rid of it. . . ." I've rarely seen that happen unless he wants to buy that business himself [laughter from the group of executives] if he's looking for a career interruption or something like that. But I don't think that happens very often. So what happens is who becomes the champion or a rat. . . . The danger is that this person can also be rejected by other operating officers because he can become a terrible threat. . . . It's a very dangerous job. You can be the noble person that saves [the company] and you may not be there.

It is critical that the champion have influence with other executives, particularly the CEO. One executive noted, "The champion will say, 'Because of my credibility, let's get rid of it now.' If the chairman has an association with that individual and believes him, he'll take it forward to the board." Another explained the risk: "I get to conduct lots of exit interviews, and I've seen examples . . . where people do come forward internally, try to champion this sort of idea, and end up on the street. And when you talk to them about what happened, it's pretty straightforward: 'I didn't have the senior guy behind me.' "

The greatest credibility may come from an individual who is considered objective. As one executive put it: "The successful divestitures I've seen have been the ones where the individual recommending the divestiture doesn't have a real stake."

Outside counsel may be sought as a form of championing. "Often there is a difference of opinion within the company [and] senior management may bring in a consultant," was one comment. Another noted, "It does help to have an outsider." An outside consultant needs to size up quickly the purpose for which the consulting was sought. A former partner of a major consulting firm explained what could happen:

The management never really wanted to divest this business even though they knew it was bad. And so if the consultant started to strike the position of, "There's no hope from here," the management would politely listen, and the consultants would leave, and nothing would happen.

In other instances, the consultant may be brought in to recommend what the CEO wants but does not dare propose for sociopolitical reasons:

I have seen situations where the chairman foresees no hope for it but doesn't want to offend the president, and there's a difference of opinion. So they say, "Let's bring a consultant in and have him do an objective study of what to do."

The experience of the chief financial officer of Consumer Products, Inc. suggested that a champion should also be prepared to implement the divestiture program:

Maybe [the president] got the gestalt. He came back from vacation and came in and said, "We have got to divest those businesses. You take over." Well maybe

I was the champion of divesting, but it was obvious to everyone that that was what should be done. I mean they just didn't make sense.

To be successful as a champion of a major decision, an executive must have several characteristics: He or she must be someone to whom the CEO will respond; he or she must be a member of the top mangement team; and he or she must have the confidence of the others on the top management team. In short, this person must have clout.

Reward Mechanisms

The modification of reward systems to facilitate divestiture is critical. It is clear that current reward systems may deter decisions to divest. Suggestions were made to change senior executive compensation to greater dependence on stock options and thus make senior management more attuned to shareholder wealth. A CFO suggested:

> One of the ways you can get the logjam moving, I think, is if the top management owns a lot of the company, has shareholder wealth, when they start making decisions for the shareholders rather than for their own ego or their own careers. That makes it a heck of a lot easier if you have a compensation system laid back for your senior executives to own a piece of the rock.

At the division level, remuneration may be dependent on a number of criteria. The usual basis for division bonuses is an emphasis on earnings growth or return on investment, which may be inappropriate or unrealistic, especially for a unit destined for divestiture. Executives explained the experiences in their companies:

> I have been through [a situation] where an individual was put into a position of having to watch cash flow. In fact, it was a divestiture where they went from sort of a bureaucratic environment to an environment where they had to meet the payroll that Friday. The heights to which a manager can rise under those circumstances are awesome. They become Ph.D.s overnight!

> We went dramatically from earnings per share, which is the classical way for companies, to totally free cash flow. . . . Now that's a change in culture! Most board members don't know what you're talking about. . . . They're all for earnings, earnings, earnings.

Goals and compensation systems can shift from year to year for various units. An executive explained:

> What's your strategic plan by operating unit? Maybe one year you want earnings; maybe one year you want to shrink the business [and] get the investment

down. Give those guys compensation plans that you thought out, and guess what? They'll figure out how to do it. . . . So the key thing, I'll maintain, is that you get the right incentive plan that you think out and leave them alone. I think you'll be amazed at what they can accomplish. . . . That's been my experience.

Structural Reorganization

Organizational units that should be divested have often been within larger organizational divisions or groups for some time. Often their original acquisition was initiated or at least encouraged by the division executive. There are implicit and explicit promises and expectations that essentially form a contract between the executives at various levels. Such contracts are effective barriers to divesting a unit. Often the reporting relationship of the unit must be changed in order to break these barriers. The restructuring occurs more frequently when several units are to be divested. In essence, the firm will sometimes make a strategic group of the to-be-divested units. These units may be noted on the balance sheet as discontinued.

Summary

This chapter has delineated the triggering circumstances or reasons for divestiture and considered the constellation of players in the divestiture process. Circumstances that trigger divestiture may occur internally at the corporate and unit levels, or they may be factors outside the firm. At the corporate level, funds shortages resulting from an increased need to service debt or to meet financial downturns in corporate performance may require divesting one or more units to provide funds for the rest of the firm. At the unit level, downturns in performance or interpersonal difficulties with executives may trigger divestiture. Potential buyers may be the management of the unit or entities outside the firm. Initiation by outsiders may occasion a divestiture decision.

It is not always clear who initiated the discussion of divestiture. Indeed, after a divestiture is complete, more than one executive may claim to have been the initiator. In some instances, unit management may initiate the discussion, more likely to propose a buy-out but in other instances to suggest that the time may be ripe for divestiture consideration.

Recommendations for Corporate Executives

What does this chapter suggest for management at various levels? At the corporate level, there are clear admonitions.

1. Executives with multiple unit responsibility (chief financial or other corporate officer, group executives, directors of strategic planning and business

development) need to be aware that divestiture is a legitimate strategic choice. As the experiences of the firms in this research indicate, divestiture no longer necessarily means admission of failure.

2. Contingency planning for divestiture should be part of the normal ongoing strategic planning process. Just as investment in a unit or acquisition is considered, so too should divestiture be formally considered. Routine planning may be fairly general and need not be written but should be verbally explicit. Further, the company should have a written set of policies and procedures that it expects to follow in divestiture situations. The existence of such policies and procedures normalizes the divestiture activity. Executives at corporate and at the unit level should be aware of these policies and procedures.

3. All units in the company should be considered divestiture possibilities. Contingency plans should be made for what-if scenarios at the unit level. Loss of a management team, a downturn in an industry, a change in technology, or an economic downturn might trigger the implementation of the divestiture contingency plan. These exigencies need to be planned in advance.

4. If the firm is entering a period when funds will be constrained, more detailed divestiture plans should be made. Funds may be constrained because the firm is servicing greatly increased debt because of an acquisition or other asset purchase or because a significant portion of the company is experiencing financial difficulties. Advance planning will enhance the value of the choices ultimately made.

5. As with any other major decision, divestiture needs a champion. The champion is usually a dissenter, at least until the decision is made in favor of the proposal. The experiences of the firms in this study suggest that provision for dissent in corporate discussion should be encouraged in order to develop the widest possible contingency plans. Care needs to be taken to protect the role of the champion of a particular orientation or decision. If it is clear that those taking the dissenting view will be brought to heel, the firm may expect less creativity in strategic problem solving. On the other hand, provision for managing the conflict between the individuals or groups representing the opposing views should be made. Such provision can be made with conflict resolution skills training, as well as provisions for "face saving" for those whose position was not supported.

Recommendations for Division or Unit Managers

Two clear admonitions appear from this chapter for unit managers:

1. No unit is sacrosanct. Every business unit of a firm is a possible candidate for divestiture. Therefore planning at both the unit level and the individual career level is in order.

2. Be aware of the risks involved in proposing a buy-out. Any unit manager who proposes the possibility of a buy-out should be fully prepared to leave the firm. There are, of course, exceptions to this general rule. The dependency of the unit on the unit manager's skill and knowledge and the ease with which that skill and knowledge can be replaced are factors. In addition, the personal relationship with key executives who may protect the unit manager in the event of an unfavorable decision or who may champion the suggestion must also be considered. The purpose, timing, and process by which a proposal for a buy-out is presented must be carefully thought out in advance, along with the personal and unit risks.

Notes

1. My difficulties in studying the divestiture process echo the same frustrations experienced by Robert Hayes more than a decade ago. See Robert Hayes, "New Emphasis on Divestment Opportunities," *Harvard Business Review* (July–August 1972): 55–64.

2. J.B. Quinn, *Strategies for Change: Logical Incrementalism* (Homewood, Ill.: Richard D. Irwin, 1980).

3. Alfred D. Chandler, *Strategy and Structure: Chapters in the History of American Industrial Enterprise* (Cambridge: MIT Press, 1963).

4. *Wall Street Journal,* July 1, 1980, p. 10.

5. Michael E. Porter, "Please Note the Location of Your Nearest Exit: Exit Barriers and Planning," *California Management Review* (Winter 1976): 21–23; Kathryn R. Harrigan, "Deterrents to Divestiture" *Academy of Management Journal* 24, no. 2 (1981): 306–323.

6. The last straw may have occurred in early 1980 when Kelly proposed an Employees Stock Ownership Plan and asked for union concessions to lower wages. The union rejected the proposition. Said Kelly, "We went to the union to get a better contract and they turned us down. I said, 'Who needs this?' " *Wall Street Journal,* June 27, 1980, p. 2.

7. See also Marguerite Wiermsa "Executive Succession, Top Management Team Consolidation, and Corporate Strategic Redirection" (paper presented to Academy of Management, August 1987).

8. In some instances, there is a difference between the announced reason for the divestiture and the extenuating circumstances. For example, the insurance company certainly did not announce the underlying reason for the divestiture as the interpersonal difficulties between the CEO-COB and the unit executive. Rather, the announcement of financial difficulties with the unit sufficed to explain that the senior executives were acting in the best interest of the firm's stockholders.

9. Some would term the Allied Bendix merger Bill Agee's sellout of Bendix.

10. See, for example, I.M. Duhaime and John H. Grant, "Divestment Decisions Involving Interdependencies, Unit Strength, and Managerial Attachment," in *Advances in Strategic Management* 3: 302–322.

11. On the other hand, one could argue that if the board had brought in new management in the mid-1970s Esmark might not have put up with the difficulties at Swift until 1980.

12. The 1980 performance of the petroleum subsidiary had slid precipitously from 1979 highs when the petroleum shortage permitted the petroleum subsidiary to contribute 50 percent of the total company's revenues and 67 percent of its profits. As it turned out, the cash generated from the sale of the subsidiary was used to purchase about 75 percent of the company's stock (about 9 million shares), which were tendered by shareholders in response to a buy-back proposal by the firm.

13. A new focus did emerge several years later under a new CEO. The chairman, the architect of the firm during the 1960s and 1970s, remained at the helm, however.

14. Thomas Moore, "Old-Line Industry Shapes Up," *Fortune,* April 27, 1987, pp. 23–32. The article focuses on Ford, Navistar, Ralston Purina, Eastman Kodak, Champion International, Hanson Industries, and Cypress Minerals.

15. This person may also have the title director of strategic planning, director of business development, or director of acquisition and development.

16. This incident was told by both the investment banker and the president of the company in separate interviews.

17. The executive apparently left voluntarily, and another executive noted that the relationships were positive several years later.

18. The CEO clearly and publicly claimed that he had initiated the idea; however, an individual with close ties to board members suggested that a particular board member actually contributed the initial suggestion.

3
Managing the Leper Colony: The Role of the Division Manager

O nce the decision is made to divest, a number of issues need to be managed to bring the divestiture to closure, among them managing the personnel, finding a buyer, and selling the unit. Managing these issues is critical to achieving the ultimate goal of positive payoffs for the seller and the buyer, as well as the unit to be sold. This chapter focuses on the first of these postdecision issues, managing the personnel, the foremost critical issue, as the executive vice-president of a major conglomerate pointed out: "The first [critical] thing is personnel. . . . How do you get people to stay, and how do you keep their morale up?"

Dealing with the personnel in a unit slated for divestiture is not an easy task, as one executive explained:

> I would say from my background [that] the handling of people in divestitures and doing it properly was probably more difficult than doing the strategic decision of you shouldn't be in this business, it doesn't fit, what prices do you want, and so forth. But in actually implementing that decision, I would call handling the people in the leper colony hardest on you emotionally, on the organization, and in the success of what we have to do.

The initial private announcement to executives in the unit to be divested can be wrenching. The head of a large unit talked about the process of informing his immediate subordinates, many of whom he had recruited from larger, more established companies as he built the unit:

> Once this thing [divestment] hit them, it was a job. . . . I spent all my time and handled it [telling them]. And they all ten acted different. . . . Some acted like it was a nothing deal, but they were dying inside. Others almost cried in front of me.

Issues of managing personnel include communicating with all personnel in the unit during the entire process and determining the role of the unit's senior managers in the divestment process. This chapter examines these two sets of issues (figure 3–1). (Managing unit personnel also includes several negotiation issues regarding treatment of personnel by the buyer; these issues will be covered in chapter 7.) This chapter draws from the current study, as well as an earlier investigation.[1]

Informing Division Personnel

All of the employees in the division to be divested must be so informed. A major decision is when to tell unit employees that their unit is to be divested. Companies handle this issue differently under different conditions. In other words, the decision of whether to tell unit personnel is contingent on a number of issues. Foremost among these is the time that the corporate parent expects the divestiture to take. The longer is the time period, the more likely it is the information regarding the divestiture will work its way through the rumor mill. One executive said, "It's been my experience that the better the manager, the more quickly he will find out [about the divestiture]."

Certainly there are good reasons for keeping the whole divestiture process known to only a select few.[2] Informing subsidiary personnel risks their deserting the ship, but not telling them risks hostility and lack of cooperation.

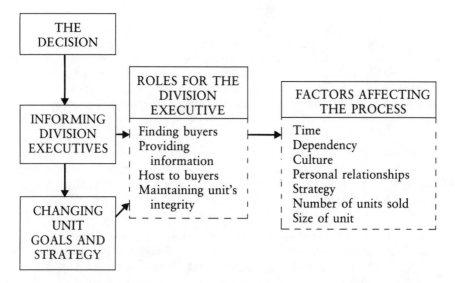

Figure 3–1. Issues in Managing the Leper Colony

The divestiture process is not short. One investigator found the process ranged from one to over thirty months, most frequently twenty months to two years. Of the fourteen cases that formed the basis of her work, she found that two required one to ten months, three took eleven to twenty months, four took twenty-one to thirty months, and five took more than thirty months.[3]

There are a number of advantages to being open with subsidiary personnel about the divestiture, including assistance in seeking potential buyers, participation in goal setting for the subsidiary during the interim period, designing appropriate compensation systems, and maintaining open communication upward of any impending difficulties in the unit.

Of all the individuals who are affected by the divestiture, no relationship is so potentially critical as the role of the unit's senior manager. Unit managers seldom play as useful a role in the divestiture process as they could. Although some of the difficulty lies with the unit manager, a great deal emanates from corporate's mismanagement of the relationship. This chapter shares the experiences of companies in our research program and that of Nees regarding the timing of telling unit personnel about the impending divestiture and the unit manager's functions. The following quotation adroitly captures the critical nature of the division manager's role: "The success of the divestment process is very dependent on the loyalty and cooperation of the divested unit's manager; he has it in his power to compromise the results."[4]

The unit manager's role has been investigated in other contexts. For example, the unit manager clearly has a political role in the resource allocation process,[5] and his or her organizational mission is definitely multifaceted.[6] At best, the unit manager's role is a difficult one. This person must meet the needs and demands of corporate and yet focus on his or her unit, its enhancement, and its survivability. As a general manager, he or she is the gatekeeper between corporate and the functioning unit and as a result is often caught in the middle.

In this chapter we assume a focus on the unit's top manager, although a number of people may be among the key individuals in the unit.

The Division Manager's Behavior

What happens to the division manager in the divestment process? The behavior of corporate toward the division manager heavily influences his or her behavior. If corporate withholds information, the company can expect resistance from the division manager. If corporate exhibits participative behavior, the division manager is more likely to give active cooperation. The possible combinations of outcomes are summarized in figure 3–2.[7]

Withholding-Resistant

Companies may prefer to keep the information secret until the deal is consummated. This attitude can be successful if secrecy can be protected, but unit

		If the corporate's behavior is		
		Information Withholding	*Autocratic*	*Participative*
Corporate can expect the following behavior from the division manager	1. Resistant	X	X	
	2. Passive		X	
	3. Cooperative			X

Source: Danielle Nees, "Increase Your Divestment Effectiveness," *Strategic Management Journal* 2 (1981): 123.

Figure 3–2. Corporate Behavior and Elicited Division Management Behavior

management has multiple channels for learning about divestiture. In one instance, the division manager caught wind of the rumor and then confirmed it. In reaction to the situation, he contacted the potential acquirer personally without his superior's consent. In the mind of the division manager, his behavior was entirely justified given the treatment he had received.[8]

Autocratic-Resistant or Passive

Autocratic behavior tells the unit manager early but expects him or her to carry out corporate orders. Autocratic behavior on the part of corporate may elicit resistant behavior or passive behavior from the division manager. The juxtapositioned comments from a CEO and a division manager capture such a situation of resistant behavior:

> *CEO:* It was unbelievable from such a good guy. We trusted him so much. Right from the beginning, we told him we wanted to dispose of the division. Our decision had nothing to do with his competence. His reaction was totally unexpected. After fifteen years, of hand-in-hand cooperation, he virtually insulted me in my office! We needed him; this business is not worth much without him. . . .

> *Division manager:* Do you realize what they did to me! After fifteen years of loyalty! That's no way to thank people! They told me, just like that, that they wanted to get rid of the division. And I was supposed to cooperate. They didn't give a damn what I thought about the idea. Sure we had problems. Who doesn't? When I started thinking about their attitude towards me, I became furious and decided I wouldn't just be a pawn of theirs.[9]

In this situation, the division manager was told the results of an irrevocable decision. Although the CEO acknowledged dependency on the division manager to retain the value of the unit, it appears that the announcement of the decision to the general manager was made without regard to his reaction. Certainly we do not know the choice of words, tone, or setting for that initial announcement, but the reaction of the division manager—anger at the betrayal—suggests the choices were not propitious. What opportunity was made for this manager to participate in the decision process? What were the expectations regarding his cooperation in the divestment process? Were arrangements made to reward him generously depending on how he played his role? Was consideration given to him as a potential buyer of the unit?

In other instances, the division manager may not react negatively or aggressively but passively respond to what is asked of him. The following illustrates the division manager's dilemma:

> I did not know how to react. Each time they asked me for something, I did it, but rather reluctantly, I must say so. I was always worrying about my future. Was I about to stay or go? I didn't know. When I asked them, they answered that they didn't know yet. . . . It was a terrible time. I couldn't make up my mind about a course of action. Hopefully I went with the division. I couldn't stand them any more.[10]

Again we see a division manager reacting to betrayal. No protection was offered to him for the personal uncertainty he faced. No provision was apparently made to help him weather the stress of this period of search for buyers and subsequent negotiation.

Participative-Cooperative

Division managers can be helpful in the divestiture process. The following two division managers talked about their role:

> Right from the beginning they [corporate management] told me they wanted to sell the division and asked for my cooperation. They said they would understand if I didn't like it but suggested I give it a thought. Although I felt rather uneasy, I decided I had little to lose; I had had to beg for funds in the last four years; they were less and less interested in my business. Perhaps another company would understand my problems better and engage more actively in the division's development. They were right, I thought, and I'd better give them a hand. The sooner, the better!

> The decision to sell was in the air. Several times the executive committee considered disengaging from my business. We were not doing too well for a number of reasons, and I knew it had to come. Personally, however, I believed there were still many things to be done. But at one executive committee meeting, the group VP said, "It's time now to divest that department; I'll come and talk it over with you shortly." When he came to visit a couple of days later, I felt nervous and didn't know what to think. In a way I understood their position.

He replied that if I was worried about my future, I didn't need to worry; there were several alternatives: I could stay with the company or with the department. I could be responsible for a new division they were setting up. He was very thoughtful and sensitive to my uneasiness. I felt greatly relieved after my conversation with him.

I have been closely associated with the divestment process all the time. Even when they found a buyer, they asked my opinion.[11]

The study from which the above material was drawn reviewed fourteen divestitures. The researcher found a participative relationship between corporate and the division manager in only two.[12] Two aspects of each situation are noteworthy. First, the two division managers had cues. They expected that something, including the possibility of divestiture, might be done about their divisions. Thus the announcement of the decision did not come as a shock. Second, each saw possible opportunities for themselves other than as division manager for this particular division. In one situation, the division manager foresaw a possible opportunity with another parent company that might have more interest in the subsidiary. Whether this argument was presented by the corporate executive or came to the division manager spontaneously is not clear. What is clear is that such a potential led him to see opportunity in the situation. Instead of reacting as though betrayed, he successfully sought a buyer for his unit. In the other situation, the parent company explicitly protected the division manager. He could go with the new parent or could be assigned a new challenge in the present corporation after his unit was sold. He too did not feel betrayed. He was cooperative in helping to evaluate potential buyers. Ultimately he became general manager of the division as a freestanding business. The old parent retained a minority interest.

The two examples suggest that if the division manager has some clues that divestment is a possibility and if he or she can see advantages in the situation, he or she can more readily accept the news of the impending divestiture. Firms in the current study arranged for generous severance compensation, restructured bonuses to recognize the unit manager's contributions to the divestiture process, committed to finding a position in corporate or outplacement help if necessary, looked for buyers favorable to current management, and invited unit management to identify and evaluate buyers. One of the firms in the study made the commitment to management that if there were two or more offers with a difference of 5 percent or less, unit management could make the choice between buyers.

Informing the Senior Division Manager

Receiving the news that his or her unit is to be divested is not easy for a division executive. After two decades of significant divestment activity among U.S.

companies, we might expect unit managers to be somewhat more immune to the impact of the news. I reflected on this issue recently, only to have an executive tell me that it is still a traumatic experience. The example of Ron Durgan at Telecommunications, Inc. (TI) is perhaps best illustrative. TI had employed Ron to acquire a set of cable companies to form the basis of a major strategic thrust for the corporation. Ron worked over nearly three years to put together the cable division. In 1986 the COB-CEO made the decision to divest the units. He came first to Ron with the news before announcing the planned divestiture publicly. Ron described his reaction: "It was a shock. I mean, that division had my blood in it. I had purchased all the units." His reaction is certainly not unique. Another executive described the typical reaction of unit heads to being told of impending divestiture: "Usually it's a blow in the stomach."

In instances where units have been performing badly, news of the divestiture might be welcomed:

> The division president wasn't surprised. I mean, he'd seen the bad performance. He knew it couldn't go on running forever as he was. In some cases, I imagine he was almost relieved because they saw the axe was going to fall someday. When it finally fell, they could say, "Okay, now I don't have to dread that anymore. Let's see how we can pick up the pieces and go on from here.

Obviously the earlier that corporate informs the division manager, the more the parent indicates it wants cooperative behavior. In the current study, when the division managers were informed varied from immediately after the decision was made to after consummation of the sale.[13] We will look at six companies: when they chose to tell the division manager and the implications of each scenario.

At least seven factors appear to relate to whether a division manager will be told early or late: the expected time to divestiture, the degree of dependence corporate decision makers perceive themselves having on the division and division executives, the corporate culture, the personal relationships between top corporate officers and division management, the strategy of the company, the number of units to be sold, and the size of the unit relative to the total firm. These relationships are summarized in figure 3–3.

In Medical Industry Supply Inc. (MISI) the established policy was to let the division managers know as soon as possible after the decision. Consumer Products, Inc., in a program of four divestments, talked to the division managers shortly after the decision. Both MISI and CPI are known as good places to work. In both instances, corporate executives indicated they undertook certain actions in the divestiture because they wanted positive messages conveyed to specific constituencies. MISI wanted potential buyers of other units to know that MISI was a firm of high integrity. The buyers were expected to come from MISI's industry. In CPI the concern was for employees remaining in the parent company.

	Appropriate Time to Inform	
Factors associated with timing of when to announce	Early (immediately after decision)	Late (after negotiations with buyer have begun, as late as postsale)
Expected time to completion of divestiture	Long	Short
Dependence of unit performance on division executive	Very dependent	Not very dependent
Company culture	Planning oriented with emphasis on being a good place to work	Portfolio oriented; planning heavily of a financial nature
Personal relationship between CEO and division head	Close	Distant
Overall strategy of the firm	Operating company related diversification	Holding company conglomerate; unrelated diversification
Number of units to be sold	Few	Many
Size of unit relative to the firm	Large	Small

Figure 3–3. Factors Associated with When to Inform Division Executives of Impending Divestment

In Tri-Diversified Corp., the CEO went to the division executive some time before he took the proposal to the board. The CEO explained:

> I needed him to convince the board that it [getting the target price] could be done. . . . I had watched his career since we bought that subsidiary. In another company he wouldn't have lasted, but here—well I understood him. When I told him, he said, "You can't sell your star pitcher!" I told him, "You may be overestimating your pitching, but in order to accomplish it [a larger program], this is what we've got to do." I told my wife. She said, "After you sell [the subsidiary], what's that nice young man going to do?" I told her after the unit was sold, there would be no place for him in [the parent company]. She thought that was terrible. . . . I finally persuaded him.

Three factors are important in this incident. First, the sale of the unit was integral to the successful restructuring of the company. Second, the CEO had spent no time in his career in the industry of the unit to be divested, while the division executive had spent twenty years there. The CEO, in other words, viewed himself as dependent on the division executive to accomplish the established goals. Finally, there existed a close professional relationship between the two men.

IEM, Inc., maintained that the company had moved to a planning culture. Divestiture "is no longer a dirty word," said the vice-president of planning, and thus "we bring [division managers] in at the beginning. We try to get it [the recommendation to divest] from the bottom up." This company had undertaken a number of divestitures and viewed most, if not all, of its units as potential divestitures.

In Diversified Foods, Inc. (DFI), a conglomerate that views itself as a holding company, division executives knew they might be slated for sale because an article appeared in the news media announcing that a number of units were for sale. The press release was not specific about which units are for sale; indeed, little in the company was exempt from sale. The executive responsible for divestiture activities was charged with getting rid of a number of mostly poorly performing small units. However, the set of units for sale shifted depending on who contacted the company and what units the potential buyers were interested in.[14]

Factors Associated with the Timing of the Decision

Clearly there is no one way of handling the timing of telling unit management. Nees's study indicated that the sooner the division manager is informed and the more roles he or she is encouraged to play, the more likely he or she is to be cooperative in implementing the divestment. Nees suggests, "As soon as the divestment is seriously considered . . . the division manager should be informed . . . [even] when secrecy is required for preserving negotiations or preventing social trouble, an appropriately informed division manager is the best gatekeeper."[15]

My research underscores this contention that division managers can undertake multiple functions, but my results mitigate Nees's strong stance. I found that several factors are important to tell division managers: estimated time to divestiture completion, dependence of the unit performance on the division executive, company culture, personal relationship between the CEO and the division head, overall strategy of the firm, number of units to be sold, and relative size of the unit (figure 3–3). Each of these factors should be considered before deciding on when to tell unit mangement of the impending divestiture.

Time: If the unit can be sold quickly, there is less need to inform the division manager. If it is expected that some time will elapse, it is advisable to inform the division manager and seek his or her approval. The longer the time period is to divestiture conclusion, the greater will be the number of people aware of the intended sale (such as potential buyers), and thus the greater will be the opportunity for the division manager to hear of the possibility. One of the division managers involved in this study received his first indication of the impending divestment from a supplier whom the parent corporation had approached as a potential buyer. The CFO of Consumer Products, Inc., underscored the wisdom of informing division personnel:

> It's amazing how much naiveté people [have] who think they can sell a company without telling their people. If you are a controlling shareholder, you can probably pull off selling the company without telling anybody. We are talking about selling a division. The buyer is going to ask the unit people, "What's going on?" you know. And people can tell [from] body English—how you treat them . . . there's nothing secretaries haven't seen. It's milliseconds until you get a call from that guy, and [he asks], "What's happening?" I don't know how it happens, but it happens before it's even been typed up. So I think corporations are enormously naive thinking their people are not going to find out.

Dependence of Unit Performance on Unit Management: Units may be dependent on their managers for many reasons. If the senior unit management is considered an industry statesman or possesses critical technical, operational, or market information or skill, the well-being of the unit may be heavily dependent on his or her goodwill. Situations where large buyers or critical suppliers with long-standing relationships with the division executive are certainly areas where the unit may be highly dependent on the continuing goodwill of the senior unit manager. In other instances, the senior unit manager may be highly regarded by unit employees. If this relationship has existed for a number of years, the morale and productivity of lower-level employees may be significantly affected by the attitude of the senior divisional executive.[16]

Circumstances where the performance of the unit is highly dependent on the goodwill of the senior executive argue for telling the senior executive early, as the following example illustrates. The chairman of the board of Tri-Diversified Corp. took three months to persuade the head of the unit that divestiture was appropriate. He judged the unit manager's positive affirmation of such a move critical to getting the board to approve the divestiture. He readily admitted that he did not know the industry intimately. In contrast, the unit manager had spent his entire career in the industry. In the chairman's words, "If Jim said yes, it would be yes. If Jim said no, I would have had a hard time convincing the board."

Company Culture: The company's culture is also a critical factor in determining when to tell the division's senior officer. In some companies, even when all other factors suggest that the division's senior officer could be informed later, the preservation of corporate values impels informing that individual early. Consumer Products, Inc., for example, prides itself on being a good place to work. Indeed all employees are referred to as "associates." In this instance, the

CFO undertook to tell all of the unit heads shortly after the decision to pursue divestiture. He realized there were potential negative effects associated with telling unit personnel early about the decision but felt that making the decision known early and incurring costs to mitigate these effects would generate goodwill among employees who would remain after the divestiture program was completed.

Personal Relationships between the CEO and Head of the Unit: Personal relationships do differ. If the CEO has been a mentor to the division head, the individual is more likely to be trusted to participate in the process earlier. For example, it was quite clear that a close relationship existed between the chairman of the board of Tri-Diversified Corp. and the unit manager. Jim Caruthers, the unit manager, had joined the subsidiary company, then a family firm, several years out of college. He had become the first noncompany senior executive and was part of the team that negotiated the larger company's acquisition of the family firm. Under Jim's leadership, the unit grew rapidly. The chairman of the board talked with obvious enjoyment about his relationship with Jim Caruthers during the years the unit was a subsidiary:

> Jim would show up at the meetings where the unit executives were making presentations to review past performance and present their plans for the future. Everyone would show up with carefully planned presentations, overheads, slides, the works. Not Jim. He'd wing it with that cigar he perennially had. I knew it annoyed the other unit executives, but I protected it. It was just his style.

The relationship between the two men, combined with the considerable respect the chairman had for the unit manager's opinion and judgment, formed a large part of the reason that the chairman drew Caruthers into the decision process so early.

Overall Strategy of the Firm: Diversified firms form a continuum from highly related (operating companies) to highly diversified (holding companies). Where the firm's units are highly related, there is more likely to be closer relationships and a culture that encourages early announcement to the senior executive of the division. Moreover, in a highly related company, the units are involved in one industry or highly related industries where word can get around. The vice-president of strategic planning for Medical Industry Supply, Inc. explained his company's careful attention to the divestiture process in these terms: "We expect to sell more units in the future, and we wanted this divestiture to be handled with high integrity. We want other potential buyers to know that when they go to buy a unit from us, that's what they can expect."

Number of Units to Be Sold: When a large number of units is to be sold, the firm realistically does not usually have the capacity, either of time or expertise, to pay careful attention to each divestiture. DFI, underwent two waves of divestitures. The first reportedly involved the sale of fifty units in 1980–1982 and the second the sale of fifty units in the 1983–1985 time frame. The company, like many other conglomerates, was fairly lean at corporate, and only one person was designated at corporate to be in charge of these divestiture programs.[17] Under the circumstances, the company had little interest in careful management of relationships with division executives of the units to be divested. If there was any incremental benefit from doing so, it was outweighed by the task of managing so many relationships. The executive in charge of the divestiture program was much more concerned about buyer identification and price negotiation.

Relative Size of the Unit: Where the unit is large relative to the rest of the company, greater attention needs to be given to the divestiture process because the financial risk is greater. In addition, the visibility of how the process is handled is greater. How the process is managed has messages for other employees, as well as for external constituencies.

Relatedness of the Factors

The factors that affect when the firm should choose to tell the division manager are not independent. In other words, they may be correlated. For example, the company culture is much more likely to be concerned with being a good place to work in an operating company with its related strategy and family atmosphere than in a holding company. In holding companies, the units are more likely to be autonomously managed and retain their own cultures, each fairly distinct from the other. In addition, the sale of holding company units may be easier to implement. A holding company can deal with the units quite independently. The company that has grown through related diversification is more likely to find divestiture more complex where synergies have been operationalized and divestiture interrupts the interdependencies among units.

Potential Functions for the Division Manager

The negotiation with potential buyers may be the most critical step in determining the unit's ultimate price; however, the functions that the division manager is expected to undertake in the divestiture process may be the most critical to determining the value of the unit. The chairman and founder of M&A Consulting Firm explained:

> There is extreme secrecy needed in the early stages in preparing for sale, i.e., before taking it to anyone. However, the division manager does have to be told. He has to be with the idea, or it would be hard to sell. If he is negative,

he can kill the deal. It is also important to get him early because at the beginning, you need to approach people who have the highest need or interest. In order to get the highest price, you have to have the people in the division with you. But the flip side of that is that we are doing this [the divestiture], and it is going to be better for you than staying with us.

It is clear, however, that the corporate relationship with the division manager does not receive as much attention as it might

Carrying out the functions expected of him or her is not always easy for the senior division executive. There are at least ten activities that the division manager can perform in the divestiture process:

1. Initiation of divestment consideration.
2. Participation in the decision process.
3. Persuasion of other decision makers, such as, the board.
4. Assistance in valuing the unit for sale.
5. Management of unit's morale and productivity.
6. Renegotiation of goals and objectives of the unit during the period of bringing the divestiture to closure.
7. Suggestions for potential buyers.
8. Potential buyer.
9. Host to visits of potential buyers (includes information gatekeeper).
10. Devising message, media, and timing for informing other employees of the divestiture.[18]

The functions that the firm wants the division manager to undertake are influenced by a number of factors, and they are highly dependent on when he or she is brought into the process—that is, told of the decision. Moreover, the tenor of the relationship between corporate and the division manager during this often stressful time is influenced not only by when he or she is told but how, where, and by whom. The remainder of this chapter focuses on what we learned about the activities in which division managers can participate in the divestiture process.

Initiation of Divestment Consideration

Do division executives initiate the consideration of divestment? In several instances, the incumbent management of the division wished to purchase the unit they were managing and initiated discussions. For example, in MIS, Inc. the division manager clearly felt he had been part of the decision to divest: "I think I was instrumental in getting the divestiture to happen. I was very supportive of it. I really believed in my heart we were better off in a different environment." And at IEM, the potential for division executives to suggest the alternative of divestiture clearly existed. The vice-president of strategic planning said that division managers were brought in at the beginning. Overall, however, initiation of divestment by division management was not the norm.

Participation in the Divestment Decision

Of all the functions that the division manager can undertake, this is probably the most doubtful for two reasons. One, there is generally considerable unwillingness on the part of corporate executives to allow or encourage the division manager to initiate the idea of divestiture. In addition, the division manager often lacks strategic information about the corporate big picture: the relative performance of other units, the potential opportunities to invest elsewhere, and corporate management's intended directions. As a result, it is difficult for the unit manager to participate in the divestment decision.

Differences as to whether unit executives were involved in the decision process appeared to relate to the company culture, as well as to the particular situation. One senior executive said:

> We have divested a large number of firms, and I don't think that any two of them have been identical, either in the structure of the deal or the timing or at what point we involve the management, or how it went during negotiations or afterwards. . . . Our approach has been to involve the subsidiary presidents pretty much after the decision has been made rather than saying, "What do you think about us selling you?" . . . Each deal is a bit different. Typically, I guess, the bottom line is we don't bring them in until we're damn certain of what we want to do.

Another individual also indicated that his company did not usually involve the unit head in the actual decision:

> [We] have a group organization. [Then] under that is a division management team. . . . In the group in which there is a divestiture candidate, we will bounce thoughts off that group individual and hopefully go down to the division. But the decision will be made at that group level. Once the decision is made, then you go down to the division level and say, "We're spinning this [unit] off."

Still another executive stated: "Do you involve them [unit executives] in the decision process? . . . I don't think I have ever seen it."

One executive explained why his company did not include the executives in the decision process:

> Typically, we will not go to the management at that time and say, "We're thinking of going somewhere else and think we probably ought to sell you." Because

unless we're fairly sure, we think that's not productive. It creates a tremendous amount of uncertainty, and we don't know what the time is going to be from the time we convey that information to the time until we can actually execute a deal. But we know that during that time is a very critical time in terms of productivity of the people. So we're concerned about productivity during the general time, and we're concerned also about what the reaction of the president, the leader of this subsidiary, is during the time when we say, "We're not sure, but we think we want to sell you." So our approach has been to involve the subsidiary presidents . . . after the decision has been made. Rather than saying, "What do you think about us selling you?" we go in and say, "We've made a determination that we want to sell the business, and we need you to help us execute that."

Generally, then, firms do not involve executives in charge of the units in the decision to divest. There were, however, two instances in which the firms were apparently open to involvement in the decision process. In one, the firm described itself as developing a planning culture. The vice-president responsible for strategic planning maintained that it had become acceptable for division or unit managers to propose that their area of operation be divested. The reward system in place recognized "stars" (cash users for growth), as well as "cash generators." One legitimate cash-generating activity was divestiture. In the other instance, it was clear that the division executive felt that he had fully been part of the decision process. Here, the long-standing relationship among the individuals appeared to play a role.

Persuading Other Decision Makers

This function was explored in the example of Tri-Diversified Corp. Just how dependent any particular corporate executive will be on the ability of the division manager to help persuade other decision makers is largely contingent on how much knowledge of the unit and its industry resides among corporate executives. The more diversified is the company, the more likely it is that the knowledge regarding the unit and its industry resides in the unit management. However, there are instances where corporate decision makers have spent a significant portion of their careers in a particular unit or with a competitor in the same industry.

Assistance in Valuing the Unit for Sale

As with the decision itself, corporate executives are largely unwilling to involve unit executives in the valuation process. One said:

Valuation, no. I would say in terms of protection [of] the shareholder values, in terms of trying to really put an appropriate price on this particular property . . . I believe the operating people often just don't have any appreciation for what the real value of the property really is. And bear in mind your decision to sell often had a lot to do with what you thought you could get in the market.

There are, however, clearly instances where the unit executives should be involved. For example:

> In the evaluation, I come up a little bit different to this extent. Many times when you're selling something, it's because it's a little different. You're working from headquarters, and while you're all good managers, you really don't know the business very well. [Therefore] as a source of information about concrete items that are present in that business and the quality of the inventory and a few things like that which the accountants had a little trouble dealing with, I think it's worthwhile to involve them [unit executives] in the evaluation of it to the extent, you know, the physical conditions as opposed to setting the price on the company. I think if they had been involved in acquisitions, those types of things before and they know the industry well, I would involve them in the valuation.

> I'm trying to draw [on how] we found out by what we did in the evaluation of some of our subsidiaries. You come up with a price, and then you dig in . . . and you say, "Hey, there's a lot of assets here which I'm sure they are not going to pay me for. They're going to pay me a multiple of earnings or not. But boy, I don't need a plant in California—that was a little far out area; now it's a suburb of Los Angeles! Hell! I can sell it for more than the whole company's worth! I'll sell the plant off first and shut that one down. I'll contract manufacture somewhere." And lo and behold, you find out in R&D you have a good little product line. The seller is not going to pay you for it, but you start running through the research list [and] it hasn't been developed but [the unit manager] knows what it's worth. So, getting ready for a sale, [remember the buyer] wants to buy an ongoing business and won't pay you for the hidden assets. And I think the unit's management knows what those things are. Those are the little things [the unit management] wanted in the future, and they are willing to help you sell those things—discover them and sell them.

A special case of evaluation occurs with leveraged buy-outs, with variations depending on who buys the company: outside investors, unit executives, employees, or combinations of these. Whether the possibility of a management leveraged buy-out should be pursued from the beginning, used as a means of last resort, or left to the unit executives to initiate is a matter of debate, as the following comments from three corporate executives indicate:

> I don't think you should offer to the management up front. I've worked a lot of leveraged buy-outs, and I think that almost should be a last resort.

They ought to bring it up to you. They ought to take the aggressive initiative on it.[19]

There was a period of time when I was 180 degrees on this point as to whether you consider it as a last resort or the first resort. . . . For some of these businesses, particularly the ones with stable cash flows and reasonably good profitability, you can get incrementally 25–30 percent more in a leveraged buy-out, and when you see that—it doesn't happen in all situations—but when in doing your homework [on] valuation, you see [that situation], I would say the worst thing you could do is to shop it to the industrial companies to get [your value] . . . and then come around and try to sell this [as] a leveraged buy-out offer after everybody in this industry knows that it's street worn. So in that situation . . . leveraged buy-out is a perfect alternative for this . . . maximized value that's going to be an alternative of first resort.

In essence, the consensus seems to be that unit managers should not be involved in actually putting the value on the business for sale, for several reasons. First, the decision itself is likely to be predicated on an expected value for the unit. Thus valuation, however implicitly, has already been part of the decision process from which the unit manager is largely excluded. Second, asking unit managers to assist in the valuation process puts them in a conflictual situation that arises partly because they may end up being the buyers. Even if the current management is not part of the buy-out, the new owner may well be their new boss. Meeting the goals of the current owner requires maximizing the price of the unit in the sale. Meeting the goals of the potential new owner requires minimizing the price of the unit in the sale. Thus setting the value puts the unit manager in a situation that is inherently conflictual.

A unit manager can be useful in valuation in two areas, however. First, if the person has had experience with acquisitions and, perhaps, divestitures in the past, his or her expertise might be valuable. Second, the unit manager should always be asked about the value of the assets under his or her control, particularly those that might be undervalued on the balance sheet and those that are off-the-balance-sheet assets. For example, real estate may be far greater than the book value, and the unit manager might be in a position to make that judgment. Further, such off-balance-sheet assets as technical skill resident in employees or expected outcomes from R&D projects currently underway might well be of considerable value. Again, a unit manager is usually in a better position than corporate personnel to make the appropriate valuation judgment.

Unit management may be thought of as an information supplier. Modern corporations are usually mutlilayered and often diversified. Thus information critical to valuation of the unit, even to the decision to divest, may frequently reside in the division, and specifically in the division manager. Corporate management cannot know everything, and the division manager thus acts as a gatekeeper or filter of information moving up through the corporation.

Management of Unit's Morale and Productivity

Critical to the value of the unit to be sold is maintaining its integrity—that is, maintaining the inherent value of the firm during the period in which a buyer is sought, negotiations are carried out, and the unit is transferred legally and operationally. Long-standing research findings indicate that productivity is not necessarily high if morale is high. On the other hand, high morale appears associated with high productivity. A major key to the maintenance of morale and productivity may well be the unit's senior manager.[20] One observer said, "One key success factor of many divestments is to preserve morale and efficiency in the division during the disengagement process."[21]

Keeping secret the decision to divest places the division manager in a difficult situation. His or her own reaction to the uncertainty must be set aside to maintain business as usual or, if the decision is disclosed to unit personnel, attempt to maintain morale and efficiency in the unit. Certainly the parent organization must be both understanding and proactive in finding ways to help the division manager manage the stress. The divestiture price is affected by unit productivity. Thus it is "very important to keep a high level of productivity. The preoccupation with secrecy is generally attributed to this concern."[22]

Renegotiation of Goals and Objectives of the Unit during the Divestiture Process

Once the decision is made to divest, corporate management may need to change the unit's strategic goals and objectives. For example, the unit may be divested because of a shortage of funds at the corporate level. If so, a unit that had been targeted for growth may have to be constrained; it may be necessary or desirable to shrink the unit, perhaps by reducing inventories, becoming tighter with trade credit, delaying asset repair or augmentation, or even selling superfluous assets. In all these instances, revamping the directions in conjunction with the unit management and dovetailing the redirectioning with changes in the compensation package is likely to be appropriate.

The need to change the unit's strategic goals and objectives argues strongly for including the unit's top executive, and perhaps other key unit managers, in the plans for divestiture. Otherwise changing the strategic orientation for the unit in midstream may be confusing. The situation may lead to suspicion of impending sale.

Changing the strategic goals and objectives may be necessary in order to effect a sale. The divestor may have to try to make the division more palatable to potential buyers. Such actions may include personnel changes, layoffs, or even plant closings. In any of these decisions, and certainly in their implementation, the division manager may be key. Some of the actions that are to be taken may be decisions made by corporate, such as the decision not to invest funds in the unit and perhaps even to shrink the funds currently invested. Other decisions may be required by the buyer; for example, a buyer may want two of the division's three plants shut down prior to purchase.[23] In the major divestment of three units by Industrial Products, Inc., the buyer did not take the unit's management in the purchase; thus IPI had to take care of trimming the unit's top echelon and staff.

Implementation of Interim Goals and Objectives

Unit management is critical for implementation of the strategic reorientation. How to encourage and motivate implementation of the changes without revealing the expected divestiture may be awkward at best and compromising of the integrity of the relationships between corporate and unit management throughout the organization.

Suggestions for Potential Buyers

The role of the unit manager in suggesting potential buyers may be a critical one. If the unit's top manager has long been in the industry, it is likely that he or she will be a valuable source for identifying possible buyers. The chairman and founder of M&A Consulting Firm explained:

> If the division manager is brought into the picture properly and early, but not so early the decision isn't sure, . . . then he has his own channels of communication. He may have someone who is very close to him. . . . He has his own way of letting it be known. . . . Again I always have to say there are exceptions. It depends upon how active the guy is in the industry and so forth.

In addition, such an individual may be expected to know the adjacent industries, such as suppliers and buyers.

If the industry is closely knit, the dependency of corporate on the management's ability to identify buyers is even more significant. Specialized units are a case in point, as the vice-president of strategic planning for Technology Conglomerate Inc. explained: "In highly specialized businesses, top management is unlikely to be as adept at identifying potential buyers as the division manager. Therefore, in [the case of a specialized unit], we asked the division manager to be deeply involved in finding a buyer."

Other factors may mitigate, however. If someone at corporate has experience in the industry, the cooperation of the unit manager is not as critical. If the industry has many participants or the unit is a kind of business currently considered attractive by many buyers, corporate will not be so dependent on unit management. For example, when the oil shortage occurred in 1979 and 1980, there were ready buyers for petroleum subsidiaries.

Three firms specifically mentioned use of their division personnel to identify potential buyers: MIS Inc. had a fairly consistent policy of asking division executives to identify potential buyers; Consumer Products, Inc. invited the participation of all four division managers in identifying potential buyers; and Tri-Diversified Corp. used public solicitations but appeared to include the top division executive in evaluating the companies that submitted bids. The circumstances under which executives are useful in assisting in the identification of potential buyers are summarized in figure 3–4.

Division Manager: A Potential Buyer?

Management may well be a potential buyer. Sometimes unit management may be the most highly motivated and most appropriate buyers, or they may be the only buyers. Such management buy-outs are often accomplished with considerable leverage: debt capital provided by the parent company or third parties. For example, corporate may want to complete the sale prior to the end of the fiscal year. If time is short, it may be in the corporate interest to assist the division management to purchase the firm. One parent firm wanted to effect the divestiture prior to the end of the fiscal year, take a loss on the unit, and thus shield a gain that had been made on the earlier sale of another unit. This parent was generous with regard to the management buy-out terms.

Management buy-outs have been considered the court of last resort; however, recent changes have occurred, especially in funds available for such purchases and the visibility of numerous management buy-out success stories. Thus many corporate executives now consider management as potential purchasers much earlier, sometimes as the first considered potential buyer.

Five companies described divestitures that took the form of management buy-outs. Of the seven divestments, only two are clearly identified as last-resort efforts to sell the unit.[24] Both units were performing very poorly and were poorly strategically positioned. In two other instances, the managers were the first and only potential buyers contacted. In one of these, there may not have been many potential buyers. However, the vice-president of corporate planning

		Small or Closely Knit Industry	Many Entrants or Not Closely Knit Industry
Knowledge of corporate executives	High	Likely not needed	Highly useful
about the industry	Low	Absolutely critical	Critical

Figure 3–4. Usefulness of Unit Managers in Identifying Potential Buyers

was sufficiently satisfied with the process that he intends to consider management buy-out as one of the initially considered options in all future divestments. In a third company, there was a long-standing relationship between the corporate CEO and the buyer. Long before he began his own firm, the CEO had worked in the subsidiary, then a freestanding multiunit company. After purchase, many of the business units were sold, most at significant profit. At the time of this study, one unit remained. The buyer had been a key executive in the subsidiary before purchase and moved to the corporate board after purchase. The CEO approached the executive even before taking the matter to his board and put his long-time acquaintance "in touch with the right people" to put together the financing.

Consumer Products, Inc. undertook a divestiture program of four units. The plans for the divestiture were made clear in the yearly session with Wall Street analysts when the CEO and the CFO gave the deadline for completion of the program. As the deadline neared, one unit remained unsold. CPI corporate executives were happy to assist the well-regarded division manager to purchase the unit. Management buyouts are covered more thoroughly in chapter 6.

Host to Visits of Potential Buyers

Unless the buyer is bargaining only for assets, he or she will want to talk to management of the unit and perhaps even a wider range of employees.[25] The unit manager's cooperation at this point can be vital. Misrepresentation of personnel talent (including his or her own) and other assets can affect the value of the sale. The attitude of the division manager and the information that he or she provides or withholds can influence a buyer's decision. Jim Caruthers, head of one of Tri-Diversified's very large divested units, talked about why his next layer of management was so critical:

> The key guys were the level below me. . . . Those ten guys were the key to the deal. Any smart guy buying anything is always either directly or indirectly . . . going to check with them [on] the quality of what they're buying, the problems, why they're selling and so on. . . . [The chairman] and I spent a lot of time talking to those ten people. . . . Actually the people that sold the company were the next layer down, not me. . . . Fundamentally when it got down to show and tells, vice-presidents handled the show and tells.

The critical nature of the unit management's interaction with the buyer alone argues for telling unit management early, gaining their confidence, and making sure that negotiators are doing everything possible within the limits of the situation to protect unit management's interests. Corporate executives choosing this procedure should let unit management know the status of negotiations on a regular basis. Unit management can be a vital and critical part of enhancing or detracting from the value of the unit in the minds of the potential buyer. Indeed no other point may be more critical than the buyer visits. At this stage, unit management begins the process of making the switch in loyalty from the old corporate parent to the new one. This time of potentially divided loyalties must be understood and confronted by corporate and steps taken to be supportive of unit management.

Devising Messages, Media, and Timing for Informing
Other Employees of the Impending Divestiture

Ultimately all employees will have to be informed; how and when are important. One firm completed negotiations the day before a gala celebration as the unit moved into new headquarters. Corporate, faced with how and when to announce the divestiture, told the employees before the news broke publicly. There was no appropriate opportunity to draw a large group of employees together for the announcement; instead, at quitting time, the unit management and corporate executives personally handed out the announcement as people left for the day. The corporate executives and unit management stayed on into the evening to answer questions. The news broke in the press the following day.

Summary

Contrary to an earlier study, this research project uncovered few instances in divestment where the division executive had been uncooperative.[26] It was clear that division executives, even in today's environment with the frequency and visibility of divestiture, still felt shock when they were told that their unit was to be divested. It is also apparent that many companies need to spend more effort thinking through how the divestiture will be handled.

Among the more critical issues to be considered is when the senior manager in the unit will be informed that the unit is to be divested. This timing heavily affects the roles that he or she can play in the divestiture process; the later he or she is told, the more roles are precluded from the repertoire. A number of factors affect the decision of when to tell the unit's senior executive: the dependence of the unit's performance on the executive, the company's culture and values, the personal relationship between the CEO and the division head, the firm's strategy, the number of units to be sold, and the relative size of the unit.

Recommendations for Corporate Executives

It is clear that there is no universal prescription regarding managing unit personnel and unit management. Some of the suggestions from the chapter for corporate executives are summarized here.

1. When to tell unit personnel that the unit is to be divested is an important decision. Timing is heavily governed by the amount of time that the completion of the divestiture is expected to take. If the divestiture is expected to take some time to completion, it is better to tell unit personnel since they have multiple sources for finding out.

2. The critical decision to be made about the division manager is when he or she will be informed. Necessarily that decision implies the role that he or she is expected to play in the divestment process. The later in the divestment process corporate management informs the division manager, the more roles are precluded. Conversely, the earlier in the process the division manager is informed, the greater is the potential number of roles.

3. The role that the unit manager plays in the divestiture can be highly critical. Careful consideration should be given to the individual and the part he or she will play in the divestiture process. Evidence suggests that the unit manager's role is often misunderstood and may actually be mismanaged. Certainly the unit manager could play more functions than are usually assigned. However, the functions that he or she undertakes are influenced by a number of factors at both the corporate and unit levels. They should be considered in planning the announcement to the division manager and in inviting his or her participation in the divestiture process.

4. Corporate should avoid deliberate exclusion of the unit manager from the divestiture process and, more important, should be ready with suggested career alternatives when the divestiture is completed—perhaps a comparable or better position with the parent firm. Difficulties constructing such an alternative arise if the parent firm is not growing, or there appears to be no suitable position for the individual in a reasonable time frame. Under these conditions, a generous severance bonus and helpful outplacement are in order. The other alternative focuses on finding a buyer who will have more interest in the unit than the current parent. Corporate might make clear that this issue is important in their search for a buyer and may include the unit manager in the search or in evaluating the candidacy of various buyers.

5. Corporate will have to decide whether to tell only the top divisional manager or to include senior managers in the announcement. Probably the best resolution of this dilemma is to tell the division's most senior manager first and give him or her the choice of when and how to inform the rest of the management team. The corporate executive responsible for informing the division manager should be ready to meet with the individuals in a group or separately, as the senior unit manager may deem appropriate. Further, the senior unit manager may prefer to tell the management team or keep them uninformed for a while.

Recommendations for Unit Managers

1. The more diversified is a company, the more likely it is that your unit will be considered for divestiture at the corporate level at some time during your tenure as unit manager. Never assume that your unit is immune from divestiture. Chapter 2 especially suggests factors to consider periodically to decide whether your unit might be divested. Such questioning is healthy and can be a basis for forming alternative strategic scenarios for your unit as well as for your own career strategy, both in the current period as well as in the longer term.

2. Firms tend to withhold the announcement of divestiture from unit personnel, including the unit manager. If you are the last to know, understand that such situations are not unusual. Corporate's decision in this matter may result from corporate's lack of experience or the corporate culture.

3. It is likely that when the announcement of the impending divestiture is made to you, you will react with shock and perhaps anger.

4. Corporate may botch its announcement of divestment to you. Careful questioning at the time can help clear up a number of potential misunderstandings.

5. In considering what functions you might carry out as part of the divestiture process, evaluate your own skills, how you are viewed at corporate, the situation within the unit, and the corporate milieu. Most unit managers can take on a broader array of functions than corporate usually outlines. Suggesting an enlargement of your responsibilities is possible but should be done with care.

6. It is unlikely that corporate will expect you to initiate the idea of divestiture. To do so requires considerable political finesse as well as clout. Two possibilities are clear. If divestiture makes sense, you might suggest the idea to someone within the dominant coalition at corporate; however, expect the credit for initiating the idea to accrue to someone else. If you initiate the idea because you are considering a management buy-out, carefully decide whether conditions are ripe for such divestiture and whether you expose yourself to too many risks as a result of such initiation.

Notes

1. Danielle Nees, "Increase Your Divestment Effectiveness," *Strategic Management Journal* 2 (1981): 119–130.

2. However, a naive assumption is that withholding information prevents the problem. Those who told us of the conflicts said that they informed division executives of the impending divestiture because the rumor mill would carry the news anyway. At least one executive stated that companies withhold the information for fear their

best executives will leave. One firm acknowledged it expected several of the subsidiary's key sales people to leave and discovered—to their surprise—that they stayed.

3. Nees, "Increase Your Divestment Effectiveness."

4. Ibid.

5. J.L. Bower, *Managing the Resource Allocation Process: A Study of Corporate Planning and Investment* Homewood, Ill.: Dorsey, 1970.

6. H.E.R. Uyterhoeven, "General Managers in the Middle," *Harvard Business Review* (March–April 1972): 75–85.

7. Evidence comes from two sources: the mid-1970s study by Nees (1981) and my own work, ongoing since the early 1980s.

8. Nees, "Increase Your Divestment Effectiveness."

9. Ibid.

10. Ibid.

11. Ibid., pp. 125–126.

12. Ibid.

13. Who initiated the decision and when it was initiated are often difficult to ascertain because more than one individual may claim to have initiated the idea of divestiture. In the overall study, the decisions to divest were initiated primarily by corporate executives. Initiators included a CFO, CEOs, and planning executives. In several instances, division managers initiated management leveraged buy-outs. However, in only two companies was there indication that the division manager had initiated the decision. Ultimately the decision was always made by corporate officers, with the need to obtain explicit board approval if the divestment were large.

14. One executive agreed that there are sharp differences in how divestments are handled in companies that are related or are run like families as contrasted to unrelated conglomerates or holding companies that are run like orphanages and where any of the children are adoptable—for a price.

15. Nees, "Increase Your Divestment Effectiveness."

16. Such a dependency argues against telling the senior executive; however, evidence indicates that after a period of dealing with their own trauma, division managers do reorient themselves to help corporate sell the unit.

17. In fact, the corporate executive in charge of the first wave of divestitures died of a heart attack. A research assistant visited the general counsel in charge of the second wave of divestitures. The hectic pace of the office indicated that the stress level was extremely high.

18. Items 5, 8, and 9 have also been identified by Nees. She combined items 4 and 7 in the role of information supplier. Nees, "Increase Your Divestment Effectiveness."

19. The same executive went on to say that executives in his company had been fired after bringing in a proposal to buy out their unit.

20. This argument might well lend support to the conclusion not to inform the unit's manager that the unit is for sale. However, corporate management will have to weigh the risk of the rumor mill's informing the unit management and the possible reaction to such information's being withheld. Unless the divestiture is to be announced publicly shortly after unit management is informed, unit management is placed in the conflictual position of having to keep information from their subordinates. Under such circumstances, the position of the unit management may well be untenable.

21. Nees, "Increase Your Divestment Effectiveness," p. 121.

22. Ibid., p. 122.

23. Ibid.

24. One company had three divestitures that were leveraged buy-outs.

25. I am differentiating here between the operational purchase of assets and the legal purchase of assets. Buyers prefer the transaction to be in the legal form of an asset purchase since buyer liability is more limited than if the purchase transaction is for stock (the purchase of the ongoing business).

26. Nees, "Increase Your Divestment Effectiveness."

4
Carrots? Sticks? Rewards? Sops? Which to Use and When

he behavior of senior executives in the about-to-be-divested unit can be critical in maintaining the value of the unit during the time to divestiture completion. Indeed the unit's senior management can add to the value of the unit during marketing and negotiation. What can be done to elicit the desired behavior? The answer to this question depends on a number of factors: the stage of the process, when the individual is informed of the impending divestiture and invited to participate in the process, and what incentives are available to administer in the situation (figure 4–1). Essentially there are four questions to ask in order to design support and compensation packages to gain the maximum cooperation of members of the unit to be divested:

1. What stage of the process is the divestiture currently in?
2. Who plays what roles in this stage; that is, what behavior is needed?
3. What incentives (including carrots, sticks, rewards, and sops) are available for use?
4. In considering company-wide equity and the intensity of need for behaviors, which of the incentives will be used?

The Stages

Organizations require different roles and behaviors of individuals at the various stages. Three stages—problem identification, alternative development, and implementation—suffice to describe the divestiture process.[1]

Stage 1: Problem Identification

In stage 1, organizations develop an awareness of the need for divestiture and (often but not always) inform managers. The circumstances that trigger identification of the need for divestment are varied and usually multiple.

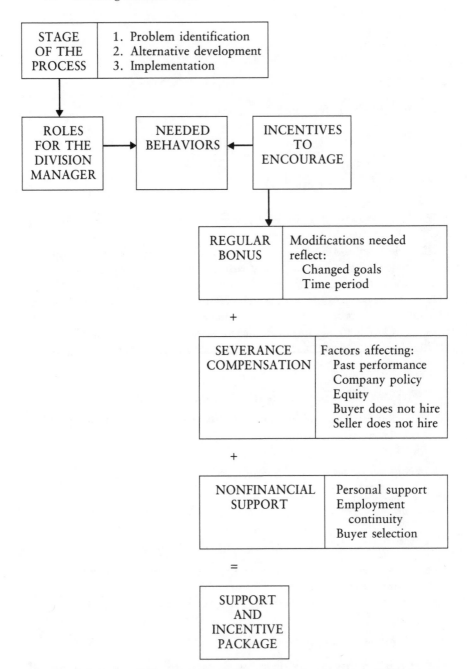

Figure 4–1. Managing the Unit to Be Divested: Incentives and Support for Personnel

Corporate, as well as the division, should view the divestiture with as proactive a stance as possible. Proactive response to divestiture is often difficult for unit management; it may not even be easy for corporate to develop. Approaching divestiture with a proactive stance is especially difficult in first divestitures, early in the process, and in situations where the subsidiary's situation is problematic. Whether corporate will develop a proactive manner depends on the reason for the divestiture, as well as the prevalent attitude in the corporate cadre (that is, the corporate culture).

Stage 2: Development of Alternatives

Once corporate identifies the unit situation as problematic, it must develop alternative approaches. Initially corporate executives are likely to consider alternatives other than divestiture. Capital budgeting approaches (such as, net present value) are useful to compare the alternatives; however, the actual alternatives must also consider the feasibility of implementation.

The divestment alternative remains problematic, as another author has noted, "Divestment is a last-resort decision, taken when other decisions have failed or when their outcome does not satisfy the decision makers. Therefore the main decision criterion is one based not on capital budgeting theory, but on return on management time."[2]

Stage 3: Implementation

Implementation has five subprocesses: negotiation with the potential buyers, internal negotiations, internal communications, external communications, and postdivestiture rationalization.

Negotiation with Potential Buyers: This subprocess has four steps: initial contact, exchange of information, general agreement, and negotiation on specific items. Sometimes there are multiple actors in this phase, and in other instances, the negotiator and decision maker is one person.[3]

The first two issues, initial contact and exchange of information, are covered in greater depth in chapter 5. The negotiation process, including establishing a price target or range and identifying and contacting potential buyers, is the focus of chapter 7. To establish price target and ranges, companies use classic financial information and analysis including financial forecasts, net book values, and multiples of earnings; however, qualitative assessment also enters into establishing a target price, choosing potential buyers, and negotiating. Qualitative issues include assessment of the unit from the potential buyer's viewpoint[4] and the new owner's expected treatment of unit personnel.

Internal Negotiations: Internal negotiations cover a number of issues, including working out the roles the unit manager will play. In some instances, unit and

corporate management may have to renegotiate aspects of the unit union contracts. In the set of firms in this study, no firms noted difficulty with union
negotiations, although there was labor representation among employees in
several firms.

Internal Communications: Usually this consists of group and individual
meetings. One of the most extensive processes for informing personnel occurred
in Medical Industry Suppy Inc. (MISI), where corporate representatives went
to each site and met with the employees. It also engaged personnel specialists
and other managers with whom unit employees could make individual appoint-
ments to talk over such issues as pension, health benefits, and career issues.
MISI prided itself on the integrity of its dealings with employees, as well as
prospective buyers.

External Communication: External communication consists of notifying the
press and significant clients and suppliers. Considerable care needs to be
exercised in choosing the timing, message, and media for informing external
parties. These announcements are part of the signaling process for both the
selling party and the buying company. Among the companies in this project,
timing of public announcements varied from postdivestiture announcements
to predivestiture announcements of multiple units for sale without specifica-
tion of particular units. Information was given selectively to buyers and suppliers depending on the perceived need to allay concerns and elicit confidence
in the unit's future business viability.

Postdivestiture Resolution: Postdivestiture issues included the need to integrate
unit personnel into the new company, as well as rationalization of the divestiture
experience by executives and unit managers in the selling company. With its
new systems and organizational structure, the new parent sometimes presented
difficulties for unit employees. A great deal of the responsibility for acclimating
unit employees, as may be expected, fell on the shoulders of the acquirer, but
the seller often helped ease the transition.

In one instance, the unit's senior executive was, to his surprise, not offered
a position with the new firm; however, his former immediate subordinates called
him when they found the new environment constraining. The unit executive
described one such situation when a former subordinate telephoned him to
express anger that the furniture and pictures in his office had just been sten-
ciled with the identification of the new company. The former subordinate felt
insulted and humiliated. The stenciling had been carried out without notifica-
tion (it was a routine procedure for newly acquired equipment in the much
larger company). The unit's former senior executive explained that the former
parent was a large conglomerate that allowed its units to run quite autonomously. His unit was a medium-sized company in its industry and without the

formality of policies and procedures of many of the larger firms. His former subordinate was thus reacting to the constraints of the new corporate parent, a much larger company in the unit's industry.

Another postdivestiture issue is the rationalization process, which occurs among managers at both the corporate and unit levels. During this research program, the researchers had opportunity to interview at a corporate site very shortly after the divestiture was concluded and then again a few months later. It was noteworthy how much clearer the rationale for divesting had become between the first and second encounters.

Rationalization also occurs within the unit and often takes the form of "We are better off than if. . ." Division managers may find their current circumstances less favorable than with the former parent. In one instance, the unit head explained that the former corporate parent had been generous with him over the years and that he was within eighteen months of retirement. Implied was that he could endure the situation for eighteen months. In most instances where unit management was dissatisfied, individuals tended to leave the firm within several months. In this instance the unit executive had elected to remain until retirement because of his ties with unit employees.

Organizational Actors

The actors in the divestiture process are many and at various levels. In this discussion, we assume a complex diversified company consisting of the levels depicted in figure 1–6. Figure 4–2 indicates the frequency with which different organizational levels were observed to play various roles in the divestiture stages. It is clear that among the firms in this study, the focal person was usually the CEO who went to the board primarily for advice and approval and who delegated various implementation activities to lower levels. In smaller companies (or where the divested unit was relatively large), the CEO was more likely to play a greater number of roles in the process. In some instances because of the CEO's preferred personal style, he or she was heavily involved in acquisition and divestment activities.

Corporate Support Actions for Division Management

It is preferable that corporate as well as the division executives view the divestiture with as proactive a stance as possible. Figure 4–3 suggests the relationship between how the situation is perceived and the expected attitude on the part of the managers.

Viewing divestiture in a proactive manner is not always easy for corporate executives. The situation is especially difficult in first divestitures, early in the

Stage in the Divestment Process	Board of Directors	CEO	CFO	Vice-President of Strategic Planning	Group President (or Vice-President)	Head of the Division
				Level in the Organization		
I. Identification						
1. Corporate difficulties	Usually	Usually	Usually	Usually	Frequently	Sometimes
2. Unit difficulties	Not usual (unless unit is large)	Usually	Usually	Usually	Usually	Usually
II. Development of alternatives	Sometimes	Usually	Usually	Usually	Usually	Frequently
III. Implementation						
1. Negotiation with potential buyers						
Initial contact	Sometimes	Frequently	Sometimes	Sometimes	Sometimes	Sometimes
Exchange of information	Sometimes	Frequently	Frequently	Usually	Frequently	Frequently
General agreement	Sometimes	Frequently	Frequently	Usually	Frequently	Sometimes
Negotiation on specific items	Sometimes	Sometimes	Frequently	Usually	Frequently	Sometimes
2. Internal negotiations	Sometimes	Sometimes (especially if large unit)	Frequently	Frequently	Sometimes	Frequently
3. Internal communications	Not Usual	Usually	Frequently	Frequently	Frequently	Frequently
4. Formal approval	Usually (unless unit is small)	Always (unless unit is very small)	Usually	N.A.	N.A.	N.A.
5. External communications	Frequently (to help formulate)	Frequently	Frequently	Frequently	Sometimes	Not usual
6. Postdivestiture resolution	Sometimes	Usually	Frequently	Frequently	Sometimes	Usually

Continuum: Always, usually, frequently, sometimes, not unusual, or never (or N.A., not applicable).

Figure 4–2. Frequency with Which Various Organizational Levels Are Involved in Stages of Divestiture

If the situation is viewed as an	Opportunity	Problem	Problem	Crisis
The manager's attitudes toward change are likely to be	Proactive	Reactive or adaptive	Passive	Reactive

Source: Danielle B. Nees, "The Divestment Decision Process in Large and Medium-Sized Diversified Companies: A Descriptive Model Based on Clinical Research," *International Studies of Management and Organization* 8, no. 4 (Winter 1978–1979): 76.

Figure 4–3. Perceptions of the Situation and Management Attitude

problem identification stage, and in situations where there are strong ties with unit management. Whether corporate will approach the divestiture in a proactive manner also depends on the prevalent attitude in the executive cadre and the corporate culture.

For board members and corporate executives, the divestiture decision and implementation is part of their ongoing responsibilities; very little needs to be done with regard to their compensation and support activities. This observation especially holds true where corporate executive compensation is heavily linked with corporate performance, that is, through bonuses tied to profits or, especially, stock options. The focus for creativity in compensation package redesign is necessarily on personnel in the unit to be divested.[5] Among the firms in this study, compensation redesign occurred for four levels of unit personnel: the head of the unit, his or her immediate subordinate managers, other managers and supervisors, and lower-level employees.

The major purpose of corporate support actions—including compensation changes, attention to employment continuity, and personal support—was to move unit executive's perception as far along the crisis-to-opportunity continuum as possible.

In approaching the issue of compensation modification, as well as other support actions for unit executives, corporate must consider three aspects of the expected context. First, the time from the decision to the time when the deal with the buyer is expected to be consummated has to be estimated. Second, the decision has to be made as to when to inform the individuals under consideration for revised rewards about the impending divestiture. Finally, the decision has to be made when to tell the various other individuals in the unit to be divested. These decisions are not independent. The longer the time period is, the more likely it is that the individuals in the unit are told earlier in the process (not necessarily earlier in elapsed time). The most difficult circumstances in this study were those when the individual was explicitly told about the divestiture early in the process and the time period to completion of the deal with the buyer was unexpectedly lengthy. The situation was exacerbated when more and more buyers considered and rejected the unit. Indeed, in these instances, the anxiety level of unit personnel could become quite high.

Informing an executive that the subsidiary he or she manages is about to be divested is troublesome. One executive recounted a particularly difficult situation:

> Ernie had come on as vice-president of Subsidiary A only two weeks prior to the board's decision to divest. He was known as a comer and well respected. He had been wooed by our original long-range plans for the operation. I went to him almost immediately with the news, and then I sat down with him and his wife in their home. It wasn't easy. It never is. They had just moved halfway across the continent. But we worked out what later he told me was a very fair compensation package. When the firm was sold, he was paid a portion because he had been involved in finding the buyer. We asked him to stay on with our company, but he went with the subsidiary. We worked out an employment contract with the buyers as part of the total package. He feels, and I do too, that we treated him fairly but it was painful, . . . painful as hell.

In Ernie's case, having corporate support actions delineated at this first meeting assisted in softening the news.

A major key to the appropriate and effective involvement of unit personnel in the divestiture process is the use of financial remuneration packages. A number of issues affect the design of these financial remuneration systems. The following exchange between two corporate executives captures some of these aspects.

> *Executive 1:* Should you create incentive systems to turn around the business before you sell it? [When] telling them [unit executives] it's for sale, should you give incentives for people to stay? . . . And the longer you stay, the bigger the bonus is so you keep management in place. Should you create incentive systems that I call "security blankets" so they don't have to fear they're going to lose their jobs, so they will stay so you can implement the turnaround [prior to] sale? . . . I would recommend strongly that you have all these questions answered so that he [unit executive] knows where the hell you are going.

> *Executive 2:* I agree on that completely because we've handled it, and we've made the mistake of handling it without having it [other issues having to do with role of unit executives] weren't even thought through.

> *Executive 1:* That's interesting—'cause more or less we came to the same conclusion. . . . I'm a believer, by the way, that you have the whole thing settled [referring to the decision and compensation programs] before you walk in the door to tell this guy the bad news.

It is especially noteworthy that these executives strongly supported having compensation packages arranged before announcing the divestiture to unit management.

Corporate support actions with regard to the division manager went beyond compensation matters in this study. Four kinds of corporate actions were observed. Two related to compensation: the first to type of compensation (severance pay, bonus, and commission) and the second to timing of payments. The other two kinds of corporate action that were part of corporate support for the division manager related to employment continuity issues and personal support. Employment continuity posed three options: selection of a buyer positively disposed toward unit management, placement within the parent, and outplacement support. The corporate actions had multiple purposes and took into consideration several issues including recognition of past employment, reduction of personal anxiety level, behavior needed or expected during the divestiture process, and facilitation of loyalty shift when the executive was to work for the new parent company. The relationships between these corporate actions and their intended purposes are summarized in figure 4–4.

Severance Pay

Corporate effected severance pay when the buyer did not have a position for the individual and corporate did not want the individual or had no appropriate position available. A unit executive explained:

> All the management people except the two mentioned went with us. So no special termination financial arrangements were necessary for other management personnel. The two management people mentioned stayed with the parent company. Any other individuals that did not go with the divested unit to the new buyer were given severance pay or offered an opportunity to move to corporate.

Regard for past performance, and especially length of employment, was recognized through the severance payment. Severance was generally based on some portion of the person's salary modified by the length of time he or she had worked for the company. Thus, an individual might get a week or month of pay for every year worked for the company. Termination might also include payout of vested pension funds or profit-sharing funds. Although not strictly severance pay, these amounts were paid at termination and functioned as severance from the employees' viewpoint. The treasurer of Medical Supplies Company explained how his company handled termination: "If the buyer didn't want them [managers] or didn't have a place for them, they got full invested retirement benefits and some sort of severance package, which usually consisted of X number of months salary."

Modifying Bonus Packages

Most firms indicated that they did not design (or redesign) bonus compensation packages explicitly to recognize the division manager's contribution to

Corporate Support Actions	Frequency of Use	Recognize Past Contributions	Encourage Usual Required Behaviors During Divestiture Period				Less Frequently Required Behavior		Comments
			Reduce Anxiety	Maintain morale and productivity of the unit	Host buyer and during due diligence visits	Assist in transition period	Help find buyer	Facilitate loyalty shift	
Kind of payment									
Severance	Always	xx	x	—	—	—	—	—	Severance is an accepted social norm and was connected with length of service and level in the organization
Bonus	Frequently	x	x	xx	x	—	x	—	Bonus systems were usually in place for management. The issues were: Should the bonus be modified? If divestiture occurs midyear, what proportion of the regular bonus should be paid?
Commission	Not usual	—	—	—	—	—	xx	—	In some instances the modified bonus was very much like a commission since it was dependent on getting the unit sold at the target price or qualitative assessment of how helpful the individual had been in the process

Corporate action	Frequency							Intended purpose
Timing of payment (usually half now and half at end of stipulated time postdivestiture)	Frequently	—	—	—	—	xx	x	It was usual to make payment conditional upon the manager's staying with the buyer for a specified period of time. If the buyer did not want the manager, he or she was released from the obligation, and the entire amount was paid.
Continued employment								
Find buyer that wants unit management	Sometimes	xx	x	—	—	xx	xx	Continuity of employment depended on whether the buyer wanted or needed the manager and (if not) the needs at corporate and how well respected the unit manager was.
Placement in parent	Sometimes	xx	x	—	—	x	—	
Outplacement	Usually (available)	x	—	—	—	—	—	
Personal support from next level of management	Frequently	x	xx	x	x	x	xx	Top management frequently recognized the need to reduce the anxiety. The issue of loyalty shift was less frequently recognized explicitly.

Note: —: no connection; x: moderate connection; xx: strong connection.

Figure 4–4. Corporate Actions and Intended Purposes

the divestiture. The reasons appeared to be either that the time to divestiture was short and the unit executive's contribution minimal or, more frequently, the bonus system in place was adequate to the situation. One firm specifically referred to the strong MBO system that was in place and the master contract that was worked out with key executives. The master contracts could be negotiated to incorporate the division manager's activities during the divestiture process. This firm did, however, occasionally design special bonuses for executives who were assigned temporary roles in subsidiaries undergoing divestment.

In one company, a set of special bonuses was negotiated for the division managers who were expected to play key roles in managing the subsidiary during the short but unsettling time of public solicitation and bidding and also during the period of transition to the new owners. In two other companies, special bonuses related to divestiture were a matter of policy. One executive explained:

> Our company has a regular bonus plan which remained in effect. If divestment occurs midyear, managers receive a pro rata portion of that bonus. In addition, a one-time discretionary bonus is worked out for the top two or three division managers. The amount of the bonus is based on corporate executives' evaluation of the effort and work put forth in getting the divestment done.

Bonuses and Setting Interim Goals

Modified bonuses were also connected to revamping strategic and operational goals for the unit during the divestiture period. The intent of modifying unit goals is to return maximum possible value to the parent company from the unit. Three basic alternatives are available: grow, business as usual, or trim. In most instances, the companies in this study either continued with business as usual or trimmed; however, at least two firms were on a growth, albeit modest growth, trend. Subsidiaries are divested for numerous reasons. The interim goals for the subsidiary are heavily dependent on these reasons for divesting.

In some instances where the subsidiary is in a growth mode, the subsidiary is reasonably self-sufficient, that is, the growth experienced by the subsidiary can be supported by its own internally generated funds. In other instances, funds are required from the parent company. Normally, however, an about-to-be-divested subsidiary does not have high priority for capital allocations. But there are instances where infusion of new capital may be useful. For example, additional marketing effort may be needed in order to give the subsidiary a jump on competitors that are expected to introduce competing products. The value of the subsidiary may be severely dampened if the new products make inroads into subsidiary sales.

Similar scenarios could be painted for advances in R&D, manufacturing processes, control systems, and new approaches to promotion and advertising. The parent company has to assess the risk of these interim investments.

The potential values for the parent firm can be evaluated by discounted cash flows of various scenarios, which include competitive reaction to various levels of capital commitment. At least one other kind of risk needs to be considered. There is little advantage in attempting to add to the value of the subsidiary if to do so severely damages the position of potential purchasers or increases the price of the subsidiary beyond the limits they may want to consider.

Trimming the firm calls for withdrawing resources in anticipation of divestiture. A subsidiary whose sales and profits are down is likely to be a candidate for trimming. Reducing funds available for accounts receivable and inventory are two commonly used initial moves to remove funds from a subsidiary. Making operations as efficient as possible is also appropriate to generate funds. Care must be taken, however, not to damage the existing sales momentum permanently.[6] If possible, sales efforts should be increased.

On one hand, an increase in sales effort is unlikely if the organization suspects an impending divestiture.[7] Top sales representatives are likely to be the first to leave since alternatives are often readily available for them. The situation is compounded if the information comes to the sales group through the rumor mill. One strategy for thwarting wholesale desertion is to make the divestiture decision known[8] and offer generous compensation packages for those willing to stay and work to increase the subsidiary's value as much as possible. A compensation package can include a restructuring of commission rates and severance packages dependent on timing and sale of the subsidiary.

Determining goals is a first step in establishing and implementing the value-enhancing strategy. One difficulty is that the objectives of the unit executives may be at cross-purposes with those of the company. If the unit executives are considering purchase, their concern may be to attain as low a value for the subsidiary as possible. Actions designed to attain maximum value for the parent company may not therefore be in alignment with unit management intent. For example, the parent company may be interested in trimming accounts receivables and inventories in order to release cash for the parent company. Subsidiary executives, on the other hand, may prefer to encourage sales growth with programs that maintain or increase the inflow of funds for current assets. A similar situation of cross-purposes may arise if the executives are supporting sale to a buyer with whom they have close ties. While no hard and fast rules are possible, confronting the alternatives and the needs of all parties is critical.

Once the basic strategy for the interim period is established, the compensation package for subsidiary executives can be modified to reflect targeted goals. If higher sales and profitability are targets, larger portions of bonus should be dependent on these measures. If free cash flow through trimming is the target, the bonus should be predicated on this performance measure. Alternatives, adapted from a suggestion by an executive in the study, are depicted in figure 4–5.

	Alternative		
Regular	Interim Strategies		Bonus Proportions
Bonus	Grow	Trim	Dependent On
33%	40%	15%	Sales growth
33	25	25	Return on assets (profitability)
33	35	60	Free cash flow

Figure 4–5. Alternative Bonus Structures

At the division level, remuneration may be dependent on a number of criteria. The usual basis for division bonuses is an emphasis on earnings growth or return on investment. Emphasis on growth or even returns may be appropriate or unrealistic, especially for a unit destined for divestiture. An executive explained the effect in his companies of modified goals and bonus plans:

> We went dramatically from earnings per share, which is the classical way for companies, to totally free cash flow. . . . Now that's a change in culture! Most board members don't know what you're talking about. . . . They're all beat in the head with earnings, earnings, earnings.

Indeed goals and compensation systems can shift from year to year for various units even in the absence of divestiture:

> What's your strategic plan by operating unit—maybe one year you want earnings; maybe one year you want to shrink the business [and] get the investment down. Give those guys compensation plans that you thought out and guess what? They'll figure out how to do it . . . so the key thing, I'll maintain, is that you get the right incentive plan that you think out and leave them alone. I think you'll be amazed at what they can accomplish. . . . That's been my experience.

On the other hand, the bonus or some portion of it may be based on corporate's subjective judgment. The following interviewer and executive interchange explains:

> *Interviewer:* So you really didn't realign salary packages except the special bonus for the division executives.
>
> *Executive:* No.
>
> *Interviewer:* How did you determine the level of the bonus? Was it based on a price or subjective evaluation?

Executive: It was subjective evaluation of who was essential. It was more by the job and what they were doing. You know, some jobs you say, "Well, if this person finds a job and leaves, we can get along without him. We can fill in or hire somebody else." [If] it was somebody like the chief accounting office, it would have been a terrible thing to have one of them leave under that circumstance and you said, "We want you to stay until the buyer has a chance to say whether he wants you or not. And if he doesn't want you, we will either keep you or we'll give you [a severance package]." In most cases it was one year's pay for having stayed on. Because otherwise a fellow would say, "I've got a chance at a job now and, if I pass that up, then you let me go, I might not have a job." So we said, "All right, to protect you against that we'll . . ."

Interviewer: And you put that in writing?

Executive: Yes. . . . We only paid a bonus if the buyer didn't want them [and] we sold them out of the job. . . . We said to them "You'll have the job, and if you don't have the job, we'll pay you a bonus."

Commission Bonus

A third type of compensation occurred in at least two instances: the unit-level executives were paid a bonus depending on the price obtained for the unit—in essence, a commission on the sale. In one case, the firm varied the bonus with the price obtained for the unit (figure 4–6). In the other, unit executives were promised the bonus only if the target price was met. A senior unit executive in this company explained the rationale behind the commission arrangement:

The top twenty people in the [unit] received some kind of settlement. It was necessary in my rationale because they would be in contact [with] people from the companies that were interested in buying the property. And we wanted them all positive as far as the way they talked about the sale and proposed sale. And, I guess, in a sense, it's buying one last minute of loyalty, because everybody wasn't like I was, who was anxious to try some things of my own. A lot of these people were career oriented and wanted to stay with a big company.

The case of the Dancer unit, related in figure 4–6, illustrates the most creative and widest range of compensation alternatives observed among the firms studied.

There was, however, serious disagreement among the companies in the study about the use of a commission-oriented bonus. One general counsel suggested that such a commission was impossible for a firm in serious financial difficulty; he used International Harvester as an example. The CFO of another firm argued that firms should base commission bonuses on the augmented price above the estimated most likely price. He pointed out that paying even up to 30 percent of the amount over the originally expected price still left the parent

Consumer Products Company had three units to be divested, which together comprised about 20 percent of the parent company sales. The restructured reward systems for the senior managers of each unit were comparable in form. The focus here is on Dancer.

During the late 1970s expectations for Dancer were high. As Ralph Henson, Dancer's division manager, put it, "We were out to tackle the world." A product that the division had acquired and developed had great promise. As it turned out, the product could not be brought to market in the manner in which the unit anticipated, and much of the expected increase in the division's sales did not materialize. Henson said, "I knew the company was for sale before anyone else did, [but] the divestiture didn't come as a surprise." It was a difficult time. Said Henson: "We couldn't look a guy in the face during the divestiture." Under such circumstances, one would expect employees to flee the unit wholesale. But of the dozen sales staff, only one left. One salesman was offered a 30 percent bonus to join another company but rejected the offer. Corporate was surprised at the response of the sales force. Henson was described by a senior corporate executive as "very hirable, very known in the industry." But he too stuck with the unit.

What made the difference? Henson and the CFO (who had primarily responsibility at corporate for the divestiture program and to whom all the units to be divested were reassigned to report) worked out remuneration packages ahead of time. The packages had several components:

1. Severance packages were designed.

2. Greater emphasis was placed on profitable growth and especially on free cash flow during the expected time it would take for the sale. The regular bonuses for the manager were revised to reflect these modified goals.

3. Corporate wanted the four senior managers in the division to help sell the division. All were offered the opportunity to earn a commission on the ultimate sales price. The commission increased as the price of the unit increased. Corporate was satisfied that all four subsidiary executives had helped to try to find buyers.

4. Retaining sales people was considered the key to maintaining the value of the company. Sales representatives were offered special one-time bonuses of 25 percent of their regular compensation if they stayed through the completion of the transaction.

Henson was given considerable latitude in revamping the company to ready it for divestiture, with one exception: the CFO mandated that the unit run lean and that inventories be reduced while maintaining full sales effort.

Dancer was the most difficult of the three units to sell; it was on the market for eighteen months, with a number of companies approached concerning possible acquisition. How did the employees react during the time? Henson put it this way, "We were out to prove the company was good."

Figure 4–6. Consumer Products Company and the Dancer Unit

firm with 70 percent of the unexpected windfall. The general counsel acknowledged the argument but pointed out that in International Harvester's situation, it would have been politically impossible to get approval from the board of directors for the payment of such bonuses.

The chairman and founder of M&A Consulting Firm also took sharp difference with the idea of a commission bonus. When asked to evaluate the idea of paying division management on the basis of the purchase price of the subsidiary, he strongly opposed the idea, reasoning that such a bonus was contrary to the implicit contract that the division manager had with the corporate firm. The manager was supposed to act in the best interest of corporate and also in the best interests of the subsidiary. Giving the unit manager a bonus based on an augmented price of the firm put him in more conflict than would otherwise be necessary.

Timing of Payment

One usual condition of bonuses was that division managers were paid a portion of the bonus some months after divestiture took place and then only if the manager stayed with the subsidiary during the transition period. A manager released by the buyer was released from his or her commitment, and the bonus was paid.[9]

Employment Continuity

All levels of unit employees become concerned about the continuity of their employment when divestiture is announced; senior unit managers are not exempt from this anxiety. Several executives talked about various aspects of corporate response to employment continuity. There were three options:

1. Moving as unit head with the subsidiary to the new owner.
2. Placement in the parent company if the buyer did not have a place for the unit executive(s) and if the current parent company was favorably disposed toward the unit executive and had an appropriate slot.
3. Outplacement support.[10]

Two executives talked about bonus payments and employment continuity efforts in their companies:

> The company takes two approaches. In some instances, it would be before the sale. They go to the people and take a more "formal approach." They tell the individuals that the people [potential buyers] to whom they have talked are likely to keep them on. [But] we will promise to protect them during that period of time. To the top people, we give a bonus.. It is a flat sum, not tied

to the purchase price. We pay the bonus in advance. If it does not work out for them with the buyer of the company, we will help them. If we cannot find them a position in corporate, we will set up a severance pay package and give placement help.

We're not always as open as we'd like to be. It's something you have to be very careful about, you know. But in this instance we decided definitely we were going to do it. We felt that within a month or so, they were going to know anyway, and so it was better for us to be up front about it. . . . And you tell a few top people that they're going to be taken care of, that they're either going to the buyer and if the buyer doesn't want them or have a job for them, we'll find a job for them somewhere else in our company. With some people, particularly going down a few steps in management, you say, "If you stay on until we terminate, we'll pay you a bonus of some sort."

Personal Support

Several corporate executives described the effort that they gave to key personnel in the form of "hand holding." They found it necessary to be supportive in many instances when they made the initial announcement. The example of Ernie is an instance where the corporate executive spent a great deal of time with the unit executive. Another unit head, whose chairman had spent three months persuading him that the proposed divestiture was an appropriate decision, talked about the lengthy time he spent with the next level of his subordinates. He went to each of the ten individually.

Late in the divestiture process, there is a need to let go of these personal relationships so that unit executives can transfer loyalty to the new parent.

Loyalty Shift

Several executives mentioned the need to recognize loyalty shift.[11] For example, one said, "Their loyalties go the other way [to the purchaser]" in explaining the need for incentive plans. Another gave explicit recognition to the need to keep division executives loyal to the interests of corporate during what turned out in two cases to be a three-year search for a buyer. The company designed specially tailored compensation packages for each executive at the beginning of the process. A third noted, "Their loyalties remain with the host company until a serious buyer comes along. The buyer says, 'I have to have private conversations with the division manager,' and we say 'Fine'. The manager recognizes that's when his conflicts begin. . . . We have to be tolerant of it [the conflict and shift in loyalty]." Another firm, however, denied there was much difficulty with loyalty shift. The executive said, "People working in the businesses are going to be working for an employer, [and there is] going to be a tendency to want that business to be successful."

The major difficulties seem to arise around two circumstances: when the division executives are potential buyers and at the time the buyer needs to begin his or her relationship with key division managers. In one instance, corporate executives felt that division executives did not act in the best interest of the parent firm, and the matter was in litigation at the time of early interviews. No other company, however, indicated any specific instances where it appeared that a division manager had betrayed the original parent company in the interest of the buyer.

Summary

This chapter has focused on the support systems that corporate put into place for unit executives. Among corporate efforts were compensation changes including severance pay, modification of bonuses, and commission bonuses. Corporate also usually took cognizance of employment continuity through buyer selection, placement within corporate, or outplacement. In addition, corporate often provided support in the form of personal relationships and time spent with the unit executive. The purposes of these support systems included recognizing past performance, encouraging required behavior, and facilitating loyalty shift. The overarching purpose was to move the unit executive's perception of the divestiture as a crisis to that of the divestiture as an opportunity for both the unit and its senior executive.

Recommendations for Corporate Executives

1. Initially unit executives are likely to view the divestiture announcement negatively. Changes in compensation, assurance of employment continuity, and personal support can be effective in helping a unit executive to view the divestiture as an opportunity.

2. Changes in compensation, assurance of employment continuity, and personal support have different intended purposes. Included are recognizing past performance, encouraging behaviors that corporate needs to effect the divestiture, and effecting loyalty shift.

3. If the new owner has no position for an employee, effort should be made to find suitable placement within corporate.

4. Sometimes employment is not possible within corporate. For these managers, severance compensation and payment of vested pensions and profit sharing are likely to be outlined in company policy. Two creative efforts can be made for such employees: assistance in investment planning and outplacement services.

5. Not all support and incentives are monetary. The outplacement services, although dollar based, are one example. The personal presence of one or more corporate executives can contribute much to anxiety reduction and shaping of behavior.

6. Openness during many organizational processes is useful, and no less so during divestiture. Openness can be manifest in willingness to listen and to provide information. Both are necessary for clear communication. Employees at every level in the organization possess information needed by the level above. Each level acts as a screen for the next level. Each level of management, therefore, should develop relationships with critical employees so that significant negative information will be readily proffered. Only through establishing such an early warning system can each level of management ensure early identification, analysis, and action.

Recommendations for Division Executives

1. Corporate executives are often novices at informing division personnel with regard to impending divestiture. As a result, they may handle the announcement badly.

2. Corporate should have considered both compensation and employment continuity issues; they may not have. If not, your initiative during the first meeting regarding divestiture, or more naturally, during a second meeting is to ask for delineation regarding these issues.

3. Your compensation will heavily depend on the roles corporate intends for you to play. Negotiation around these issues is appropriate but must be handled with care.

Notes

1. Danielle B. Nees, "The Divestment Decision Process in Large and Medium-Sized Diversified Companies: A Descriptive Model Based on Clinical Research," *International Studies of Management and Organization* 8, no. 4 (Winter 1978–1979): 67–93.

2. Ibid., p. 78.

3. Nees observes differences in bureaucratic versus organic organizations. Ibid.

4. Nees aptly puts the findings from her study: "Thus, contrary to what has been stated in much of the literature on divestment, the divestors do foresee the advantages of divestment from the buyer's viewpoint. They do so not with sophisticated financial tools, but rather, in qualitative terms." Ibid., p. 83. She suggests no definite price is fixed at the beginning but only a minimum level below which no proposition will be considered. In this study, that minimum level was usually book value.

5. The personnel to be considered include individuals who might receive special temporary assignment to the unit to help implement the divestiture.

6. Unless a reduction in sales can increase the profitability of the entity.

7. If the subsidiary has increasingly poor performance, there is often rumor of divestiture in any event.

8. There are, of course, instances where secrecy of divestiture plans may be necessary.

9. None of the executives interviewed noted that this had been an issue. However, I did not ask explicitly about it. Most firms are concerned that unit personnel are treated fairly with regard to compensation. When there is doubt, the issue appears to be resolved in favor of unit personnel, especially those in senior positions.

10. Often the use of office space and a secretary are critical to finding new employment. Such facilities need not be provided on company premises if the parent company finds having employees of divested subsidiaries around after divestiture impossible for insurance reasons or awkward. For executives or some sales employees, maintaining certain club privileges or attendance at key industry conventions may be highly useful in helping in a past employee search for new employment.

11. The research program identified a few instances where the first time a subsidiary manager explicitly knew his unit was slated for divestiture was when a corporate executive called and said, in essence, "You're sold." However, none of these instances was investigated from the division perspective."

5
Marketing the Unit

T he parent company has decided to divest the unit, has informed the unit management, and has designated who is to be in charge of the process of selling the unit. The set of critical tasks ahead involve marketing the unit to maximize value. The task as carried out by the firms in this study involved a number of phases, including deciding whether to use outside help, establishing a price, identifying potential buyers, signaling the impending divestiture, and putting together the information package (figure 5–1). As we shall see, the process of marketing a business unit has analogies in the proverbial 4Ps of marketing, as suggested in figure 5–2. There are numerous combinations of approaches to the various phases of marketing. In some of these phases, clear patterns arose; in other phases, patterns did not arise, although the experiences of the firms give us insight into the range of possible alternatives.

Outside Help: Bane or Blessing?

There is considerable controversy about the use of outside help: investment bankers, consulting firms, brokers, and, for smaller firms, lawyers and accountants. The following comment by the chairman of M&A Consulting Firm lends insight into the various kinds of advisers and the roles they may play:

> [Depending on] the traditional relationship of the CEO and those people, . . . it takes a different route. Many times the selling firm will give it to an investment banking firm, one on Wall Street or a local firm, and the investment banking firm will prepare the company for sale—meaning they will do the analysis, presentation materials and so forth. . . . Another [source of outside help] are brokers and finders. That's a jungle. That's a dangerous route. But sometimes the individuals involved know someone who is a broker or finder . . . [or] investment banker or whatever . . . [or] sometimes they will take certain people that they realize would be good prospects themselves. By and large it takes an intermediary . . . unless it's something that has been sought after by others before.

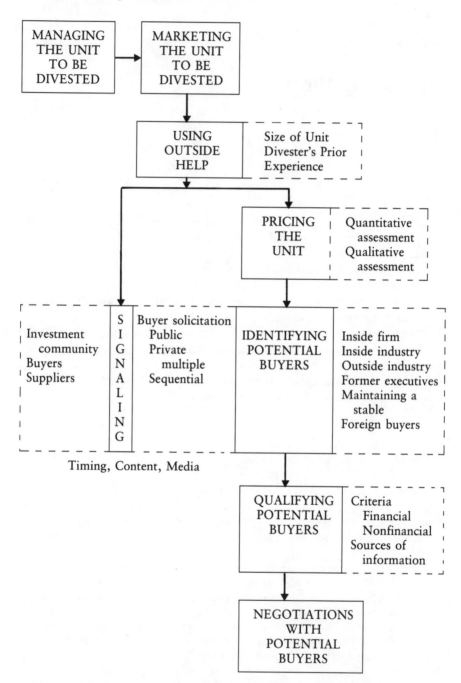

Figure 5–1. Marketing the Unit to Be Divested

Product: The unit must be defined and sometimes restructured to prepare for the sale.

Price: The acceptable price floor and a target price must be established. The ultimate price is determined by the negotiation process and is a result of the seller's original costs and estimate of market demand, as well as the reality of buyer demand for the unit.

Promotion: The company must identify the potential customers to determine what media and message to use to reach them.

Place (or distribution channel): The firm must decide whether to use inside or outside expertise at the various stages. In addition, there are decisions to be made about whether the unit's availability for sale should be made open to the public or, at the other end of the spectrum, if potential buyers should be contacted privately and sequentially. This process is part of what this chapter refers to as signaling.

Figure 5–2. Marketing a Business Unit: Analogies with the Four Ps

Whether the firm will in fact turn to outside help depends on several factors. One vice-president of strategic planning of the large and successful Technology Conglomerate stated succinctly, "Whether we get help depends on size." The buyer of one unit talked about a natural resources company from which his firm had purchased a unit:

> The selling company did not use an investment banker or any other outside consultant. . . . I personally feel, in many cases, a selling company would get a better price if they sought the advice of an investment banker or an outside person who specializes in mergers and acquisitions. Sometimes people in large corporations think they are very knowledgeable in the merger-acquisition area, and they attempt to do things themselves.

However, the use of investment bankers does not always turn out well. The vice-president of strategic planning of Technology Conglomerate explained:

> Those that we have had help with have typically not turned out well. The investment bankers—there are [different] types and they're organized to do divestitures—most of them tend to make everything into a federal case. There are swarms of young MBA types trying to get all sorts of data. . . . Recently we had [several] units for sale. It was a problem. We finally took them off the market. . . . I find it better to handle little ones myself.

Whether the company needs outside help depends upon the size and complexity of the transaction. In addition, the company must consider the expertise

		Size of Unit	
		Large	*Small*
Degree of experience with divestitures among corporate executives	High	Use advisers for selected transactions where some aspect is unfamiliar	Do not need advisers
	Low	Definite need for outside help	May use advisers for first one or two transactions

Figure 5–3. Using Outside Advisers: Relationships between Unit Size and Experience of Corporate Executives

of current corporate executives. The larger is the transaction, the more likely it is an investment banker will be used. Several executives sounded a note of caution, however. They expected that investment bankers might tend to target a price lower than the company could expect. The implication was that investment bankers need a margin of safety to ensure completion of the transaction. Figure 5–3 relates the size of the transaction and the expertise residing in corporate executives to the decision to utilize outside advisers.

Why does size make a difference? The major issue is the risk to the parent firm. The larger the size is, the more complex the transaction is likely to be, and thus the greater the risk posed to the firm. As the experience of the firms in this study indicated, however, the larger was the parent corporation and the more frequently divestiture had been carried out, the more likely the firm itself was to have the needed expertise. Are outside advisers needed when the firm has expertise? According to the former vice-chairman of a nearly $1 billion firm, "When you get the consulting report, you realize you knew 90 percent. But the consulting firm gives you that comfort of the 10 percent."

At what stage to use outside help is a critical decision. Figure 5–4 summarizes the various roles outside advisers played in the companies in this study.

Pricing the Unit

Precise values cannot be put on units because their values are contingent on what the buyer is willing to pay and what the seller is willing to take. If the buyer's range and the seller's range overlap, there is good chance they will come to a mutually agreed upon price. As we shall see, however, price is not the only issue sellers consider. Other factors, both quantitative and qualitative, must be identified, managed, and negotiated.

Usually firms do spend effort in-house on financial evaluation of the unit prior to sale. How is price established? A vice-president of business development

Stage or Task	Frequency of Use of Outside Adviser	Comments
Identification of divestiture candidates	Not usual	Will use consultant to evaluate total company portfolio. Analysis may lead to divestiture
Financial evaluation	Usual	Will use outside consultant to check analysis done inside
Informing division personnel	Unusual	No case existed in this sample
Finding buyers	Frequent	Especially if there are no readily available buyers
Initial contact	Usual	Especially if parent does not want the impending divestiture known outside a small group at corporate
Negotiation	Not unusual	May want for comfort or use for sticky issues that the two parties do not want to confront directly
Transfer of unit	Unusual	May use for advice but not for implementation

Figure 5–4. Frequency of Using Outside Advisers in Divestiture

for a $700 million company explained how his group established the price for a management buy-out transaction:

> We looked at it from several different ways. One was to take cash flows from the business that we had seen in recent years on the assumption that these should dramatically improve without putting in more cash. We made some assumptions about the future of the business, and we discounted those back to a present value. We also took a look at the assets and had in mind a certain value of what the assets would be worth and see whether that would be worth more than the discounted cash flow.
>
> It was a fairly straightforward kind of thing. A relatively low-return, no-growth business that wasn't going anywhere with us, in which there was an entrepreneur in [the buyer] who had a vision of its value that was higher than our vision of its value and that enabled us to get together on a price.

Several different approaches were usually combined to come to a range within which the divesting company will agree to negotiate. The following methods were suggested by executives involved in this study:

1. Comparing comparable units being sold.
2. Use of financial projections.
3. Market value of assets (especially real estate).
4. Need for good fit with the buyer.
5. Run cash flows from the buyer's perspective (for example, include reduced overhead and addition of new product lines).
6. Use of book value. (This method is especially critical if the unit is experiencing red ink. In these cases, executives recommended always starting negotiations above book value and working down. Companies do not like to take a book loss.)
7. Multiples of earnings.
8. Multiples of book value.
9. Expert estimates.

Usually analysis of a unit has been part of the periodic review process. The decision to divest may or may not be accompanied by a special analysis of the unit's situation; however, the formal announcement of the decision is likely to be preceded by such a focused analysis. The analysis usually falls into two categories: rational qualitative and rational quantitative.[1]

In a qualitative analysis, the attempt is made to delineate the areas where there are potential synergies between the subsidiary and the rest of the organization (figure 5–5). The addition of other subsidiaries provides an opportunity for a global analysis of the fit among the various company operations. Entities that do not fit are not necessarily slated for divestment, however. The qualitative analysis may indicate an attractive opportunity that does not fit but in the judgment of the board and/or executive committee is sufficient to warrant using the current subsidiary for a significant future focus for the firm.

The steps in quantitative analysis are briefly outlined in figure 5–6. Output from the quantitative analysis may include the expected net present value of keeping the subsidiary, the internal rate of return, and the selling value of the subsidiary at various points in time.

The decision whether to divest is not, of course, synonymous with the analysis. Sometimes the decision to divest is made prior to carrying out the analysis.[2] Regardless of whether the decision to divest is preanalysis or postanalysis, however, the top echelon of the company is usually involved.[3]

The following sections on pricing a unit examine the alternatives of book value, market value of the assets, net present value, and expert estimate. A final section underscores the need to conduct the valuation from the point of view of both buyer and seller.

Steps:
1. Delineation of critical variables in parent company's current strategy.
2. Delineation of critical variables in subsidiary's current strategy.
3. Evaluating the fit between the two

An example is given below:

Strategic Factors	Parent	Subsidiary	Points of Synergy
Marketing:			
Kinds of customers			
A	+ + +	+	*
B	+	+ + +	*
C	—	+ +	—
D	+ +	—	—
Media used			
X	+ +	+	*
Y	+	+ + +	
Channels of distribution			
M	+ + +	—	—
N	+ +	+ +	* *
O	+	+	*
Manufacturing:			
Materials used			
A	+	+	*
B	+ +	+ +	* *
C	+	+ + +	*
Processes used			
X	+ + +	+	*
Y	+ +	+ +	* *
Z	+	+	*
R&D activities			
A	+ +	+	*
B	+	+	*

Note: + + + heavy reliance; + + significant but not heavy reliance;
      + some reliance; — do not use.
      ** considerable synergy; * some synergy; — no synergy.

Figure 5–5. Steps in the Qualitative Analyses for Divestiture

1. Projection of pro forma income statements and balance sheets for subsidiary (projections may include sensitivity analysis for several scenarios, including different growth rates, sudden changes in raw material costs, labor costs, or interest rates).

2. Projections of cash flow: including income after tax + depreciation + other noncash expenses − (increases in net working capital + increases in fixed assets).

3. Application of appropriate discount rates: firm's cost of capital if risk is about the same as current firm; a higher rate if the risk is deemed higher; or determination of the internal rate of return if subsidiary is held in perpetuity or if subsidiary is disposed of in various years.*

*This latter analysis suggests the value of the subsidiary to the parent firm and the sensitivity of its value to various divestiture timings. Another approach is to use sensitivity analysis on the internal rate of return. This approach was used for Dancer, a subsidiary of Consumer Products Company; the analysis is presented later in this chapter.

Figure 5–6. Steps in the Quantitative Analyses for Divestiture

Book Value

The book value is not usually a problem to identify but may have little bearing on the actual value that the selling firm can expect from the buyer. Book value is often the lowest price that the selling firm will consider. Anything below that, and the seller must record the transaction as a loss. Firms prefer not to take a book loss. If they must, they are likely to consider timing the divestment of another unit at a time when it will show a gain so that the gain and a loss can be matched in the same fiscal year.[4] In some cases, firms set aside a reserve for such a loss when they put units to be divested in the category of discontinued businesses.

Book value to the selling firm is essentially the total value of the assets less the liabilities owed to anyone but the parent firm. Thus the book value to the selling firm may include both equity and long-term debt. Consider Dancer's balance sheet in figure 5–7. While the book value for Dancer was $2.2

Assets		Liabilities and owner's equity:	
Current assets	$2.5	Current liabilities	$1.4
Plant, property, and		Long-term debt	1.0
equipment (net)	1.9	Owner's equity	2.2
Other	.2	Total	$4.6
Total	$4.6		

Figure 5–7. Dancer, Inc. Balance Sheets, December 30, 1983 (in millions)

million, the minimum value that the parent wanted to realize for the company was $3.2 million, which consisted of the accumulated retained earnings and the contributed capital by the parent in the amount of $2.2 million and the long-term debt in the amount of $1.0 million provided by the parent company. The $3.2 million thus formed the floor of the price that the parent was willing to accept. In actuality, the parent company would have been unwilling to accept $3.2 million in early 1984, the year the decision to divest was made. At that time, Dancer was expecting significant sales growth from a new product line. The actual value of the company would depend on how the new product line performed in the marketplace.

Market Value of the Assets

The market value of the assets is essentially the liquidation value of the firm or the sale of the firm's assets. Liquidation value presupposes the firm does not continue as a going concern. In some instances, the market value of the assets may be considerably more than the book value. This situation may occur if unit assets have appreciated in value. Property values especially need to be checked, as do buildings, plants, and offices.[5] In some instances, the value of intangible assets may be considerably more than appears on the balance sheet—for example, the value of the patents associated with products. In other instances, the value of discoveries not patented, the unit's customer list, its distribution system, or the value of its brand name may far exceed the balance sheet value. If any of these values turns out to be significant, the book value is certainly not acceptable as the minimum price for the unit.

Whether the unit is worth more "dead" than "alive" is also a matter of judgment. The value of the alternate uses to which property and plant can be put may be considerably more than the value of operating the firm. Therefore the liquidation of the unit might well be considered, or consideration might be given to separating the assets financially and legally. The significantly appreciated assets can then be converted to alternate use by the parent, or the potential new owner could be invited to pay for their value. Such separation takes some preparatory effort by staff experts from finance and accounting.

Fuqua Industries, Inc. confronted real estate evaluation issues with Martin Theatres, a company J.B. Fuqua purchased in the late 1960s. Fuqua sold the last remaining piece of Martin in 1982. At the time of purchase, Martin Theatres consisted of three segments: movie theaters, a number of properties (especially drive-ins), and two television stations. Since some of the assets were incorporated into companies of their own, the predivestment separation was not as onerous as it might have been. Throughout the period of ownership, however, Fuqua had selectively sold most of Martin's drive-in locations. The locations had been purchased at the edge of towns in the 1950s and early 1960s. During the late 1960s and into the 1970s, many of the drive-in properties rose rapidly in value as they became surrounded by suburbs of growing towns. It was not unusual for the drive-in properties to be sold for four to ten times their original purchase price. Indeed, in some instances, strips of the drive-in that fronted on major roads could be sold for very high multiples and the interior land held for a longer period for continued appreciation. Finally, when the two television stations were sold for significant profit, the profit was carried into the retained earnings of the subsidiary's balance sheet. The buyer, knowing of the transaction, asked whether the profits from the television stations could be taken out of the retained earnings. Presumably the parent corporation did declare a dividend to corporate.[6]

Real estate is an area where hidden value might exist in a unit. As the Martin Theatre example demonstrates, the divesting firm should exercise care in establishing a minimum value. Executives charged with evaluation must consider the possible areas on and off the balance sheet where hidden value might exist. A potential buyer might be interested in the ongoing business and not the hidden assets. Dealing with this issue is one aspect of cleaning the unit up for sale. As one executive put it,

> You can get that business shaped up for sale. And if the unit executives are participating in the divestiture process, they think up ways to clean up the ship before it's sold. The divesting firm can then get a higher price rather than [corporate] letting the buyer have the unit at a bargain price and then the buyer cleans it up later on. . . . [The buyer] wants to buy an ongoing business and won't pay you for hidden assets. I think the unit's management knows what those hidden assets are. They are the little things the unit management wanted in the future and unit management will be willing to help you discover those things and get rid of them.

Net Present Value

The value to the firm is the present value of the future net cash flows plus the terminal value. Most experts suggest using sensitivity analysis, calculation of at least three scenarios of the net present value. One of these scenarios should correspond to the worst possible expected case, one should correspond to the most likely case, and one should correspond to the best possible expected case. The basic financial projections are likely to be available from the most recent strategic plan submitted by the unit.

In the analysis of Dancer that follows, the parent firm used sensitivity analysis and internal rate of return and ran various scenarios. The sensitivity analysis presented here, however, demonstrates the internal rate of return depending on what year the sale took place and given the assumptions.

In 1984 the estimated value of Dancer, including what was expected from the new product line, was calculated as indicated in figures 5–8, 5–9, and 5–10. The company used an internal rate of return approach instead of present value.

What do we need?
1. Develop cash forecast (10 years)
2. Calculate terminal value:
   Assume divestment at terminal
      Net asset value approach
      Market value approach
   Assume continued operation and new product line as perpetuity
3. Value the opportunity cost of not selling:
   Cash flow not received as the results of a keep decision
   Market value approach

Method:
1. Calculate the internal rate of return (IRR) of keeping the subsidiary through various periods of time.
2. Compare the IRRs giving consideration for risk differentials.

Figure 5–8. Calculating Dancer's Internal Rate of Return

Figure 5–8 outlines the methodology employed. Figure 5–9 gives the cash flows for the subsidiary from the time of this analysis in 1984 through 1992. Figure 5–10 compares the results of Dancer with two other subsidiaries. The final figure in this series, figure 5–11, outlines the company's conclusions after the analysis.

Earnings Multiple

Another way of ascertaining the possible market value of the firm is to determine the multiples for which similar firms are currently selling. If the unit is part of an industry in which there are freestanding public companies, it is likely that one or more have been sold recently enough that the multiple of the sale is relevant. If there have been recent private sales, discrete inquiry might be made of contacts, or a consultant might be engaged.

Care must be taken to ascertain that the earnings of the unit to be divested and the firm chosen for comparison are comparable. For example, if the unit being divested is heavily supported by debt obtained at nominal rates from the parent corporation, the earnings of the unit should be adjusted to reflect a market rate for the debt. Transfer prices should be examined to see if they are at market rates. Raw materials or component parts purchased from another subsidiary, for example, might create difficulties in establishing comparable earnings and cash flow from the unit.

Another caution is also in order. If the unit's activities are to be restructured in some way in preparation for sale, modifications will necessarily be made in the financial projections. Strategic and operational changes in the unit will require the cooperation of its management. In addition, the revised financial projections are also very likely to require their input. Such inquiries lead naturally

	Actual 1983	Forecast (millions of dollars)								
		1984	1985	1986	1987	1988	1989	1990	1991	1992
Sales	9.0	12.0	16.0	20.0	25.0	30.0	35.0	40.0	45.0	50.0
Assets	5.0	6.6	8.7	10.6	13.2	15.6	18.2	21.0	24.0	26.8
Current liabilities[a]	2.0	2.6	3.5	4.4	5.5	6.6	7.7	8.9	9.9	11.0
Earnings (AT)	.4	.55	.8	1.0	1.3	1.6	2.1	2.4	2.7	3.0
Cash Flow:										
Earnings after tax	.4	.55	.8	1.0	1.3	1.6	2.1	2.4	2.7	3.0
Δ Assets (increase)		(1.6)	(2.1)	(1.9)	(2.6)	(2.4)	(2.6)	(2.8)	(3.0)	(2.8)
Δ Current liabilities (decrease)		.6	.9	.9	1.1	1.1	1.1	1.1	1.1	1.1
Free cash flow		(.45)	(.4)	0	(.2)	.3	.6	.7	.8	1.2
Investment	3.0	4.0	5.2	6.2	7.7	9.0	10.5	12.2	14.1	15.8

[a]Assumed 22 percent of sales.

Figure 5-9. Cash Forecast for Dancer

Scenario I:	Expected Price in Comparing potential divestment in 1992 versus 1983		
	IRR[a]	1983	1992
Dancer	26 percent	Eight times	Ten times
Subsidiary A	17 percent	Book value plus $.5 million	Eight times earnings
Subsidiary B	8 percent	Book value	Book value

Scenario II:	Comparing potential divestment in 1987 versus 1983		
	IRR	1983	1987
Dancer	32 percent	Eight times earnings	Ten times earnings
Subsidiary A	7 percent	Book value plus $.5 million	Book value plus $5.5 million
Subsidiary B	9 percent	Book value	Book value

[a] Internal rate of return if subsidiary was held until 1992 in the first scenario and until 1987 in the second scenario. The calculations of the basic financials for subsidiaries A and B appear as appendixes 5A and 5B.

Figure 5–10. Divestiture Timing Scenarios for Three Subsidiaries

to concern on the part of the unit management and underscore that the unit management should be informed regarding the potential divestiture.

Expert Estimate

Experience with buying and selling firms leads to the development of an understanding of the market reaction to the unit. For example, the CFO of Dancer's parent company had been a principal in a small but successful New York investment banking concern. In establishing values for the subsidiaries to be sold, he was asked the estimates. In essence, he could assess the situation and give a reasonable guesstimate of how much a potential buyer might consider paying for the unit. The earnings multiples in figure 5–10 were the results of his expert estimates. Similarly, the vice-president of business development for Diversified Conglomerate Inc. indicated that the firm had always engaged in considerable hard analysis, but as time went on, corporate executives found that their own estimates were as much on target as the results from hours of working with the numbers. The value of formal analysis should not be underestimated, however, as the senior vice-president of strategic planning for

If the opportunity arises and if funds are needed, the suggested order for divestment would be:

1. Subsidiary A
2. Subsidiary B
3. Dancer

Suggested timing for each subsidiary

1. Subsidiary A:
   If held through 1987, then hold to 1992. IRR declines to a low of
      7 percent in 1987 and improves to 17 percent in 1992.
   Low IRR relative to risk indicates divestment should take place at the
      first strategic opportunity.

2. Subsidiary B:
   Little IRR sensitivity to timing of divestment.
   Low IRR (7–8 percent) relative to risk indicates divestment at first
      strategic opportunity.

3. Dancer:
   Hold through 1987 and reassess fit and compatibility with corporate
      missions and objectives at that time.
   IRR (32 percent) sufficient to offset risk.
   Consider divestment in 1987–1988 as IRR is lower in 1992
      (26 percent).

Little timing or decision sensitivity to various multiple or price scenarios.

Little decision sensitivity if future value approach is utilized in calculating discounted rate of return for Dancer and others.

Figure 5–11. Divestment Timing Proposals: Conclusions from the IRR Analysis

Food Products, Inc. pointed out: "I can't underestimate the amount of what I would consider hard financial analysis behind the scenes prior to negotiations."

Valuation from the Buyer's Point of View

Before entering into negotiations, the seller should consider the potential value of the firm from the buyer's point of view. The attempt to value the unit from the buyer's point of view should take into consideration possible synergies that the buyer might be able to effect. The value of the unit will be different with different buyers. For example, one of the buying firms reduced overhead by not taking the senior management with the division. In other instances, the buying firm may have the resources to add a new product line. Thus the seller must reevaluate the unit for each potential buyer.

The firm should have a clear idea of where the released funds will be best invested. One of the firms was positive where the funds from the divestiture would go: "We said to ourselves, 'Let's get our money out of that unit and put it into a new business activity.' That's when we decided to sell the business—not in pieces but in total."

Finding the Potential Buyers

How does a firm find a buyer? Four aspects of the process are salient: who conducts the search, the process of finding buyers, the source of leads, and qualifying the potential buyers.

Who Does the Search?

In the firms in this study, the CEO, the CFO, staff executives, group executives, and managers of the units to be divested might be involved in the search for the buyer. In some instances, one person was involved; in others, multiple people. Generally the person chosen knew the unit and could be expected to identify readily potential buyers. One observer who had broad exposure to the process explained a difference between larger and smaller firms.

> There is a variety of ways of identifying buyers, again depending on the individuals. Often executives in the divesting firm will talk to their lawyer if it's not a huge company. If you are talking about a Fortune 500 company, that's one thing; . . . a big company often has a whole department that does it mechanically. . . . Lawyers are the conventional advisers to a private company. A company that doesn't have in-house staff will use lawyers, bankers, and accountants. Investment bankers aren't necessarily the best finders of business buyers, but they are the ones that are often the most confidentially relating to the chief executive officer in the decision making.

In the set of firms in this study, no clear patterns appeared. One buyer of a divested unit explained that key geographical executives were charged with the responsibility:

> Only corporate executives in [headquarters] were encouraged to look for possible buyers. Regular personnel in the company were not involved in a major decision like that. It is usually best to have the executives find buyers, negotiate, and so forth. When you get too many people involved, problems develop like conflict of interest, productivity, rumors, and so forth. . . .

Another executive vice-president explained why in his firm the group vice-president looked for buyers:

The group VP was generally the one that was given the main thrust of looking for a buyer. The feeling was that he knew the industry better than anybody else in the corporate office. We figured he knew that generally you're better off selling to somebody in the industry.

The manager in charge of the unit to be divested can often be a useful source of potential buyers. However, involving the division manager in helping to find buyers can have both positive and negative outcomes, as the following comment illustrates:

> I think having the division manager involved does two things. In the first place, . . . employees obviously have more respect for their leadership when the leader can explain why there is a logical reason for the divestiture . . . [so] you don't discourage the division manager . . . [but] contacting potential buyers has to be done at the top level. It has to be orderly. You can't have people running around saying, "How would you like to buy our company?"

Whether the search is conducted by someone internal or external to the firm, attempt should be made in the initial phases to identify the potential list of buyers so that, the chairman of M&A Consulting Firm said, "they can analyze which is going to be the best for all concerned."

No matter who searches for buyers, the task can be frantic, as the following illustrates:

> Let's take the R&G unit. That was a big one. That was our biggest problem. R&G had so many units overseas, and overseas was where they were suffering even greater losses than they were at home. . . . We made a couple of overtures to some people, but it didn't seem likely that we were going to sell all of those overseas units to one buyer. We were going to have to sell them locally, country by country. We couldn't very well depend on the local people there because they were so far from the headquarters and from our corporate attitude, that it almost had to be somebody from here doing it. So the Group VP for R&G went over to Europe and made numerous contacts and stayed lengthy times going from one place to another trying to sell the various pieces of R&G. That was a very discouraging thing because they were small businesses. They were not doing well, you know, and then there was language, customers, all those differences.

The Process of Finding Buyers

Among the firms, at least five methods of identifying buyers occurred: public solicitation, private multiple solicitation, sequential solicitation, management buyout, and opportunism. An examination of several factors suggests the circumstances when each was appropriate (figure 5–12). Public solicitation occurred

| | Characteristics of Divested Unit | | |
Solicitation	Size	Performance	Number of Buyers Expected
Public	Large	Good	Many
Multiple private	Moderate	Moderate	Many
Sequential private	Large to small	Poor to moderate	Few to moderate
Opportunistic	Varied	Varied	N.A.

Figure 5–12. Type of Solicitation and Characteristics of Divested Unit

when the unit was large and successful, and the number of interested parties was expected to be high. Multiple private solicitations tended to occur when the unit was moderately large and moderately successful and the number of potential buyers was estimated to be large. Sequential solicitation occurred when units' size varied from large to small, performance varied from poor to moderate, and the number of interested buyers ranged from few to a moderate number. When the buyer initiated, the divested units varied in size and performance.

Public solicitation usually entailed the firm's clear announcement in the *Wall Street Journal* and other news coverage. (Figure 5–13 contains Beatrice's announcement in 1983.) In the case of Vickers, Esmark openly invited bids from qualified buyers and in fact held an open house in several areas of the country where potential buyers could examine documentation relating to Vickers's operations and assets. Open solicitation creates the situation for a lot of "tire kicking," however. If the unit is not doing well, the expectation of buyers may be that the firm is announcing a giveaway. Early in this research, one of my associates visited a firm after it had been made public that the company intended to sell multiple units. My associate found a harried member of the general counsel's office who had been charged with fielding the inquiries, qualifying potential buyers, and negotiating the transactions.

Public solicitation, as one executive vice-president said, can result in being "deluged with people that think that they're going to get a super bargain." Another executive in a major conglomerate demonstrated evidence of stress in his initial (negative) interaction with an interviewer. Later in the interview he explained the source of his harried feelings:

> I got about nine deals cooking and, you know, in the divestiture business when a company decides to change its direction and concentrate on specific core businesses, the decision of this one and that one or that one [is] to be sold happens over a long period of deliberations . . . and it's a difficult situation.

James L. Dutt, chairman, president, and CEO, said that during the next two years, Beatrice will divest itself of fifty companies with combined sales of $900 million. It will sell mostly cyclical, capital-intensive companies, Dutt said, and will consolidate its remaining businesses, step up marketing, and emphasize internal growth over acquisitions.

The charges include a $75 million divestiture reserve; a $190 million write-down of good will, mostly for Tropicana Products Inc., and a $15 million charge to finance a voluntary early retirement program. The charges will produce a fourth-quarter loss, Dutt said. . . . Nevertheless, Wall Street applauded the move. . . . Beatrice rose $1.124 to $23.125.

A strategy of extreme decentralization and growth by acquisition built the company in the 1950s and 1960s from a small dairy concern into a conglomerate boasting 9,000 products and 435 profit centers. When Dutt took over Beatrice in 1979, he tampered with the success formula only timidly, announcing that Beatrice would sell companies as well as buy them.

Mr. Dutt proceeded to unload some disappointing Beatrice units, including Dannon Co. Altogether he sold about sixty companies representing sales of about $1 billion. The 1981 annual report indicated that asset redeployment program had been completed, but the company's earning growth was sluggish. Beatrice is planning to consolidate domestic profit centers into a much smaller number of units and will ultimately end up with fifty to seventy businesses.

To illustrate his point, Dutt used the example of Beatrice's candy business. Though Beatrice has six candy companies with "excellent growth records," he said they cannot compete against the candy giants because they are managed independently of each other "and even compete against each other." Under the reorganization, the six companies making candy canes, mints, taffy, licorice and candy bars will become one company instead of six profit centers. Though the candy factories will still be scattered across the country, such functions as marketing, sales, and distribution will be centralized.

Source: Meg Cox, "Beatrice Foods to Take Charges of $280M," *Wall Street Journal*, February 17, 1983, p. 56.

Figure 5–13. Example of a Public Announcement of Multiple Divestitures

The stress was clearly evident in the office of a recently appointed general counsel. He was charged with the responsibility of managing many divestitures for which his firm had made an open solicitation. He told the researcher that his predecessor had died of a heart attack. The process of finding a buyer may be one of trial and error, mixed with a little bit of luck, as a senior executive of a major conglomerate explained:

Executive: What happened was a stroke of luck in a way. The group VPs were trying to find buyers for the particular division. As I said, in particular our man was spending a lot of his time in Europe. Meanwhile, once the announcement was in the paper, we were deluged with people saying, "I would like to buy all of it," or "I would like to buy a piece." Those inquiries came here to this office. It was very troublesome in that nine out of ten of them had no capability of buying. . . . We have one man who has a title director of corporate development who normally buys and sells little units for us. He usually would talk to them on the phone or meet with them. With many it takes just one conversation or one meeting to eliminate them. That initial contact takes them out of the running. . . .

Interviewer: So the initial cutoff was whether the person was capable of consummating the deal?

Executive: Yes, that he did have the money, that he could do it, and he did have enough knowledge of the business to do it. And so on. After that the next step was to start to talk and give them some information. We gave financial information. That's one of the advantages of announcing you're going to do it. Then you don't have to say, "Well that's confidential. I can't let you have it." We could put out information. It didn't take long after that for some of them to say, "Well, it's worse than I thought. I don't want it," or "I can't handle it." or to have them say, "Well, I'll pay you X dollars," and you say, "Well, that's such a ridiculous price, we won't even consider it."

The experiences of firms studied suggest that they need to think through the effects of making the impending divestiture public as a method of inviting solicitation. Timing of the announcement also needs to be carefully thought out.

A more limited mode of addressing multiple potential buyers occurred in the following case:

[The seller had a business described as] in a very good financial position. . . . It was a very small part of the parent [e.g., $12 million in sales while the parent had more than $1 billion in revenues]. . . . The unit was not having any great difficulties. . . . The selling company sent out an opportunity package, which included all the information on the company, to about 100 people in the United States and overseas. They asked interested buyers to contact them. In addition, the selling company also contacted some suppliers, competitors, and a few other people they knew personally. We were sent an opportunity package. The selling company did business with [a bank in the same city where the unit was located], and the bank was informed about the parent company's selling subsidiaries not involved in the company's primary line of business. I have done business with the bank for a great many years, and this is the reason why I was able to find out about the divestitures. Subsequently I bought this unit.

Most divestitures were the result of the parent company's decision and subsequent search for a buyer; however, opportunistic approaches by the buyer may play a role in more divestments than is readily apparent.

Sources of Buyers

The sources of buyers vary considerably, sometimes coming from predictable sources and other times from unlikely sources. Figure 5–14 suggests characteristics

The firm needs to identify the buyers for whom the unit will have the most value. If the firm has little or no experience doing divestitures, it should probably use an investment banker or broker for screening and elimination, as well as initial approaches. Competitors, near competitors, suppliers, and customers are usually those who will find the unit of most value; however, they are also the potential buyers with whom antitrust difficulties might be most likely. There should be an attempt to find a complementary fit between the unit for sale and the buyer. Criteria that might be considered in identifying potential buyers are companies for which the purchase would:

1. Enlarge market share.
2. Enlarge product line.
3. Entail forward (thus a supplier) or backward (a customer) integration.
4. Enlarge distribution channels.
5. Mean a geographic expansion.
6. Offer opportunity for manufacturing capacity expansion.
7. Offer opportunity for process technology.
8. Enable acquirer to obtain valuable patents.
9. Enable two companies to combine marketing efforts and obtain efficiencies.
10. Enable buyer to obtain trademarks or brand recognition.
11. Enable buyer to obtain R&D capability.
12. Enable buyer to obtain service capacity.
13. Provide complementary products for buyer.

Source: Peter N. Walmsley, "Divestiture Planning," in James R. Gardner, Robert Rachlin, and H.W. Allen Sweeny, *Handbook of Strategic Planning* (New York: Wiley, 1986), pp. 13.8–13.9.

Figure 5–14. Guidelines for Finding Buyers

of potential buyers. Among the firms in the study, there were three primary sources of buyers: inside the firm, outside the firm but inside the industry, and outside the industry. Firms may locate buyers from files they keep on entities that have approached them previously. In addition, foreign firms may become buyers.

Inside the Firm: One of the best sources of suggestions for potential buyers is the participants in the subsidiary; however, offering the subsidiary first to the executives managing it may be a wise internal political move because such an offer appears to give the division executives as well as other employees a sense that they have been dealt with fairly. One company arranged an attractive buy-out package at the cost of about $500,000 less on a $3 million transaction than they had hoped to find on the open market but felt that the contribution to company morale was worth the cost. Insiders to the firm—either the executives managing the entity or others within the parent company—are viable possibilities.

In a firm active in management leveraged buy-outs, the vice-president of corporate development explained how the former general manager of the unit had ultimately become its owner:

> Gordon Finch had been general manager of the unit before it became one of our subsidiaries. After we acquired the unit, Finch became corporate president and then vice-chairman. He didn't involve himself much in the unit over the decade he was at corporate because he was so much involved in the set of diversified product lines that made up the conglomerate. Finch's younger son, Tom, however, had started working in the subsidiary in his teens. Then in his early thirties, Tom Finch had worked in a number of various positions in the unit. Sometime in 1980, our corporate chairman said to Gordon Finch, "You really ought to buy the unit for your son Tom." As it turned out, that is exactly what happened.

Corporate provided funding assistance for several of the management leveraged buy-outs. The assistance was in the form of:

> Help in finding equity interests. For example, one manager nearing retirement was not interested in purchasing the firm but was invited to help find the buyer. Ultimately the company found a buyer who had available funds and was putting together a portfolio of companies. The buyer gave 20 percent of the equity to the management if they would stay with the company after purchase.

> Direct loans. Dancer, for example, was partially funded by a loan from the parent company. The loan was on attractive terms, including payments dependent on future sales and/or income levels.

> Retention of equity interest by the parent—for example, as Esmark did in the case of SIPCO, one of the firms remaining after the restructuring of Swift.

If the current management team has no interest in a buy-out, another option is to make finding potential buyers financially rewarding to them—perhaps payment in the form of a finder's fee, bonus, and/or generous severance package. A unit head who stayed with the new owner said, "Our previous corporate owner was very generous to me over the years, and they arranged for an attractive package for me here." This unit executive, within two years of retirement, obviously appreciated the efforts of the divesting firm. The main effort, of course, should be to make the package in the interest of negotiations, the divesting company, the subsidiary executives, and the buying firm.

Outside the Firm But Inside the Industry: Whether looking inside the industry makes sense depends on the concentration of the industry. If the unit is large relative to its industry and the competitors who are potential buyers are also relatively large, there may be difficulty with the FTC, although this difficulty has eased somewhat in recent years. In the following example, the purchase expanded the buying company's product line in a logical manner:

> One of our units made products that didn't fit with our main business. There was another company in the same industry. Our unit was the "Cadillac" and the other company was the "Chevrolet." We took a gutsy move. They had tried to buy one of our other businesses, so we kind of knew the guys. We asked one of the senior executives to meet us at a [major area] club. We said, "Did you ever think of buying us?" Oh, yeah, great idea was their reaction. I said, "Well, can you make a decision by Monday? You can't beat the price. If you do decide yes, I'll go back to our corporate executives and see if they'll sell it to you." . . . That was a gutsy move. [CFO of medium-sized consumer products company]

The incident is an example of a horizontal combination that made considerable sense. Indeed, it is with buyers with whom the unit has some logical connection and potential for synergy that there is opportunity for the highest price.

Insight into the fit of a particular divestiture with a buyer comes from the divestiture of a component manufacturer to a heavy equipment conglomerate. The buyer's treasurer talked about why his firm was interested in the component manufacturer:

> The unit became available to us after several years of our wanting such a company. We were buying these major components from the unit all along. . . . Generally we have been in the heavy equipment business for a 100 years, and most of our manufacturing activity started out in the Northeast. The unit is located about fifteen to twenty miles away from our facilities so there has always been a close relation between the product lines of the companies. As the unit came down the acquisition track over the years, we were always in the bidding process, but [we] were never willing to pay the price for this piece of property . . . so the chain is original company, two other owners, and now us.

In this case, the treasurer of the heavy equipment manufacturer pointed out that his firm had identified itself much earlier as a potential buyer. His firm had been a competitive bidder when the seller had acquired the unit in an earlier transaction.

In still another instance, the divesting firm identified the leading company in the industry as a potential target. The attraction, as the vice-president of strategic planning explained, was the distribution system:

> We thought [the leading company] would look at it as an opportunity. There was nothing bad about our unit. Indeed, it is unique. Our unit's distribution system is the envy of the industry. We felt that the strength of our distributors would be attractive. We had engaged investment bankers to tell us who might

be the best buyer. We went to management of the unit. [We said], "We are going to sell you guys. We need you to cooperate with us." The guy who is the
unit CEO became its CEO in 1967. He is about retirement age, and his son
has been working in the unit for ten to twelve years. The son was the next
in command. And so they worked with us to try to sell it to [the leading com-
pany]. That didn't work. [There was] one other company in the industry that
we tried.

In both of these examples, the source of the buyer was from within the
industry. Other sources include suppliers and customers, that is, related industry links. In addition, firms looking for particular kinds of opportunities
(for example, growth or turnaround opportunities) should also be considered.
In other instances, potential buyers have approached the firm in the past and
are potential buyers today. Finally, the selling firm may want to consider using
a business broker or investment banker to find a suitable buyer.

There were only two units among the companies that had locations abroad.
One of these units was the R&G divestiture already described. The second
unit was sold to a leading competitor. The corporate vice-president of strategic
planning in this second firm explained why his company was interested in selling and why the buying company found the unit an attractive opportunity:

> We had no fit and no synergy with the four units. It was not really a decision
> for us to get out of the business. Quite the contrary, we used the money from
> that divestiture to support our domestic business and other things. The unit
> was a business that didn't fit us and that was not performing up to standard.
> The buyer, on the other hand, had some real interest.
>
> What happened was this. The transactions involved businesses in four
> foreign markets. I'll call them Number 1, Number 2, Number 3 and Number
> 4. The buyer had wanted to get into Number 1 for a long time. It's a small
> country, but we were in the number one spot, so that part of the purchase
> was nice for the buyer. They were in Number 2; we weren't. Foreign market
> Number 3 was a very major market, but that part of the unit was probably
> the lowest item on their totem pole. However, we said, "You take all of the
> units or none." But that unit gave them a manufacturing position in Number
> 3 market. Another U.S. competitor was number one there. . . . We were both
> in market Number 4, but when they combined their unit and ours, I think
> they became number one in market Number 4. So they had some reasons.
> They were essentially buying market share and buying customers.

Another inside-the-industry or related opportunity is diversified companies
that have purchased similar units before and may have a strategic group focusing on a set of related industries. How does one find such opportunities? Perhaps
one clue came from the description of one of the great traders of all time, the
CEO and founder of a $1 billion conglomerate. As an observer put it, "His only

recreation is reading 10-Ks far into the night." The story is apocryphal but illustrates the breadth of the CEO's knowledge of a wide array of companies. This founder and chairman can readily identify potential buyers for his units, as well as companies he may want to buy.

Outside the Industry: Several alternatives exist for prospective buyers outside the industry. Outsiders seeking to diversify their own portfolio of subsidiaries is one possibility. Outsiders seeking a freestanding company is still another. In at least two instances, units were sold to investors.[7] The vice-president of corporate development for one firm explained how one of these buyers was contacted:

> Al, the buyer, was an entrepreneur, a venture capitalist and an investment banker. I had never met him except on the phone but he sounded very nice. One of our fellows was telling him about two other industrial businesses we are in the process of selling. Al said he had a firm in Kansas. So our man said, "We got a unit for sale in Kansas." Al has a miniconglomerate, and he brings management in for a large part of the action. They just love him. He says, "You run it." He has them in for 20 percent or something. Al sent out a man and he went through it. . . . We are going to close sometime in December.

Former Executives as a Source: Former executives may be potential buyers. The senior vice-president of a major conglomerate discussed how one former executive came to buy a large, ailing unit:

> One of our former executives brought in a would-be buyer from outside the United States, a conglomerate with a lot of different businesses. They said, they'd like to buy some businesses, or, in particular, R&G. We had one or two meetings with them and it became clear they thought, as did many of the [potential] buyers, we . . . were ready to give the business away. They were looking for a real ridiculous price. We said no. . . . We felt that we were giving a bargain, but it was not as much as they wanted. So we said to [the conglomerate firm] that it didn't seem that there was any point in carrying on with discussions further. At that point, our former executive said, "Well, you know, maybe I'd buy that business. I'm retired, and I haven't got anything to do, and I like a little challenge."

Another example involved Ralph Johnson, a former executive of Medical Industry Supply, Inc. (MISI). Through a series of acquisitions, Medical Industry had put together a specialty unit largely under Johnson's guidance. Johnson left MISI in the late 1970s. He first went to a large conglomerate, where he headed up a competitor unit. Then he joined ABC, Inc., a smaller conglomerate. ABC had a similar but weak unit. Johnson convinced ABC to buy MISI's specialty unit as part of his longer-term strategic plan to build a totally integrated major firm within the specialty industry subsegment. This MISI divestiture was completed in 1982. Executives from MISI and from the unit shared their perspectives on how the purchase by Johnson came about (figure 5–15).

Maintaining a Stable: If the company is known to be an active divestor, the flow of inquirers from various sources will be substantial. Even firms that divest at least occasionally are likely to have inquiries from time to time from firms interested in specific units or simply units in general that might be for sale. A file on these inquiries should be maintained because they can provide a source of potential buyers for units to be divested in the future. Moreover, records might be kept regarding the inquirers' interests and qualifications in order to facilitate prioritization when a unit is actually for sale. One of the executives referred to this set of past inquires that he maintained as a stable. Another said, "Over the years we have accumulated a large stack of letters from people who say, 'If you ever want to sell, let us know.' "

Foreign Buyers: Foreign buyers are often interested in entering the U.S. market. These buyers may be more difficult to find but can potentially provide a premium price. Only one example with a foreign buyer was involved in the study, and the sale was precipitated by the foreign manufacturer, which had decided to buy the U.S. marketing capabilities distributing their products.

The usual difficulties of negotiating with individuals from another culture were evident in this case. It was readily apparent that the president of the U.S. firm felt considerable stress at certain points in the negotiation in not understanding clearly what the buyer really wanted. It was also clear that the buyer was targeting a good price for the unit—that is, a good price from the buyer's point of view. The foreign buyers had held over the U.S. executive's head the possibility of establishing their own company or buying another; thus, the U.S. company would have lost the product line, which was considered key to the unit's success. The unit had been acquired a number of years prior, and the CEO readily admitted that he did not want to rebuild the unit as he had had to do shortly after the original purchase. Although he indicated he was satisfied with the ultimate price, he clearly would have liked to have had more leverage with the unit's buyers. Ultimately his satisfaction came not from price but from negotiation of employment conditions for the management, who remained in charge of the unit under the new owner.

Qualifying the Buyers

Identifying the potential buyers is not enough; they must also be qualified financially and nonfinancially.

Vice-president of corporate development, MISI: We had been contacted periodically by various buyers who had an interest in this unit, including ABC. Ralph Johnson, one of our former executives, was over there, and Ralph said, "If you ever want to do something, I certainly would like to take a look." And so we made the contact.

President of the specialty unit (who went with the unit from MISI to ABC): Ralph and I were friends in the business from almost the day I came on board in MISI. He'd been there sixteen years when he left. I left after seventeen years, but he and I did business together when I was in MISI's Division A. We did business together when I was at MISI's Division B and he was at MISI's Division C. We're basically the same age. He's maybe a couple of years older. Then when I moved back here as president of MISI's Division D, I reported to him. We both live in the same town. Our families are friendly. So we stayed in touch. We often talked about what he was trying to do and what I was trying to do. Then he moved again to ABC. And ABC really did have a desire to build world wide [industry of the unit to be sold] companies because they have about a $150 million position in [industry of the unit to be sold]. So Ralph went there to take over their group, which contained several companies. The first thing he suggested was they should approach us about buying our division. Their division was not particularly well managed. They had no corporate management team like we did, and the business was going downhill.

I think trust facilitates; I mean, ABC was so anxious to do the deal and Ralph was anxious to do the deal that I think that it facilitated the negotiation. There is one more player who you're going to meet this afternoon that's interesting also, and that's Doug Husted. At one time, Ralph was the president of our group and had four divisions—the four I mentioned. The presidents of those divisions reported to him. I was one of them. Then he had a controller for his group and a business development person. The business development person was Doug Husted. Now when Ralph left MISI, he took Doug with him. When Ralph went to ABC, Doug said, "I've been with Ralph long enough, and I want to go back to MISI. I'm coming back to work with you." He joined me as my group person. . . . Doug came back for the stability of MISI, and six months later he was involved in the analysis to divest the business to, of all companies, ABC and Ralph. That is kind of an ironic twist of fate, but it facilitated the thing also because Doug knew Ralph so well. He knew what ABC had because he'd been in the business for several years. Doug had been around MISI, so he was also a key player in working out the strategies, and he's an excellent strategic thinker and really was supportive of the deal. So we had a lot of people on the same wavelength. I think that's rather unique. I mean, I think the proximity of Ralph in terms of living here in [major city] but working for ABC in [a city about one hundred miles away]. Him having his office in suburb A, our office being in suburb A. Doug having worked for both of us. All of those things helped facilitate the process.

So we at MISI were looking at our portfolio to see what made strategic sense. Finally we concluded we shouldn't try to sell parts of the portfolio. We should either sell all of the unit or build with it. And that was the ultimate decision. But in a real involved conversation, regarding anything could go, anything, nothing [was] sacred. The only one we never thought about selling was Torno because it was terrific in terms of growth, return on investment, and profitability . . . [but] the group VP argued that it didn't make sense to stay in the one specialty business and sell three others. And then ABC was smart enough to say, "If you don't include Torno, we won't take the other three." That was a smart thing to do. So all of a sudden there was no debate. Torno was sold with the other three units.

Interviewer: Did Ralph buy the group for the management?

President of the specialty unit: Yes, I think that was part of the story. . . . He knew the players. . . . ABC was getting advice from key organization consultants who were saying, "You need some management in this specialty unit." ABC's company is weak in top management. . . . So that was very helpful to Ralph when he was able to go in and sell that fact that, "Oh, by the way not only does this MISI unit fit strategically, but we're really going to upgrade the overall quality of the management organization because we're bringing in a bunch of guys that we think can make the contribution whether it's here or some other places at ABC." It was a boost. So yes, that's part of the story that was used to sell the deal.

Figure 5–15. MISI's Divestiture of Major Unit to ABC, Inc.

Financial Qualifications: Financial qualifications are preeminent; the buyer must have the ability to consummate the deal. No aspect of a potential buyer will make a seller lose interest more quickly than the possibility that the buyer might not have the necessary financial resources. Indeed, given the effort and stress that must be invested in negotiations, no other aspect should be more strongly considered.

With publicly traded firms, the financial information is readily available for analysis. Determining financial ability for private companies, investor groups, or individuals is more difficult. The seller may ask for information and references and may also make discrete inquiries in the banking community. Assessing the qualifications of a buyer is a stage in the process where outside help might be employed to assist with the gathering of the appropriate but not always easily obtainable data.

Nonfinancial Qualifications: Nonfinancial qualifications cover a range of issues, including integrity in the negotiations and the manner in which the buyer is expected to manage the unit after the sale. Concerning the integrity of the potential buyer, a senior consultant with over two decades of M&A experience provided the following insight:

Interviewer: It appears there are two aspects that determine if a firm even wants to approach a buyer, that is, do we want to have anything to do with the individual? The first is financial. The other aspect has to do with something I'll call integrity, and it has to do with whether we, the selling firm, even want to have anything to do in negotiation with that potential buyer. Would you comment?

Interviewee: That's quite common. I mean the first one (financial qualifications) is obvious. Yet is should not be. Potential buyers should not be totally discarded if the appearance is that they are not in a position to do it. In today's world we have leveraged buy-outs. . . . You got to recognize that there's been a total change in bank attitude in terms of financing acquisitions. They are always willing to finance on what you're buying. But now they are willing to finance on what you may divest. . . . The new element of the banking situation is that they loan more than the balance sheet worth of the thing you're buying because there is something there that can be divested that's worth more than the book value.

Interviewer: What about the integrity issue?

Interviewee: Well, across the table, I would say a lot more than you think. If something is very hard to sell, it may very well modify the divestor's opinion because they need to sell it. But I find it rare that someone sells to "a bad guy," especially if they have any feeling for the people that were in the division or subsidiary. But you have to recognize that in some instances there is the responsibility to stockholders as well as to the other employees that are in the remaining part of the company. If you have to sell something and that's the only buyer, then you have to consider that. Then that person would be very careful in my opinion and would have all kinds of safeguards to make sure that it was not a problem.

The issue of integrity, however, can go by the boards when a unit is difficult to sell and the buyer is willing to pay the price. The vice-president of business development for a major conglomerate shared an unpleasant experience of negotiating with representatives of another firm. After several frustrating episodes in which the vice-president felt that the other firm was dealing with less than integrity, he withdrew his firm from the negotiations. Later the potential buyer returned and wanted to reopen negotiations. "We told them," said the vice-president, "That that was our price and they could take it or leave it. They took it."

Besides integrity, the seller is often interested in how the unit will be managed after the sale. Nonfinancial considerations vary; however, clearly high in priority are how the buyer will deal with the employees, especially management, and whether the unit will be harvested or milked.

How the buyer will deal with the employees is especially important to operating firms that have family cultures. It is even more critical to firms that pride themselves on being a good place to work. The message that the seller took care to protect the employees of a divested unit can be a powerful one to underscore a basic tenet of a culture. The message can be underscored through the seller's choice of buyer with whom to negotiate, as well as negotiation of employment contracts.

A word of caution must be noted here. Protection of employees is at best difficult where it is clear that the unit's employment body must be reduced. If the unit is experiencing a downturn in the market, the decision for the seller is whether to reduce the number of employees prior to divestiture or negotiate the price accordingly and let the new buyer do the layoffs. The matter is difficult for either party since for morale, it is better for the buyer to require the seller to "clean up" the unit. Yet, it is usually in the seller's best interest to leave that unpleasant task to the buyer, time permitting. In the case of externally caused factors, such as a market downturn or technology changes in process, there is pressure for the seller to undertake the reduction in work force and leave the buyer unencumbered to move ahead. A buyer of a unit explained the rationale of the seller for choosing his company as the ultimate buyer:

> The selling company reviewed the proposals that all of the potential buyers were required to submit and started to negotiate with people they thought they could work out a transaction with. The selling company wanted to sell the company to someone who would pay the best price, all cash, plus have the financing and organization to carry on the business in the future. We fit these requirements. We were able to purchase the company over other people because our final proposal was the best one, plus they felt we would be fair to the employees and be successful in the future. . . . Four people wanted to purchase the company. They negotiated with each one and gradually narrowed the choice down to one, us.

There are nonfinancial issues other than how the buyer will treat employees. They include issues of reputation in the marketplace and ease of dealing with the buyer after the divestiture transaction is completed. The treasurer of Medical Products, Inc. made these issues explicit:

> There would have been prerequisites for considering any buyer. One would be, How would they handle our products and our reputation in the marketplace? And we envisioned that there would probably be a protracted set of dealings after the actual closing. It's always a matter of who would be relatively easy to work with. Those are things that could have disqualified a buyer. And, we looked at price and the ability to pay that price.

If paring the work force is imminent because the buyer will be able to effect synergies not available to the seller, the roles are reversed. Depending upon circumstances, the buyer may still wish the seller to do the layoffs. It is much more likely under these circumstances, however, that trimming the work force will not be appropriate until legal, financial, and operating performance of the unit has been transferred. The onus is usually on the buyer under these circumstances.

What can the seller do? First, where there is a choice of buyers, the seller can make the deliberate choice among the potential buyers and let the management of the unit know that such a deliberate choice was made. Management should be asked for their opinion about potential buyers. Indeed, one selling firm made a commitment to unit mangement that they could choose between buyers provided the prices were within 5 percent. In addition, choice can be made on the basis of external information; perhaps the buyer is in a growth mode and is likely to continue that orientation with the new purchase. Or it might be made through observation of how the buyer has handled prior acquisitions.

Second, the protection of at least the management employees can be a matter of negotiation. The choices of the seller around this issue—and indeed those of the buyer—can set the tenor of the whole deal. Level of pay, bonus systems, length of contract with guaranteed pay, golden parachutes, or other similar arrangements for severance pay in the event of subsequent sale or liquidation, as well as various perquisites, are legitimate negotiation points. The seller should at least evidence having tried and the buyer should evidence having allowed at least some success for the seller in the negotiations. The buyer must simultaneously protect the general policy of the new parent with regard to compensation levels and the morale and preferences of the management of the new unit. There is often a trade-off.

It is not the responsibility of the seller as to what happens to the unit after the transaction is completed; however, there are several reasons why the selling executives might wish to give attention to the buyer's plans. One reason has already been given: the impact of the subsequent events on the seller's continuing employees' attitude and morale. But there is another reason. The average time that a unit has been held is slightly more than eight years. During that time, the unit and the parent have had a relationship. It is not unlikely that there has been a high expectation for the unit at some time. Parent executives thus have some personal investment in the future of the unit. Although this emotional attachment must be diminished if the divestment is to be consummated, it is nonetheless present and must be considered. There are buyers who purchase units to dismember them either quickly through liquidation or through harvesting or milking of the unit. Such reputations can be identified. Time spent making inquiry may reveal important damaging—or supportive—facts.

Signaling

In addition to the issue of who might buy the subsidiary, the decision must be made to make the potential sale publicly known (known as signaling), or keep the transaction quite secret until the consummation of a contract can be completed. Whether to make the process fairly open or keep it fairly quiet depends on a number of factors, including reason for divesting, the knowledge that potential buyers might already have of the subsidiary, the duration of time from the decision to formal contract for purchase, and the desire of the parent company executives to keep the news quiet.

The experiences of the firms in this study revealed the importance of signaling for effective implementation of divestment. Both internal and external signaling are important. With regard to external signaling four issues emerged as crucial: signaling to potential buyers, signaling to the investment community, signaling to customers and suppliers, and timing and content of signaling.

No public announcement should be made before employees are informed. Most companies made sure that employees were told, although at a few, division management found out about the impending divestiture from suppliers and customers or even potential buyers who may have been approached quietly by the corporate parent. The individual making the announcement, the words chosen for informing division personnel, and the choice of location are critical for maintaining the integrity of the unit, both before the divestiture transaction and after. A senior executive in a major conglomerate talked about why his firm does not make public announcements:

> We do not announce like many companies [and say], "We're gonna sell this thing," and then get 59,000 tire kickers. I usually select companies that I think might be interested, contact them myself, and just discuss it with them in general terms to see if they're interested. Then if they are interested, I arrange meetings, and we take it from there. Now many, many companies just make a public announcement. We're gonna do this, this, and then they just wait for the phones to ring. I think that's the wrong way to go because it gets all of the tire kickers in. It gets some people upset. It takes too long a time, and you got people traipsing through and all that kind of stuff.

The importance of signaling to potential buyers is captured by the maxim, "A good divestor is a good marketer."

Signaling to the investment community is generally made with an eye to raising the stock price of the firm. The form of such announcements is critically dependent on the frequency and size of divestment (figure 5–16). Where divestment size is relatively large, signaling takes the form of specific announcements regarding the unit. Where size and frequency of divestment are low, announcements refer to the strategic orientation of the firm. In the case of frequent divestments, both kinds of announcements—strategic orientation and periodic announcements—are found.

Issues of timing emerge as central during signaling to the investment community for strategy-driven firms. For firms in this sample, signaling sometimes preceded the search for acquirers. In other firms, the announcement might be

Frequency of Divestment	Size of Divestment Relative to Firm	
	High	*Low*
High	None in sample	Strategy-related and/or periodic announcements
Low	Extensive, specific to the divestment and strategic reorientation	Strategy-related announcement

Figure 5–16. Signaling to the Investment Community

made after the deal was closed. In the case of holding companies, signaling was not deemed important because the investment community expects such divestments. In the case of firms in the process of strategic transition, signaling issues were not explicitly considered, though typically these firms signaled after the divestment.

Marketing the unit involves maintaining the integrity of the unit, including relationships with suppliers and customers. Insight into maintaining relationships with customers came from the vice-president of strategic planning for Technology Conglomerate, Inc.

> You call the customers personally, the key customers, major customers, and important ones. I went out and visited them, so that [they would] know what was coming. They knew that the unit was in trouble. We tried to keep those people informed. The SEC regulations prevent you from telling some kinds of people before the actual sale date. . . . When you get to the day—or the day before, depending on SEC regulations—before you can tell some of them, you need a lawyer, and you need him right beside you. Get to your customers as fast as you can. Get to the vendors. . . . For example, you need to know about leases, leased equipment, etc. I want a snapshot of where we are on a certain day.
>
> Vendors and special customers get quite upset. It is a problem, and there is confusion. No matter what you do, you can't help that. Customers and vendors, however, are different. Vendors will say to themselves, "I was going to go on vacation, and there went 3 percent of my business." Once you have told them, it is a process of repeated reinforcement and answering questions.

Announcing a divestiture to customers can be a wrenching experience, as one of the executives pointed out:

> I think CEOs seem very worried about telling people about when they are going to divest and what they are going to tell their customers. I have seen CEOs absolutely panic when they were selling a big subsidiary percentage wise. In one instance, 60 percent of the business was one customer, and the firm that was doing the divesting was absolutely panicked about telling that customer. They did tell the customer, however, and the customer expressed gratitude that they let them know early.

The Information Package

As part of the marketing effort, firms generally put together an information package on the unit or units to be sold. They may be quite elaborate or consist of a few pages in a looseleaf binder. In general there are at least three stages of information supplied to potential buyers. The first stage may take the form of a general description of the business and may contain abbreviated financial information. The intent is to test the interest of potential buyers. If buyers are interested and qualified, a fuller description of the business is made available. Indeed, an information package at this stage may essentially be a prospectus. The final stage, when the selling firm has narrowed the field to three or four potential buyers, consists of field visits and probably conversations with the management of the unit to be divested.

The treasurer of one of the companies talked about the process used in his firm:

> We would send out a package of information on the company, give some financial history, simply put together a prospectus and circulate [it] to people who we felt would have an interest. . . . We asked people to keep it confidential, but I'm sure that it became known.

Summary

This chapter has covered a number of aspects of marketing a business unit. The analogy between the proverbial four Ps of marketing and the process of marketing a unit are clear. The chapter suggests that the process is complicated and cumbersome, especially when there are multiple divestitures ongoing at the same time.

Many deals hit snags somewhere in the process; however, the selling process can go smoothly, as the following comment illustrates:

> Generally [it went smoothly because] the selling company wanted to sell it, and that made it very easy. It was not a difficult deal because it was something we wanted to buy, and the other company wanted to sell it. So it was a pretty easy fit, and there weren't many people buying things like that in that area.

Recomendations for Corporate Executives

1. The process of selling a divestiture must be treated as a marketing program. Thus, the application of the four Ps is appropriate. That is, the product (unit to be divested) must be defined, the price target or acceptable range established, the distribution channels to be used (intermediaries or inside personnel) selected, and the means of promotion (or signaling) determined.

2. Pricing involves both quantitative and qualitative factors. Net present value approaches are generally used as a basis for coming to a price target or range; however, book value, comparison to comparable firms being sold, expert opinion, and market value of assets should also be considered. As the firm becomes more experienced, it is likely that corporate personnel

will develop the expertise to "eyeball" a situation and establish a price within an acceptable range.

3. Pricing a unit should always consider the potential value to the buyer. Thus, the possible synergies that the buyer may effect may increase the value of the unit.

4. Whether the company should use external intermediaries to assist in the sale of the unit depends upon several factors. One is the degree of experience in corporate. Many large companies active in acquisition and divestment have sufficient expertise in corporate staff. In addition, the size of the unit is critical. Larger units usually portend more risk for the company and therefore require a greater level of expertise. (Figure 5–3 summarized the conditions under which outside intermediaries may be appropriate.)

5. External communication (promotion or signaling) is critical. How the company will go about letting potential buyers know that a unit is for sale should be thought through carefully. (Figure 5–12 suggested the conditions under which public announcements versus multiple private solicitations versus sequential private solicitations of buyers are appropriate.)

6. External communication must also be considered for suppliers, customers, and the investment community, since each of these groups has an impact on the ultimate value of the unit and corporate.

7. Identifying potential buyers is a task unto itself. Possible buyers include executives from inside the company, companies outside the firm but inside the industry, companies outside the industry evidencing interest in entering the industry, investor groups, former executives, and companies that have approached the company previously.

8. Qualifying buyers involves financial considerations as well as nonfinancial issues. Financial considerations are foremost and focus on the buyer's ability to consummate the deal. Nonfinancial considerations encompass the buyer's intent with regard to the unit, including strategic and operational plans, as well as probable treatment of employees. The potential working relationship between the buyer and seller may be important if a continuing relationship is expected.

Recommendations for Division Managers

The functions expected of division managers depend on corporate preferences. It is clear, however, that the value of the unit heavily depends on the actions of division management. Division management's input may be requested at any point in the marketing of the unit. The intent of the suggestions in this section is to enhance the value of the unit during the sale process and the value of the division management to current corporate management, as well as to potential buyers.

1. Who are possible buyers that might have interest in this unit? How would I approach them informally if I become aware of the possibility of divestiture? What potential buyers would I suggest to corporate if asked?

2. What is the market value of this unit? Because division management is closer to industry action, it is possible to stay more current than corporate with such issues as the selling prices of comparable companies, the market value of various unit assets, the value of various assets that may not be reflected readily on the unit balance sheet (such as patents, expertise among personnel, expected fruition of product development, or marketing activities), who is buying or selling what, and the strategy of various industry entrants, including suppliers and buyers, as well as competitors.

3. It is unlikely that division management will be involved in external communications with the investment community, but certainly division management should consider the possible effects of divestment on suppliers and customers and the best approach to an effective communication program with these entities in the event of divestiture.

4. How to present the unit to prospective buyers in such a way as to enhance the value of the management team (including oneself) and how to manage personal feeling and emotions if the potential buyer is not likely to be positively disposed toward current division management must be considered.

Appendix 5A: Cash Forecast for Subsidiary A

	Actual 1983	Pro Forma (millions of dollars)								
		1984	1985	1986	1987	1988	1989	1990	1991	1992
Sales	9.0	12.6	17.6	24.7	34.6	37.7	41.0	44.8	48.8	53.2
Assets	5.1	8.4	11.0	14.5	18.7	18.9	20.0	21.3	22.3	23.1
Current liabilities	1.6	2.3	3.2	4.4	6.2	6.8	7.4	8.1	8.8	9.6
EAT	.2	.25	.35	.6	1.0	1.3	1.6	2.0	2.5	3.2
					Cash Flow Pro Forma					
EAT	.2	.25	.35	.6	1.0	1.3	1.6	2.0	2.5	3.2
△ Assets		(3.3)	(2.6)	(3.5)	(4.2)	(.2)	(1.1)	(1.3)	(.9)	(.9)
△ Current liabilities		.7	.9	1.2	1.8	.6	.6	.7	.7	.8
Free cash flow		(2.3)	(1.3)	(1.7)	(1.4)	1.7	1.1	1.4	2.3	3.1
Investment	3.5	6.1	7.7	10.0	12.4	12.0	12.5	13.1	13.3	13.4

Appendix 5B: Cash Forecast for Subsidiary B

| | Actual 1983 | | | | Pro Forma (millions of dollars) | | | | | |
	1983	1984	1985	1986	1987	1988	1989	1990	1991	1992
Sales	10.8	12.8	15.2	18.1	21.5	23.3	25.1	27.2	29.3	31.6
Assets	12.0	13.8	15.6	17.3	19.5	21.3	23.2	25.1	27.3	29.8
Current liabilities at .09 × sales	1.0	1.2	1.4	1.6	1.9	2.1	2.3	2.4	2.6	2.8
EAT	.7	.8	1.0	1.2	1.5	1.6	1.9	2.0	2.2	2.5
					Cash Flow Projections					
EAT	.7	.8	1.0	1.2	1.5	1.6	1.9	2.0	2.2	2.5
△ Assets		(1.8)	(1.8)	(1.7)	(2.1)	(1.8)	(1.9)	(1.9)	(2.2)	(2.5)
△ Current liabilities		.15	.25	.2	.3	.3	.2	.1	.2	.2
Free cash flow		(.8)	(.55)	(.3)	(.3)	1.	.2	.2	.2	.2
Investment	11.0	12.6	14.2	15.7	17.5	19.0	20.7	22.5	24.5	26.8

Notes

1. The use of the term *rational* does not preclude consideration of intraorganizational political issues. Indeed individual decision makers do take into account the political factors. For example, the chief financial officer of Consumer Products Company was responsible for making the recommendation to divest to the board of directors. He took into consideration who among the board members had vested interests in the original decision to acquire. Various scenarios were then possible for increasing the chances that the board members would accept the divestiture recommendation. The basic options he might have considered included obtaining the support of other equally or more powerful members of the board to force or persuade the individual with vested interest in the past and individually educating the board members or executives of the difficulties encountered with the subsidiary with the intent of getting their participation in designing the solution (divestiture). Ultimately he chose to carry on informal conversations on the golf course during the course of the three-day meeting.

2. When the unit is at least marginally profitable, the firm's decision to divest is often predicated on the price the executives think they can obtain.

3. This observation does not negate instances where executives from within the subsidiary might initiate a possible buy-out, either on their own account or on behalf of parties who have approached them.

4. The reverse is also true. A firm that sells a unit where it shows a gain should consider, if possible, the sale of a unit where it shows a loss and match the two transactions in the same fiscal year. The most celebrated instance is Esmark's sale of Vickers and Swift.

5. Equipment values seldom appreciate.

6. Marilyn L. Taylor, "Martin Theatres," Field Studies Program, University of Kansas, as presented to North American Case Research Association, 1987.

7. Investors can include investment bankers, venture capitalists, and conglomerate builders.

6
Management Buy-outs

T he 1960s was the Age of the Conglomerate. The 1970s was the Decade of Divestiture. The 1980s is likely to be known as the Era of Leveraged Buy-outs. The milieu in the early 1980s led to a sharp increase in the number of management leveraged buy-outs (MBOs), and the phenomenon was not confined to the United States. This chapter considers the general experience in the United States, with a brief look at Great Britain and Europe, and then moves to compare the specific experiences of the set of MBOs in this study.

There are external factors as well as internal conditions that have led to aggregate outcomes, as well as outcomes for the individual firms (figure 6–1). Both are examined in this chapter, as are firm-level outcomes and the aggregate MBO experience and trends.

Definitions

Three terms are usually associated with the leveraged buy-outs: LBOs (leveraged buy-outs), MBOs (management buy-outs), and MLBOs (management-leveraged buy-outs). In some instances all three are the same. An LBO is a leveraged acquisition, one that is financed with a significant amount of debt. The purchaser usually relies on the sale of assets or cash flows from operations to pay down the debt. As leverage declines, value accrues to the equity holders, often producing spectacular returns. Not all LBOs give management a piece of the action, but many LBO financiers feel that it is an important aspect. Jerome Kohlberg, a founding partner of the well-known specialist buy-out firm Kohlberg, Kravis, Roberts (KKR), believes that management participation "makes for tremendous motivation. It puts everybody on the same side of the table. That is their incentive and we as investors really require that."[1]

LBOs first attained widespread use in the United States; they have become increasingly popular in the United Kingdom, and are beginning to occur in

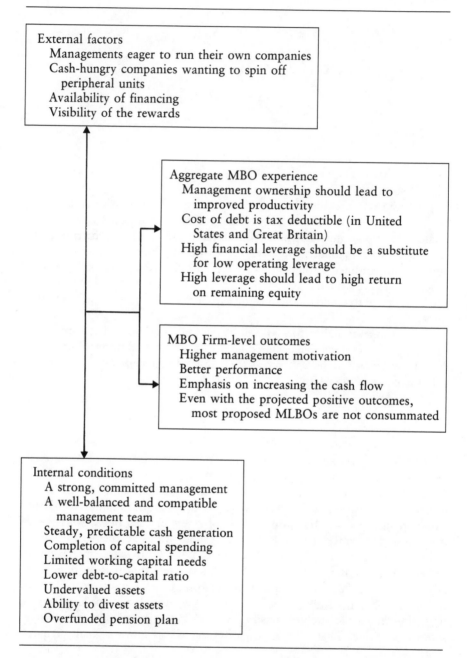

Figure 6–1. MBOs: Relationships between External and Internal Factors and Firm-level and Aggregate Outcomes

some European countries as well (table 6–1). LBOs have varied from total company LBOs to business units. The underlying financing has come from a wide range of players. The kinds of companies have varied, and the size has ranged from $1 million to more than $6 billion. LBOs can be accomplished by outside buyers, as the celebrated case of Beatrice Companies illustrates (figure 6–2). The Beatrice transaction is the largest LBO to date. It involved the KKR purchase of Beatrice Companies for $6.5 billion in 1985 with the involvement of a management team that had formerly headed up Esmark.

An MBO occurs when a company or a subsidiary is purchased by the people who run it. The sellers or prior owners could be a large corporation that desires to divest itself of a subsidiary that no longer fits its long-term strategic plan, an individual owner who wishes to retire, or any other group that desires to terminate its ownership position by selling to the existing management. There are various forms. Earlier small MBOs tended to take place at a discount to assets. These transactions had less need of leverage than is occurring today. MBOs can be accomplished without leverage, although it is rare for management of units to have sufficient capital to effect a buy-out without debt capital or equity capital from a venture source.

MLBOs are a special case of MBOs and LBOs. They are both effected by management and carried out through the means of debt capital. This chapter focuses primarily on MLBOs, although the experience of MBOs and LBOs is used to sketch the milieu in which MLBOs are effected today. (The terms MBO and MLBO are used interchangeably in this chapter.)

Table 6–1
Buy-outs in Europe and the United States,
1982–1986 (Estimated)

Austria	0
Belgium	20–30
Britain	950
Denmark	4
France	N.A.
Holland	125
Italy	10
Norway	27
Spain	0
Sweden	10
Switzerland	N.A.
United States	1,050
West Germany	9

Source: Mikael Ahlstrom et al., *Mergers and Acquisitions Monthly*, Nottingham Centre for Management Buy-out Research.

Beatrice has been described as "once one of the best-run food processing companies in the world [that fell] victim to executive power struggles and misguided management ambitions, winding up in the mid-1980's as a huge but unwieldly potpourri of businesses ranging from rent-a-cars and bras to luggage and soft drink bottling plants."

Current chairman of the now-private company is Don Kelly, one of the investors in the transaction. Experts expect Kelly and other investors to make as much as a ten-to-one return when they take the company public, presumably within three to five years. Kelly was chairman at Esmark before its takeover by Beatrice, then headed by James Dutt. Kelly and a group of Esmark officers attempted to take Esmark private. However, Dutt made a higher offer for Esmark, and Esmark became part of Beatrice.

The final deal for taking Beatrice private was $6.4 billion, with $3.5 billion from a banking syndicate headed by Citibank, Bankers Trust, and Manufacturers Hanover plus $2.5 billion junk bonds arranged by Drexel's Milken. Beatrice ended up with total debt of about $7 billion and annual interest charges of $480 million, more than operating cash flow could handle. Lenders required Kelly to repay $1.45 billion within eighteen months through divestitures. To generate the needed cash, Kelly sold Avis car rental for $250 million, Coca-Cola bottling operations for $1 billion, and International Playtex bra and girdle business for $1.25 billion. Commenting on the lender's push for cash, Kelly noted, "First they did everything they could to get us to borrow money from them. Then they did everything they could to get us to pay it back right away." In actuality, however, slimming the company down quickly after the buy-out was probably essential in terms of manageability, as much as debt service needs.

Source: Stephen Quickel, "MBO: Warnings Fail to Dim LBO Dazzle," in *The Lucrative World of Management Buyouts, A Supplement to Euromoney and Corporate Finance*, (December 1986): 20–29.

Figure 6–2. The Beatrice Buy-out: A Profile

The nature of deals has changed in recent years. Early MBOs were subsidiary operations that had been shopped by the parent without success. When a third-party buyer could not be found, management became the buyers of last resort. More recently, MBOs have been undertaken for wider strategic objectives. One recent impetus has been raiders. Management may launch a successful counterbid to beat off an unwanted approach from a raider. These MBOs, usually referred to as LBOs, have often been of total companies and are highly leveraged. Financial institutions usually provide most of the funds, which is predominantly debt. Management can put up a small proportion of the purchase price but still end up holding a majority equity stake.

The U.S. Experience

Early in the 1980s, MBOs were invariably last-resort sales. The pattern was described thus: "In the early days many of the proposals put up were unsellable ones—parents trying to dispose of subsidiaries for which no third parties could be found."[2] Indeed, until mid-1985, most buy-outs were distress sales of subsidiaries by ailing parents, disposals of unwanted peripheral operations, or family-owned companies seeking to avoid succession crises.[3] The situation changed markedly by the mid-1980s. Four broad factors contributed to the change: managements eager to run their own companies, cash-hungry companies wanting to spin off peripheral units, availability of financing, and visibility of the rewards.[4]

Entrepreneurial Management

From 1982 to 1986, the number of buy-outs doubled. Their popularity stemmed from an increase in entrepreneurial spirit in the United States. Increasingly managers have wanted to own their own companies, with the accompanying risks and rewards.[5] Observers, including the managers who buy and financiers who underwrite, have noted a desire among managers to own their companies and control their own destinies. In an era of deconglomeration, there emerged a two-tier U.S. economy where everyone wanted a piece of the ownership pie.[6]

The noticeable surge of entrepreneurialism can be attributed at least in part to the baby boom. The low birthrate during World War II gave initial baby boomers little competition for jobs in the mid-1960s. But subsequent baby boomers have found the management ranks clogged,[7] and MBOs have become one way around the clogged ranks.

In addition, the current generation has had less concern with financial risk. One executive of an institutional leader in the buy-out boom noted this aspect when he stated, "People are willing to take risks. There is a whole generation which has never felt economic pain."[8] Among those interested in LBOs, "Corporate managers themselves are by far the most enthusiastic buy-out players."[9] Even institutions that fund the transactions have been fervent supporters. A Citibank executive said, for example, "[We] believe that a business will be most successful if it is run by the people who own and understand it best."[10]

Abundance of Units Available

Opportunities for MBOs have come from several sources, including receiverships, family businesses concerned about succession problems, and units of larger companies. However, "divestments [of units of larger companies] have been the most common source of buy-outs and could get more prominent as the general boom in takeovers and mergers produces new corporate groupings which need to get rid of freshly acquired activities. . . . Divestments now account for two-thirds of all buy-outs, up from just over half at the turn of the decade."[11]

An abundance of units was available in the mid-1980s. The number of divestitures was spawned in an era of restructuring. Companies often claimed to sell the units because of "strategic considerations." Observers suggested, however, that

larger economic forces [have] generated the growth of LBOs. At the beginning
of this decade, industrial America was entering a period of wrenching adjustment, challenged by inflation, recession, and corporate raiders at home and
by Japanese and other competitors abroad. Diversification, once thought to
be the panacea to cyclical slumps, became regarded as heresy, as companies
learned to concentrate on what they did best. Corporate restructuring and
refinancing became an urgent priority, rivaling the industrial reorganization
of the U.S. in the early part of this century. Suddenly businesses were up for
grabs, often undervalued and underperforming, and a new breed of managers,
transfixed by the idea of equity stakes and shared profits, was quick to spot
opportunities.[12]

Another factor contributing to the restructuring was the undervaluing of
companies, especially those that were diversified. The problem was particularly
rampant in the early part of the decade when the bull market had only partially corrected fifteen years of real decline in share prices in many companies.[13] In many instances, these companies undervalued the units that made
up the company.

Abundance of Funds

There was also an abundance of funds as midsized banks and other financial
institutions sought better return on loans and investments. Large banks,
securities houses, and LBO specialist firms have also hunted for deals, fees,
and equity opportunities. Indeed, there has been so much money available that
dealmakers chose to bypass the tax-exempt U.S. pension funds because they
are highly visible and slow moving. By the mid-1980s stock multiples made
leverage much less attractive, but there was still a great deal of debt funds
available.[14]

There have been biases, including the assumption that if a company could
be bought on a leveraged basis with its own cash flow, it must be undervalued.
For example, as recently as 1985, Nathan Collins, executive vice-president of
Valley National Bank of Arizona told a national meeting of bankers, "LBOs
are bad financing. To lend someone their equity and expect them to earn their
way out of it is contrary to all banking principles."[15]

Visibility of Rewards

The visibility of rewards has also had an impact on the units and financing
available. From these examples, "Managers . . . are learning to be more aggressive. They are being spurred on by the publicity given to the fortunes made
by buy-out pioneers who have become millionaries through floating their
recently bought-out businesses on the stock market, sometimes as little as eighteen months after the acquisition."[16]

The Experience in Europe

In Great Britain, the buy-out surge was similar to the American experience in several ways: the evolution from sales of last resort to opportunities for managers, the increase in the number of divestitures, and the increase in entrepreneurial spirit.

Like the United States at the opening of the 1980s, the buy-out in Britain was at best a last-ditch attempt to sell a company. By middecade, it had become one of the fastest-growing parts of the takeover scene.[17] Management buy-outs were also catching on fast in Europe. In the late 1970s, MBO transactions there were used mostly to save companies from liquidation. By middecade, they were used so that firms could spin off unwanted but still profitable or salvageable businesses:[18]

> In spite of the difference in size and vocabulary, the buyout boom on both sides of the Atlantic is being kindled by similar forces. After years of growth through acquisition and given fresh impetus by the present wave of mergers, many conglomerates are now looking to rationalize by ridding themselves of non-core businesses. They argue that in increasingly global and fast moving markets, it makes sense to concentrate all their resources on mainstream activities. Indeed, in 1986 an estimated 80 per cent of U.K. buyouts arose from planned corporate restructuring.[19]

Divestitures from U.S. firms were also a source of buy-outs from 1983 to 1986. (See table 6–2.) Middecade insight suggested that the United Kingdom could expect a number of American-owned subsidiaries that operated fairly autonomously to become buy-out candidates.[20]

The increased interest on the part of managers stemmed in part from the visible encouragement of private enterprise by the Thatcher government. One observer suggested, "It is a cultural change. There is a growing awareness among

Table 6–2
Sources of Buy-outs in the United Kingdom

Source	1986	1985	1984	Pre-1984
Divestiture by U.K. parent	61.2%	65.5%	62.5%	52.8%
Family or private	10.2	16.6	6.0	20.5
Receivership	3.1	1.4	10.7	17.9
Divestiture by foreign parent	8.2	9.5	12.8	7.0
Privatization	2.0	2.4	2.0	1.8
Overseas divestiture	15.3	4.1	6.0	N.A.

Source: John Coyne, Mike Wright, and Ken Robbie, "UK Buyouts Grow in Complexity," in *The Lucrative World of Management Buyouts*, Supplement to Euromoney and Corporate Finance (December 1986): 41–45.

U.K. senior managers that there are opportunities to purchase the company they have run for a number of years, and in the process achieve a reasonable level of affluence."[21]

This British activity remains unabated. A recent survey in the United Kingdom indicated that there were 245 buy-outs in 1985 with a total financing of about £1.2 billion. This number of buy-outs was more than double the 1979 activity. The 1985 buy-outs included thirty-three for more than £5 million compared with an average of £500,000 for management acquisitions five years ago.[22] The first ten months of 1986 had about 166 deals, totaling about £1 billion. In first-quarter 1987, activity in management buy-outs was dropping. Ultimately, however, the first half of the year value topped £800 million ($1 billion), and the total 1987 activity was expected to exceed the 1986 record of 260 deals worth £1.2 billion.[23] Indeed, by 1987 most large U.K. companies had had experience with buy-outs as a way of making divestitures. Using LBOs to take firms private, however, had emerged only recently.

MBOs were spreading to other parts of Western Europe as well.[24] Several factors, summarized in figure 6–3, play a part. However, in other countries

---

1. *Favorable tax and legal rules and regulations.* Belgium, Denmark, Sweden, and France prevent companies from using their assets to obtain loans. Treatment of interest as a tax-deductible expense varies by countries. Norway, Belgium, Italy, and Spain do not allow the interest deduction at all. Sweden allowed the deduction for one year. France liberalized restrictions in 1984.

2. *A suitable supply of companies.,* With no government-owned industries and an active trading market for companies, the United States has the most favorable climate. However, observers expect family firms in West Germany, France, and Belgium to come up for sale in the near future.

3. *Available financing.* The United States has plenty of money for management buy-outs, and Britain follows suit. The 1987 estimate of funds awaiting U.S. companies was $60 billion, three times the value of 1986 buy-outs. There was money for small buy-outs in Britain, but financing for larger buy-outs came available only in the late 1970s when American firms such as Merrill Lynch and Citicorp Venture Capital moved into the British market. Thus, British financing to some degree was spurred by U.S. money.

4. *Interested management.* Entrepreneurship increased under the Thatcher government and enjoyed a revival in the United States. However, European country managers were either ignorant of the opportunities or averse to the risk.

5. *An active stock market for companies.* Investors need a way to exit readily. A number of countries qualify, including Britain, France, Holland, Switzerland, Sweden, and West Germany.

Source: "On a Slow Boat from America," *Economist*, January 3, 1987, pp. 57–58.

Figure 6–3. Factors Needed to Effect Management Buy-outs

in Europe, there has been little tradition of sharing ownership with managers, and unfavorable tax regulations make it difficult to find funding (for example, in some countries there is no tax recognition of interest and no active secondary stock market so investors cannot exit LBOs readily).[25]

Outside the United Kingdom, the Netherlands was most active, with 130 MBOs from 1980 to 1985; the majority of these buy-outs of small units from Dutch parents. Most of the funding was debt. Nineteen (15 percent) were buy-outs from a foreign parent, with eight coming from U.S. public companies.[26]

The main barrier in France has been unfavorable tax treatment on interest payments. There was some tax change in 1984 but also a number of restrictions accompanying the changes. As a result, the 1984 tax revision was not expected to encourage management to pursue owning their own units. Nevertheless, in many European countries, company owners are reaching retirement age with no apparent successor. They may well become buy-out targets.

Characteristics of MLBOs

Sound leveraged buy-out candidates have the following well-defined set of characteristics:

1. A strong, committed management.
2. A well-balanced and compatible management team.
3. Steady, predictable cash generation.
4. Completion of capital spending.
5. Limited working capital needs.
6. Lower debt-to-capital ratio.
7. Undervalued assets.
8. Ability to divest assets.
9. Overfunded pension plan.

Management

The CEO of Chase Investment Bank underscored the importance of the quality of the participating management team when he stated, "The quality of management is more important than any income statement or balance sheet."[27] Other observers also suggest that the involvement of managers as owners is critical. The assumption is that managers who own their companies work harder and more productively than those who do not.

Management ownership has sometimes produced startling results. In some instances, sales and earnings improved dramatically for no identifiable reason soon after managers bought a company from its former shareholders. Under such circumstances, reasonable questions may arise concerning the responsibility of management toward the former shareholder wealth.

Commitment of management to the buy-out may be judged in several ways. Creditors, however, generally want managers to invest a significant portion of their personal wealth in the equity of the new firm. In other instances, the industry stature of the unit management or their expertise may be enough for the investor to undertake the risk of financing the buy-out.

The Management Team

The management team members must be competent to manage the various business functions. The team should therefore include individuals with marketing, production, and financial skills. One person may have two or three of these skills, but it is unlikely that one person will be able to handle all three.

The compatibility, stability, and commitment of the management team is crucial, a point underscored by a member of Peat Marwick's Great Britain office:

> We are picking up people already thinking about it. If management has not already got it [leveraged buy-out] in mind, they should not be doing it. A buy-out turns on management incentive and reduced overheads. We have advised people who have not been up to it. Usually what we have tried to do is to say, "You have someone in your team who might not be able to take the pressure. Do you really want them on board?" The whole team has got to be capable. The need is usually to combine leadership from the chief executive with good support from the managers in charge of finance, production, and sales.[28]

Cash Flow

Earnings are important; the company should have a strong, stable earnings history. Even more critical is a predictable free cash flow stream (earnings plus noncash expenses less capital needs). The potential buy-out candidate does not have to be a business that will be immediately profitable, nor is the debt ratio the key. Rather, the key is the ability of the purchasing group to cover the principal and interest payments. The company therefore must be a strong cash flow generator. Preferably it should be able to cover debt payments by a two-to-one ratio.[29] In addition, cash flows must be reasonably steady. Thus, highly cyclical businesses are not usually good LBO candidates.

A member of the investment banking community has pointed out that neither "are interest rates the key thing. It is cash flow. While profits are important, cash flow is much more so because that is what you need to service debts and to start to repay them."[30] An ideal MLBO candidate often has a well-defined niche in its market and thus is not under earnings or funding pressure to find such a niche. In addition, the company must not be at risk of technological obsolescence.[31]

Low Capital Spending Requirements

Companies subject to high funds needs for capital expenses are low on the list, as are those in high-growth businesses, especially if additional capital is needed to fuel the growth. High-tech companies are equally difficult because of business risk and unstable earnings. Low-tech businesses with solid earnings, quality management, and strong market share make the best candidates. Further, capital-intensive businesses are usually not appropriate since many are already heavily leveraged or pose risks should fixed assets need to be replaced or should a growth spurt occur.[32]

Limited Working Capital Needs

Usually working capital needs can be met by decreasing the current ratio somewhat, that is, stretching the accounts payable. Indeed an important source of funding for seasonal needs is often suppliers. In addition, suppliers may agree to stretch payables for a period of several years if management makes a concrete proposal demonstrating a period of growth with its attendant positive consequences for the supplier. The ideal MLBO candidates, however, usually have low increased working capital needs because of the slow growth of the firm. Thus ideal MLBO candidates are not usually exciting companies. One observer described the ideal candidate as "a boring company . . . that operates in a flat industry, [and] needs minimal investment."[33] Ideal candidates are "by their nature . . . [in] well-established business products which are not able to expand markets dramatically."[34]

Low Debt-to-Capital Ratio

The unit to be purchased must start out with debt capacity. Thus already highly leveraged units are not usually good candidates. However, since most of the units in MLBO transactions are business units of larger companies, debt leverage is not usually a problem. Debt on the business unit's balance sheet often consists of funds supplied by corporate. The division or business unit's interest expense is thus an intracompany funds transfer. The funds supplied by corporate generally need to be replaced by debt funds from other sources.

Undervalued Assets

Undervalued assets refers to the difference between book value and market value of the assets. Where the business unit has older multipurpose assets as contrasted to single-purpose assets, the market value of the assets is often higher than the book value. This difference eroded in the mid-1980s, however, as the prices of MLBOs rose.

Ability to Divest Assets

Lending institutions, particularly the senior secured lenders, prefer to see easily marketable assets. Businesses in service industries are usually undesirable because they have a lower level of assets and therefore not enough collateral. Divisions that consist of several business units that might exist in their own right are potentially good MLBOs since the units may be sold to generate cash.

Overfunded Pension Plan

An overfunded pension plan is applicable for total company buy-outs or for larger subsidiaries with their own plans. Under these circumstances, the firm may be able to use the excess pension funds to assist in the purchase of the company. A company can often meet its pension obligations by purchasing defined benefit annuities and may find that the premium is less than the funds accumulated in the pension fund. If this is the case, the funds may, under appropriate circumstances, be diverted to other uses, such as capital asset purchase or repayment of debt. When a unit's pension plan is overfunded, a MLBO may become the catalyst for absorbing the overfunding into the parent company.[35] Most business unit divestitures are included under the total corporate pension plans. Under such circumstances, the excess in pension funds is not usable.

Sources of Funds for MLBOs

The managers targeting a buy-out do not usually have the necessary capital; however, they believe they can run the company better as owners. Under the circumstances, they prefer not to seek significant equity from other sources. Therefore leverage is sought. Can the proposed deal be financed with long-term debt? The answer depends on the amount of equity to be contributed by the management group, the amount of short-term debt available to the firm, and the degree of business risk and stability of cash flows.[36]

The funds for MLBOs have come from several different sources. Commercial banks usually supply the main source of funds in the form of senior debt. Investment bankers and insurance companies are the most frequent sources of subordinated debt. Equity comes from all types of investors.[37] The subordinated debt is referred to as *mezzanine debt* and often has warrants or options attached, in addition to interest well above senior debt because of higher risk. U.S. insurance companies have been large providers.

A typical funding package may include 10 percent equity (with as little as 1 percent from management), 20–30 percent subordinated debt (outer limit, 40 percent), and 60–70 percent senior secured debt (bottom limit, 45 percent).[38] The amount of leverage varies by deal. For example, large U.S. buy-outs have involved eight or ten times debt to equity.[39] The average leverage

The example here is the core business of Mettoy Corgi Toys, which made the traditional Corgi die-cast toy vehicles. The managing director and several other managers presented the idea of a management buy-out. The parent company was in receivership. A major motivation for approval of the MLBO was the expected effect on local employment. The financing package was as follows:

£1 million equity with £140,000 from management.

£860,000 convertible preferred shares from Electra Venture Capital Fund.

£1 million in selective financial assistance from the Welsh (government) Office in three installments.

£400,000 long-term loan from 3i (an investment banker).

£500,000 overdraft by Lloyds bank.

Source: Robin Reeves, "Waltes: Control Brought Closer Home," *Financial Times,* October 10, 1986, p. 4.

Figure 6–4. Illustrative Funding Package for Recent U.K. Buy-out

ratio is about two to one.[40] In the United Kingdom, the ratio of debt to equity in MLBOs have been about five to one.[41] Normal leverage in Britain is about one to one, with interest cover at about four to one.[42] Figure 6–4 demonstrates a funding package for a U.K. buy-out.

Equity participants look for a 30 to 50 percent return over a three- to five-year period. Through 1986–1987, most expectations were met. For example, John Canning, Jr., president of First Chicago Venture Capital, indicated that his firm earned $50 million on $3 million investments in five years. Further, the bank had lost in only two situations out of seventy and had usually increased value by six to eight times. Security Pacific Venture Capital targets compounded pretax returns of 20 to 75 percent.[43]

Funds Availability

Well-planned MLBOs that meet the criteria outlined have found a plethora of funds awaiting them. The primary reason for the interest is the extraordinary gains that have often been made and the lack of visible failures. Through 1987, experience indicated only 10 percent of the companies failed.[44] Buy-outs that went bad were rare. There had been small failures, but the larger buy-outs had not succumbed as frequently.[45] Thus, for venture capitalists, the buy-out was less risky than a new deal.

The milieu in which the MLBOs have taken place includes lower interest rates and a bull market. For most players, a major enticement was the possibility of increasing their return on their debt interests and then exiting by cashing in equity holdings later. From 1982 to 1986, conditions were almost ideal for LBOs as borrowing costs declined and equity prices climbed. Even the October 1987 crash did not dampen the momentum for any length of time.[46]

Sources of the capital include commercial banks, investment bankers, and venture capitalists. Banks generally take senior debt issues, and investment bankers and venture capitalists take on subordinated debt with higher yields and warrants or options attached. Interest rates have been variable. Each of these players has a somewhat different motivation for participating in buy-outs.

Banks

Banks are not looking just to place loans. Rather, they seek a long-term relationship with clients. In addition, participation in MLBOs allows banks to play in territory long reserved to investment bankers by the Glass-Steagall Act (GSA) since the GSA disallows commercial bank participation in the securities market. Banks, however, do scrutinize MBO deals carefully.[47]

Investment Bankers

Traditionally Wall Street firms made their money conducting transactions as agents. By the mid-1980s they increasingly did deals for their own accounts; the risks were higher, but so were the rewards. Returns would run in excess of 50 percent per year where fees of upwards of 1 percent did not compare.[48]

In addition, "junk bonds" became a legitimate financing tool. Junk bonds are noninvestment-grade corporate debt instruments that bridge equity and senior debt. They are securities downgraded by the rating agencies to BA1 or lower for Moody's and BB-plus or lower for Standard & Poor's. The junk bonds were pioneered by Drexel Burnham and were original issues with interest rates 3 percent higher than top-rated bonds. By the mid-1980s, the spread went to as much as five points. Observers expected that 25 percent of Drexel's revenues and a higher proportion of profits came from junk bonds. Specialists like Drexel were ready to take significant proportions of this lower-tier debt. As a result, there were many more companies that would not have previously qualified for a predominantly leveraged solution.

The use of junk bonds was not free of controversy; indeed, in 1985, it appeared that the Fed might effectively paralyze their use. However, what was a minor activity turned into a profitable niche for Drexel. Drexel started the trend in 1984 of using high yields to finance takeovers of major U.S. companies and funded such takeover specialists as Boone Pickens, Saul Steinberg, and Victor Posner. Drexel's management buy-out partner was often KKR.

One major bank chairman cited three reasons for investment bankers' participation: "Big corporations started to sell less-than-investment-grade bonds publicly. Second, institutional-type buyers were willing to downgrade portfolios because inflation forced them to find ways to improve their returns on investment. Third . . . sufficient capital had to be devoted to market-making in quantities to provide a liquid aftermarket."[49]

Venture Capitalists

MLBOs have been viewed as one of the safest investments that the venture capital industry can make. Unlike start-up companies, buy-outs have a history and asset base plus a set of known managers.

Management

Managers' personal investment provided as little as 1 percent of investment, although the amount of the investment may be $1 million or more. Managers do not have deep pockets, while the other players often do.[50]

Results of the MLBO Trend

The results from MLBOs are evident at both the individual firm level and the aggregate level. This section examines what happened to MLBO firms and the MLBO trends in the mid-1980s.

Outcomes for Firms

At least four outcomes appear to occur with MLBOs: higher management motivation, better performance, emphasis on increasing the cash flow, and even with the positive outcomes, most proposed MLBOs do not reach consummation.

MLBOs had been a success through the mid-1980s. One expert viewed them as "one of the most encouraging and dynamic things happening to business in the U.S."[51]

Higher Management Motivation: Investors urged managerial ownership. One institutional investment executive explained, "It is a basic human instinct. . . . If you suddenly find you are working for yourself and making a lot of money, you think as an owner and your attitudes become sharper."[52] Indeed, there was concern if business units were purchased to be freestanding units or as part of an investor's grouping. The performance of non-owner managers of such units could deteriorate markedly. But, spotting good buy-out potentials includes more than just identifying good management and making them part owners.[53]

Better Peformance: Several factors, including motivated management, appeared to contribute to increased performance. Publicly owned companies or business units that were part of a publicly owned company often became laden with burdensome corporate overheads and requirements that drained the company financially, a point underscored by Michael Jensen when he suggested that LBOs were "an absolutely ingenious invention. Public companies can grow fat and sloppy. LBOs compel managements to trim them down and shape them up so the debt can be paid off."[54] A senior managing director at Manufacturers Hanover suggested that managers "do better and work harder because they are freed from a more bureaucratic environment and the need to focus constantly on near-term earnings."[55]

Emphasis on Cash Flow: In the early period following an LBO, emphasis must be put on improving cash flow in order to service the debt. One group executive of a major institutional investor noted, "The corporate jets go in the first hour. It's amazing how quickly a lot of the fluff blows away when the managers are also owners."[56]

The firm generally finds itself bound by creditor restrictions: no payment of dividends or issuance and exercise of stock options during the first five years, little expansion into other lines of businesses, sinking fund repayment of long-term debt, an investor seat on the board of directors, and mandated monthly operating statements. The squeeze of restrictions can be burdensome. If, however, the company survives this early period of servicing the debt load, managers are likely to find themselves with significant personal fortunes.

Typically the early years have had a heavy emphasis on paying down the debt. But servicing the debt should not be at the exclusion of capital investment. The heavy leverage would not affect the health of a company if the business had a steady cash flow, including stable revenue streams from high-quality customers and immunity to sudden changes in the market, intense competition, and rapid technological change, and if it had good assets.[57] Thus companies that require high levels of capital for R&D, new product development, and innovation are usually not suitable LBO candidates.

Most Proposals Do Not Happen: Evidence suggests that of every ten proposed buy-outs, only two have been finalized. Most of these failed at the first hurdle when the accountants concluded that the deal was "unbankable." Tom Wilson, head of a Price Waterhouse buy-out team, commented on this aspect of MBOs: "Two or three of ten drop out at this stage. . . . Tax considerations can often determine the structure of acquisition, the assets acquired and even the success or failure of the whole enterprise."[58]

In short, then, with MOBs, management ownership should lead to improved productivity. The cost of debt is tax deductible (in the United States and Great Britain). High financial leverage should be a substitute for low operating leverage. And high leverage should lead to high return on remaining equity. For buy-outs, the finish line comes several years later when the company is sold or taken public for significant capital gains.[59]

The Aggregate Experience

By-mid 1987 there had been six aggregate outcomes of the MLBO phenomenon: the failure rate was low, buy-outs had become larger, the number of buy-outs was increasing, prices were increasing, the quality of the transactions was likely decreasing, and the time to exit was becoming shorter.

Low Failure Rate: One observer noted, "So far there have been no disasters. This is partly because buyers have chosen their companies carefully. They seek low price/earnings ratios, stable earnings, and saleable assets. They want mature companies with no big capital commitments."[60] Other estimates of failure rates for small buy-outs are about 14 percent, much lower than for other kinds of venture capital ventures.

First Chicago Venture Capital has made seventy such investments. Two failed, primarily because of unforeseen events. In one instance, the industry was deregulated, and in the other a new competitor arrived.[61] Through mid-1987 at least, "LBOs appear to have an almost unblemished record."[62]

Larger Transactions: LBOs are becoming larger. In the past, they typically were under $100 million, but Kohlberg, Kravis, Roberts, and Forstmann Little were arranging deals for over $500 million. W.T. Grimm & Co.'s data indicate that the average price of transaction rose from $3.8 million in 1978 to over $100 million in 1985. The situation suggests that "leveraged deals have now been legitimized."[63] Indeed, leading merchant banker KKR claimed winners out-numbered losers, with annual returns averaging 46.8 percent.

Increasing Number of Transactions: Although estimates vary, the consensus seems to be that U.S. buy-out deals jumped fourfold, to a total of $19.6 billion in 1986. Some debt to equity was as high as eight to one. U.K. management buy-outs topped £1.2 billion ($1.7 billion) for the first time in 1985. In this milieu, Michael Stoddart, chairman of Electra Investment Trust, which ran a £260 million buy-out pool with Candover Investments stated: "More people are realizing that a management buyout can be a good way of selling a company. This is becoming a way of life that we will see getting even more es-tablished over the next three or four years."[64]

Increasing Prices: With so much money chasing deals, prices are going up. Indeed, there have been fears that corporate vendors are asking too much.[65] Early in the decade, companies were bought at three to four times earnings; by 1986 the multiples were eight and even ten times. With prices going up, there were more deals where cash flow could not service the debt. In essence, the participants were banking on the growth in stock price rather than on solid cash flow projects or the collateral of the assets. Under these conditions, ex-perienced players were becoming selective in their investments.[66]

Decreasing Quality: Although the LBO groups went over the companies carefully, observers have suggested a deterioration in the quality of deals. W.T. Grimm has calculated that prices of companies purchased in LBO deals in 1979 were an average of ten times earnings, in 1983, prices were 18.6 times earnings. In addition, the equity component of LBOs is declining.[67]

Decreasing Time to Exit: Time between the buy-out and taking the unit public is getting shorter. In 1986 it was about two years.[68]

Dangers of MLBOs

In spite of the prevailing euphoria concerning MLBOs, there are concerns. The potential dangers include a significant LBO failure; a serious recession, stock-market downturn, or rise in interest rates; restrictive legislation; fallout from insider trading scandal; and the new tax law, which takes away the ability of new owners to redepreciate acquired assets.[69]

Stephen Diamond, senior vice-president at First National Bank, suggested: "In the next down tick many of these things [LBOs] could come undone." And Nicholas Boglivi, vice-president of M&A at Citibank, stated, "I'm surprised it hasn't happened already."[70] If the market falls, the smaller funds are likely to suffer the most since they rely more on flotation (exit through taking a company public). But other observers indicate that the economic cycle will not knock out a lot of companies because the cycles are shorter than that needed to build up a business. The larger funds expect to do the needed building of the businesses in which they have an interest.[71] By early 1988, however, no significant MBO failures had taken place.

External Environmental Issues

Federal Reserve chairman Paul Volcker sounded an alarm about the excessive use of junk bonds: "As the end of 1986 draws near, the great American buy-out binge continues unabated. Huge amounts of low-quality debt keep piling up on buoyant balance sheets."[72] In early 1986, the Fed was ready to issue limits on junk bonds, although their issuance was slower than earlier in the decade ($17 billion in junk bonds issued in 1984 and $15 billion in 1985). Insider trading scandals, such as that involving Ivan Boesky, have also been an issue. Boesky and other members of the arbitrators' community "make their fortunes by buying stakes in vulnerable companies which they thereby help to put 'in play.' "[73] The arbitrators have fueled the controversy. In addition, in early 1986 there was the danger of tax overhauls damaging to movement and no guarantee that further reforms were not forthcoming.

Internal Conditions

The major argument against highly leveraged acquisitions is that they leave the new firm with a high ratio of debt to equity and a low ratio of profits to interest due, a situation that threatens to make the business vulnerable to interest rate movement and business downturn.

With buoyant market conditions, such deals can be negotiated cheaply.[74] Thus rates of return are bound to go down. Further, firms are burdened with increasing debt loads, a concern to many. The situation is exacerbated by the fact that "managers are not always aware of the real value of their companies and sometimes are all too ready to accept the price demanded by the parent."[75] Observers suggest that deals for MLBOs are overpriced.[76] Peter Goodson, vice-president of Kidder Peabody has summed up the situation: "Just because you can get the financing doesn't mean it's a good deal."[77]

Few MBOs have gone bust, although some managements are finding the debt load onerous. Others have had their credit ratings lowered. In September 1986, down ratings of bonds exceeded upgrades by 43 percent.[78]

There are also other concerns about the strategic and operational effects on LBO companies. If pressed by debt service needs, companies might slash R&D budgets and modernization programs or sell valuable assets to meet the debt requirements. Indeed, "buyouts may be criticized as not creating any new businesses and just revitalizing old ones."[79] Another question is whether the spectacular improvements in performance that are reported come from business and economic performance or from reductions in corporate overhead and reductions in interest charges by reducing debt with asset sales.

"None of these dangers, however, seems to have curbed the prevailing appetite for privatization."[80] Why? As noted earlier, Mark Solow, senior managing director of Manufacturers Hanover Trust, a leader in the buy-out boom has suggested that there are currently people willing to take risks.[81]

The MLBOs in This Study

There were nine MLBOs among the firms in this study (table 6–3).[82] Three were units divested by Consumer Products, Inc. in 1980–1981. Two of the MLBOs were divestitures by Conglomerate, Inc.[83] In all, then, six parent companies in this research study had experience with MLBOs.

Comparison with General MLBO Characteristics

In comparing the nine MLBO cases in this study with the descriptions and conclusions suggested earlier in this chapter, three characteristics of the MLBOs

Table 6–3
Characteristics of MLBOs in This Study

Year of MLBO	Name of Parent[a]	Name of Subsidiary[a]	Management Initiated?	Shopped?	Management[b]	Profitable?
1980	Consumer Products, Inc.	Eyewear, Inc.	Unknown	Yes	Team	Unknown
1980	Industrial Products, Inc.	Small Consumer Products, Inc.	Yes	Yes	Team	Moderately
1981	Consumer Products, Inc.	Medico, Inc.	No	No	Team	Yes
1981	Consumer Products, Inc.	Dancer, Inc.[c]	Yes	Yes	Strong leader	No
1982	Major Food Conglomerate	Industrial Small Parts, Inc.	Yes	No	Strong leader	Yes
1982	Conglomerate Inc.	Entertainment Services, Inc.	No	Some	Strong leader	Moderately
1983	Petroleum, Inc.	Container, Inc.	Yes	No	Strong leader	Yes
1984	Private Co. Inc.	Laboratories Inc.[c]	Yes	No	Team	Yes
1985	Conglomerate Inc.	Consumer Packaging, Inc.[c]	Yes	No	Team	Moderately

[a]Names are disguised.
[b]Team = balanced team; strong leader = leader with many years of experience with the unit or the individual had effected a turnaround of the unit.
[c]Turnaround by current management team within three years prior to MLBO.

are salient. First, it is clear that most of the MLBOs were not highly profitable. Indeed, five of the units had undergone turnarounds under the existing management within three years prior to the MLBO. The unit with the lowest profitability at the time of the MLBO was the breakeven situation in Dancer. Three were at least moderately profitable. Only Medico was considered a profitable, solid growth firm. Second, each of the MLBOs had either a balanced management team or a very experienced CEO.[84] Third, all of the units were purchased on a highly leveraged basis. In all of these respects, the units were similar to other MLBOs in the United States.

The comparison of the early MLBOs with the later MLBOs in the study is of interest. The four earliest (1980 and 1981) management-initiated MLBOs were units that were well shopped by corporate management before serious consideration was given to unit management as a buyer. In essence, these early MLBOs were sales of last resort. The pattern then changes for the five most recent MLBOs included in this study (1983, 1984, and 1985). Only Entertainment Services, Inc. had been shopped by corporate management, and then only lightly. The experiences of these companies suggest that MLBOs had become an acceptable divestiture option. This conclusion, too, is in keeping with trends.

Six of the MLBOs were management initiated. Comments drawn from the interviews with the heads of these units support that MLBOs had become a more acceptable divestiture option.

Early Management-Initiated MLBOs: The two early management-initiated MLBOs were shopped initially. These companies were Small Consumer Products, Inc. (a former unit of Industrial Products, Inc.) and Dancer (a former unit of Consumer Products, Inc.). Although both were shopped by corporate management, the circumstances were quite different, and the experiences confronted by the management teams also differed. The management of Small Consumer Products, Inc. initiated a proposal before any shopping activities began. When they were turned down, they helped to sell other related units and also assisted in marketing their own unit to potential buyers. The unit head of Dancer, on the other hand, helped to bring the unit to breakeven in order to get it ready to sell. He also helped to identify potential buyers. Only as corporate's deadline for completing the divestiture program drew near did he propose a MLBO.

Small Consumer Products, Inc.: The parent company, Industrial Products Conglomerate, Inc., made a deliberate strategic decision to sell its consumer products' divisions and focus on its industrial products. Ross Johnson, head of the division Small Consumer Products Inc., had a strong, positive relationship with his corporate chairman. Johnson first sought to buy all of the consumer products divisions. He explained what happened:

Our management group said to each other, "Okay, let's try to buy all the consumer business, because they don't fit with what corporate wants to do. So we approached the CEO, and he said, "Fine, if you can put it together." We went to [a major investment banker] and some others. [The investment banker] agreed to finance us. We would have ended up with a very small piece of the equity but at least it was buying the business. We would have ended up with 12 1/2 percent. It would have been a big operation, and we could not have swung it on our own. The investment banker agreed to finance it. We got the bank debt and presented an offer to the CEO. We had every indication he was going to accept. Well, something happened. I don't know exactly what it was. Maybe he felt he could get a better deal by breaking it up, but out of the clear blue sky, he said, "I've decided not to sell the divisions intact. I want to break them up, and I want you to sell the pieces." I didn't like that very well, and none of the management team did. So we basically said, "Look, you need our help to get it sold. We'll help you sell these businesses, but we want to be able to buy our own division, Small Consumer Products, Inc. We want a shot at our own division." He basically said, "Fine." So we helped him sell the other divisions and proceeded to work on buying SCPI. Because we had turned our division around, it was making money and had a pretty good track record.

Dancer: Dancer was a particularly difficult unit for Small Consumer Product's corporate management, as the corporate director of financial services indicated:[85]

We tried to sell Dancer to a number of companies, but remember that it was a company with several specialty products. We finally sold it to Tom [the unit head] and pretty well all the salespeople. Those that wanted to could exchange their profit-sharing money and their severance pay for equity. We took some personal guarantees from the employees. If Dancer goes down the tubes, we don't stand to get much, just recourse against the assets.

Several buyers looked at Dancer, but neither in whole or in part did the unit fit into their operations. One potential buyer who had considered the unit made the following comment regarding Dancer: "We can ingest anything. Digesting it is the problem." Tom Hanson, president of Dancer, described the unit as "a very complicated little company." Among its difficulties were that it had experienced serious financial problems for three years, it had no product with a significant market share, and the one significant product line had been sold.

The corporate chief financial officer for Small Consumer Products, Inc. talked about the difficulty the corporate parent encountered and how it readied the unit for sale:

A product that we had expected to be a winner didn't go so we sold that product line to a major company. . . . When the product didn't go, I essentially said to Tom Hanson, the president of Dancer, "Look, Tom, you got to at least break even. I don't care about the profit." So he went to work, and he came back and cut $1.5 million out of the overhead without doing any damage to their ability to keep sales up. He didn't make a profit, but he broke even, and the unit turned cash. He cleaned it up so it could be purchased by him or by someone else.

In addition, Dancer did not have the R&D capability to produce its own products. Rather, it had used a search and develop strategy to put together its product line. These serious strategic and operational difficulties made Dancer difficult to sell.

The president and CFO had clearly made a commitment to the financial community that the divestiture program would be completed by the end of 1981. Only Dancer remained of the units targeted for divestiture. With time running out on the parent company's timetable, Tom Hanson approached the company with the idea of an employee buy-out. The proposal was accepted.

Later MLBOs: Container, Inc. (1983), Laboratories, Inc. (1984), and Consumer Packaging, Inc. (1985) were also management initiated. In the first two cases, it was clear that corporate management had not actively considered divestiture prior to the management buy-out proposal; however, the reason that management saw the unit as a potential buy-out differed across the three companies.

Container, Inc.: This MLBO was proposed by the investment banking company that put together the financial package for it. When the idea was first presented to the president of Container, Inc., he indicated little interest. After two or three days, he returned to the investment banker. Together they drew up an MLBO proposal and subsequently sought out the corporate chairman. The deal was ultimately approved.

Laboratories, Inc.: The MLBO of Laboratories, Inc. was headed by an entrepreneur who had wanted his own company for some time. Ed Versaw, president of Laboratories, explained how the MLBO came about:

> I began planning the move from a large corporation to my own business approximately three years before I actually did it. I set criteria for the acquisition, screened potential candidates, and I only saw owners of companies meeting those criteria. I spent long hours reviewing financial statements, D&Bs, and examining markets that the companies competed in.
>
> In the midst of my efforts, Private Company, Inc., where I was director of business development, gave me responsibility for a troubled subsidiary—Laboratories, Inc. About eighteen months later, I had successfully turned around this subsidiary but was still unsuccessful in locating my potential acquisition candidates.

As Laboratories, Inc.'s sales and profits grew, I recommended to Private Company, Inc. more aggressive capital infusions to stimulate continued growth of the unit. The recommendations were declined because Private Company, Inc. management felt the unit was not a particularly good strategic fit.

So I began thinking the potential acquisition candidate I'd been looking for might be right before my eyes. It wasn't an obvious notion, however, because Private Company, Inc. almost never spins off a subsidiary and never had an employee of the company actually buy one of its subsidiaries.

Consumer Packaging, Inc.: When his corporate parent made a large acquisition, the president of CPI felt strongly that his unit, which was relatively small and had been in the lower quartile of profitability for some time, would be slated for divestiture. He initiated his proposal before corporate made a concrete decision about the unit:

Now in 1984 Conglomerate, Inc. was selling other divisions. I have some good friends at corporate. [He named four men with whom he had previously worked or whom he had hired into the company.] . . . So, I knew what was going on. Conglomerate, Inc. didn't see that any subsidiary of less than $50 million really fit into their plans . . . so other divisions started being sold.

I called my friend [one of the four men] and said, "Jack, I got a lot of vibrations that Consumer Packaging does not fit into Conglomerate's plans, and if CPI is going to be sold or if you have been thinking about it, obviously I hope you have enough allegiance to me to talk to me first." And Jack said, "Well, I'll be talking to [the corporate president] about this, and I'll get back to you." So Jack called back and said, "If you have some ideas, why don't you come on down?" So I went down—I guess that was in the spring of 1985—and said, "I think I can do it." And Conglomerate corporate management was very gracious. They are very proud of Conglomerate organization. They said, "Listen all we want out of the deal—all we want out of any of these dispositions—is no book loss—and that's zero—no book loss and no paper. Now if you can do that deal, come back and talk to us about it."

And that deal was not that difficult to get. So thirty days later, we had an agreement, and Conglomerate never shopped the company with anybody else. They gave me the opportunity to put together a deal. I put together the deal, and it was done.

The experience of the first two units suggests that at the beginning of the decade, even when unit management initiated the possibility of an MLBO, corporate management shopped the unit before turning to the management proposal. Second, the experience of Dancer suggests also that earlier in the decade, management was more likely to consider an MLBO only if corporate management had been unsuccessful in finding a buyer. The comparsion with the experience of the later MLBOs suggests that both unit management and corporate management have come to accept MLBOs as a viable divestiture option.[86]

Management Initiation of MLBOs

Two sets of circumstances were associated with the companies included in this set of MLBOs. The first set related to the ripeness of the corporate situation and the second to the relationship between the unit management head and corporate management. There were six characteristics of the situations that rendered the corporate circumstance ripe for an MLBO:

1. The unit did not fit strategically. Either the corporation had undertaken a recent strategic reorientation, or the unit had apparently never fit.
2. The parent had incurred a high debt ratio as the result of a recent acquisition.
3. The parent had been unsuccessful at finding a buyer for the unit.
4. The unit was low in profitability relative to other units in the parent's portfolio.
5. The unit was relatively small.
6. Investment bankers identified the unit as a potential MLBO.

The experiences of the MLBOs are summarized in table 6–4.

Other than item 6, the circumstances listed are not markedly different from those leading to divestiture to outside buyers. What circumstances led corporate management to consider an MLBO? We might speculate that the entrepreneurial bent of the unit management was a factor. Indeed, in three instances, the management had made moves to own their own firm. These moves predated the MLBO. Only in the case of Small Consumer Products, Inc. was this entrepreneurial fervor known. One factor does hold in all cases: the strong, positive association between unit and corporate management. Unit management were well regarded in each case. This is not too surprising since each unit head had been with the unit for a long time and the profitability level of the unit was at least moderate or unit management had effected a turnaround of the unit in the recent past (within three years). (See table 6–5.)

Corporate Circumstances Ripe

The approaches that the MLBO unit heads used in approaching corporate management varied but essentially revolved around pointing out that the unit no longer fit. We have noted at least six different circumstances that prompted unit management to consider their unit as a potential MLBO candidate and elaborate on four of them here.

Small Unit Mandating Little Corporate Attention (Container, Inc.): According to Container, Inc.'s CEO, his company never fit with its parent corporation. It had been acquired as an entry into the packaging industry, but the

Table 6–4
Management-Initiated MLBOs: Unit Management's Reason for Initiating

Year of MLBO	Name of Parent	Name of Subsidiary	Reason for Initiating
1980	Industrial Products, Inc.	Small Consumer Products, Inc.	Parent company had undertaken strategic reorientation. Unit no longer fit. Parent had high debt as a result of large acquisition. Unit management's bent as an entrepreneur was an issue known to corporate executives.
1981	Consumer Products, Inc.	Dancer, Inc.	Parent company had been unsuccessful at finding a buyer. Time was short on targeted deadline for completing divestiture program.
1982	Major Food Conglomerate	Industrial Small Parts, Inc.	Parent company underwent a strategic reorientation. Unit was relatively low in profitability. Manager had tried to buy unit before it was acquired by MFC.
1983	Petroleum, Inc.	Container, Inc.	Investment banker initiated on unit management. Unit president was nearing time of mandatory retirement under corporate policy and "liked to make money."
1984	Private Co. Inc.	Laboratories Inc.	Unit president's recommendation of additional investment in unit was denied because of lack of fit. Unit president was looking for a company to buy. Had already looked at many firms to purchase.
1985	Conglomerate Inc.	Consumer Packaging, Inc.	Unit head saw that corporate was beginning to sell smaller units with moderate to low profitability.

materials it used did not afford any synergy with its parent, Petroleum, Inc. The long-time head of the unit explained how he convinced the CEO of his parent corporation to consider the unit as an MLBO:

> I went to the chairman of Petroleum, Inc., and I told him we had no synergism. I was never cut out to be a big corporate man. I like to make money. . . . I wanted to keep on working at this [he was within several months of retirement]. One of the partners in the investment banking concern and I went in to see the chairman. I told him we had 22 minutes of his time if he worked 250 days a year. I would like to buy the unit I had managed for so long. . . .

Table 6–5
Characteristics of Unit Head's Relationship with Corporate

Year of MLBO	Name of Parent	Name of Subsidiary	Nature of Relationship
1980	Industrial Products, Inc.	Small Consumer Products, Inc.	Unit head had been responsible for turnaround of another unit and putting the MLBO unit in profitable shape. Strong positive relationship with CEO.
1981	Consumer Products, Inc.	Dancer, Inc.	Unit head was well respected among corporate management. Viewed as a strong manager. Helped to bring unit to break-even in order to get it ready to sell.
1982	Major Food Conglomerate	Industrial Small Parts, Inc.	Head of unit had come with the original acquisition many years previously. Unit had not had any difficulty under his leadership.
1983	Petroleum, Inc.	Container, Inc.	Head of unit had come with the original acquisition many years prior. Unit had not had any difficulty under his leadership.
1984	Private Co. Inc.	Laboratories Inc.	President of MLBO was a corporate officer charged with turning the unit around. He did so successfully and then proposed the MLBO.
1985	Conglomerate Inc.	Consumer Packaging, Inc.	Unit head had successfully turned unit around to moderate profitability after corporate sold a major item from their product line.

He had sold several units [and he said], "If you are crazy enough to try to do that at age sixty-five, I will help you do that." . . . I asked him, "Do you have the power to say yes or no?" He said, "No, the executive committee of the company has that power." I asked "Do you have influence on the committee?" His answer was, "Sizable."

Convincing corporate executives to sell the unit to the management team was not difficult. In addition to the misfit of the unit, two other circumstances prompted the initiative. First, a regional investment banking company suggested to unit management that their unit might be an appropriate MLBO deal. Second, the president of Container, Inc., who had worked for the company most of his career, was facing mandatory retirement at the end of the calendar year. This combination of circumstances lead to management initiation of the MLBO.

Major Strategic Reorientation (Small Consumer Products Inc.): In the case of Small Consumer Products, Inc., the parent company made a strategic reorientation away from consumer goods into industrial goods where it was felt there would be better margins. The point of departure was the acquisition of a large industrial manufacturing company. The president of Small Consumer Products, Inc. explained:

> When they bought [the large industrial manufacturing company] . . . we saw an opportunity. We had talked all along about the possibility of a leveraged buy-out. Since I had done a leveraged buy-out in the early 1970s, the idea was constantly in the back of my mind to do it again. I had talked to my unit CFO about a leveraged buy-out. I saw this thing happening at corporate with [the large industrial manufacturing company]. I reported to the corporate CEO. When they bought the industrial manufacturing company, I was given all of the consumer businesses to manage. . . . The entire group was a $450 million sales volume operation. After the acquisition, all of a sudden none of these consumer products units really fit that well.
>
> The sale of the consumer products units was precipitated only after Industrial Conglomerate, Inc. bought [the large industrial manufacturing company]. That acquisition gave us the opportunity. We knew immediately that with that much debt and knowing the CEO, he was going to want to get out of some things. So we were just johnny on the spot and capitalized on the situation by approaching him on it.

The case of Small Consumer Products, Inc. is of particular note because Ross Johnson, head of that unit, tried to buy a unit of Industrial Products before he was employed by the company. After Johnson considered and rejected buying a particular unit, IPI's CEO offered him a position at corporate. Johnson accepted and shortly after became head of the division that included Small Consumer Products and another smaller unit. Still later, he helped to sell a set of companies and finally effected an MLBO on Small Consumer Products, Inc., a portion of the division that he had headed up for several years.

Acquisition of the Parent Company by Another Firm (Small Consumer Products, Inc.): The management team purchased SCP Inc. from Industrial Products in 1980. In 1982 they sold SCP Inc. to MIC Inc. Even as a subsidiary executive of MIC Inc., Ross Johnson had interests in an MLBO. At one point his interests included MIC Inc. as a total company buy-out. Johnson explained:

> I approached Ralph [MIC's chairman and CEO and] I said, "What about letting us put together a buy-out on MIC Inc., the total company?" And I guess I didn't push it hard enough. At that point, it would have been good to have done that. But the stock started to increase in value, and in a short time it went up so much that it no longer made sense as a leveraged buy-out. The chairman and I got to be pretty good friends, and I said, "Ralph, if you ever

want to sell Small Consumer Products, Inc., if it doesn't really fit and so forth, I would like to have a chance to buy it back." And he basically said, "If I ever reach the decision, you'll have the first chance. I'll definitely let you guys have a shot at it." And he said, "I can understand why you like to be independent because I have been independent. I can feel that." He was very emphathetic. He and I talked about that, I would guess, every time we had a general management meeting. I would bug him on it. I'd try not to be obnoxious, but I would say, "Ralph, I just want you to know if you ever want to sell, we would like to be independent again."

And, you know, I think probably I wouldn't have stayed a lot longer anyway. It didn't look like we could buy the unit back. Just to continue running it [as] the general manager was getting less and less challenging. I was really getting bored, particularly in the third year . . . but then I got an inkling that maybe there are rumors on different people buying MIC Inc. and so we said, "Well, maybe we ought to wait this out and see what happens." There was always an excuse to wait a little longer. There were a couple of times I frankly thought about just bailing out. I'm sure [the unit CFO] did. I know [the unit marketing vice-president] did. But somehow we always said, "Well, maybe we ought to hang in a little longer." After the first two years, I felt our moral obligation was completed. The third year got to be pretty tough. But then NAT, Inc. announced they were buying MIC Inc. . . .

Then we really were a stepchild. So again our management team kept saying, "This may well work out. Here's a golden opportunity." I approached Ralph again, and he said, "Well, Ross, I told you that I would give you first chance. And I'll talk to the president of NAT, Inc. I think you have that right." It came [out] in the conversaton that he had told the president of NAT, Inc. that he had told me that if Small Consumer Products, Inc. was ever sold, we should have the first right and that he had made me that promise. So again he was living up to a moral commitment, which he didn't have to do at all. This conversation was early on in the process, and we thought, "Well, maybe that will happen, and maybe it won't." We went to a couple of meetings with NAT, Inc., and we knew it was the end of the road if we had to work under NAT, Inc. because their management style was totally different from Ralph's. It went back to worse than Industrial Conglomerate, Inc. It was total centralized control and total interference. . . . Very clearly and immediately we saw that. It gave us the incentive that we either buy the business, or we are going to be gone anyway. So we had very little to lose by forcing the issue.

We then went to NAT, Inc. . . . And it took months to get to this point, but they said, "Yes, we can sell you." We thought that they were very tough people. We knew that if we went in too low, we'd never get the business. We went in at what we thought was a very full price but asked them to carry a significant part of it back, hoping that maybe they weren't as focused on discounted cash flow value and maybe they would look at the total dollars as opposed to the method of payment . . . which it turned out was the right strategy. . . . If we had gone in one penny less than book value, I don't think they would [have sold us]. . . . [He talked about how the management team wanted to get the price below book value and NAT, Inc. refused to budge.]

The team countered with full price but more carryback. Also NAT, Inc. refused to take some contingent liabilities. They wanted a "neat and clean" transaction. We had determined in our own mind, the four of us, that if they shopped the business, we were not going to be part of it and that we would simply leave. We had nothing to gain by doing that, and we weren't going to sit around waiting to see if they would then sell it to us after it was shopworn. I think they knew that. I think Ralph brought that issue to their attention. We had been through that experience with our first parent company.

Reorientation of the Parent Company (Industrial Small Parts, Inc.): A similar situation occurred in the Industrial Small Parts, Inc. MLBO from Major Food Conglomerate, Inc. The parent company changed strategy, and the president of Industrial Small Parts, Inc., knowing that his unit had slower growth in profits than the parent company preferred, expected his unit was slated to go. He wasted no time: "I went to [the chairman], and I told him I had been private and I had been public, and right now in my career, private looked better. I told him I was interested in buying some businesses."

Evidence of Misfit (Laboratories, Inc.): In the case of Laboratories, Inc. the head of the MLBO was a corporate officer. One of his assigned tasks was to undertake a turnaround of Laboratories, Inc. He succeeded in the turnaround and then tried unsuccessfully to get corporate management to invest more aggressively in the unit. He explained the circumstances leading up to the MLBO initiation:

> As Laboratories, Inc. sales and profits grew, I recommended to Private Company, Inc. more aggressive capital infusions to stimulate continued growth of the company. The recommendations were declined because Private Company, Inc. management felt the company was not a particularly good strategic fit.

Unit Management's Contributions to the Unit

In addition to the situations being ripe for divestiture, the unit heads of the MLBOs had all contributed significantly to their units. As noted in table 6–5, four unit heads had accomplished a successful turnaround. In the other two cases, four unit head had been with the moderately profitable unit since the time of its acquisition.[87] Three of the cases are particularly illustrative of the efforts of the unit heads to effect turnarounds: a turnaround after downsizing (Consumer Packaging), rebuilding the unit (Small Consumer Products, Inc.), and a turnaround to breakeven, a case of a continuing unit head after disaster (Dancer).

Turnaround after Downsizing (Consumer Packaging): At Consumer Packaging, Inc. the president cleaned up the unit for Conglomerate, Inc. before proposing a buy-out. Two years later, he took over as head of the unit. Within a year, the chairman of Conglomerate, Inc. made a handshake deal for a major portion of Consumer's product line. The president of Consumer Packaging first found out about the divestiture of the product line through a customer. Nonetheless, he willingly took on the challenge of downsizing his division:

> Well in 1982 the problem was, how do you downsize a $45 million company to a $20 million company because we'd just sold over half of our business. . . . So we closed warehouses, . . . terminated a lot of people. We had to cut our G&A roughly in half. That was a challenge. Nobody at corporate got too bogged down in these details. What they liked was the $6 million over book they got for this product line. They said, "Okay, Len will work out the details." That was fine because I thought I could, and I didn't really want their help anyway. 1982 and 1983 were not profitable years because we had all the severance pay to worry about, leases running forever. You can imagine the expenses in downsizing a company and trying to be fair with everybody. Everybody that I separated, we gave them six months' severance.

The severance was his idea rather than company policy:

> With these two divisions I would do this and then say, "This is what I did with the people we had to let go." The president would say, "Fine." Other divisions have done it very differently.

Turning the Unit Around (Small Consumer Products, Inc.): At Small Consumer Products, Inc. the situation was very similar to that at Consumer Packaging. The president explained the set of circumstances that led to his heading up the unit:

> I sold my first company. Then I looked for another company to buy for almost a year, but I really didn't find anything that made sense. During that time I had gone to Industrial Products, Inc. and talked to them about their small parts division because I knew small parts. But after I looked at the numbers, I said, "It's not going to make it. There's no way that this can be a stand-alone business." I got to know the chairman of the company from this contact, and he kept talking to me about working for him. . . . So I went to work for Industrial Products, Inc. as corporate vice-president of finance with the understanding that if a line job opened up, I would get the first chance to look at it. This job of heading up the division that included the small parts unit opened up one week later. . . . We took the small parts business back to breakeven. It had been hemorrhaging millions in losses a year, and we brought it back to break even, but frankly, never made it really profitable.
>
> In [the small consumer products] part of the division, we had a good name, good market position, good market share . . . Industrial Products, Inc. didn't understand consumer marketing. They had fragmented, small product shares.

I knew I had a major rebuilding job if I took the division, but it looked interesting and challenging so I told [the CEO] I wanted it. I came down here as president of the division. It was losing money; it had lost $12 million or $14 million the year before. . . . It was running out of control—too many plants, lack of inventory control. . . . It would put products on the market without adequate testing. There were quality problems, too many products at a point in time, too much organization, too much overstaffing—you know the classic things.[88]

Turnaround to Breakeven (Dancer): Dancer's unit head had been with the unit for a couple of years when it suffered a disastrous set of years with the failure of a new product line. Dancer's president willingly helped to bring the unit to break even and also helped to identify potential buyers.

Finding Financing

Most of the MLBOs were sold at book value. A major goal on the part of corporate was that there be no loss to report on the sale of the unit. As noted, all of the units were highly leveraged. The financing came from several sources, including management's personal capital, management personal debt, outside investors, investment bankers, debt from local banks, debt from the parent company (usually subordinated), and guarantees of debt from the parent company. The sources of financing and profitability levels are indicated for the MLBOs in table 6–6. The MLBOs are ordered by the difficulty they encountered in finding financing. The four most difficult circumstances occurred from 1980 to 1982 and the three easiest from 1983 to 1985. The experience of these MLBOs is in keeping with the general observation that financing for MLBOs has become more readily available. Comparing the firms that experienced difficulty in finding financing with those that experienced the greatest ease in finding financing reveals additional factors.

Lack of readily available financing affected the early MLBOs, although the difficulties these MLBOs encountered emanated from other issues too. Dancer, the most difficult of the MLBOs, had to rely almost totally on its parent corporation. The unit management of Small Consumer Products had a firm goal of maintaining control of the equity interest. This objective plus pressure from personal relationships between one of the investment banking firms and a corporate board member contributed to the difficulty in getting financing. Entertainment Inc. found several doors blocked, in at least one case because of gloomy predictions concerning the industry. Medico found persuading local banks difficult in spite of solid performance and significant potential growth.

The three firms that had the greatest ease in finding financing appeared to share one factor in common: close links with the sources of funds. Consumer Packaging's CEO had close relationships in the banking community. Container, Inc.'s MLBO was initiated by an investment banking firm. In the case of

Table 6-6
Sources of Funding, by Company

Year	Unit	Profitability before Turnaround[a]	Profitability at Divestiture	Source of Funding				
				Personal Funds	Outside Investors	Investment Banker	Bank	Parent (Guarantee)
1981	Dancer	Negative	Breakeven	X				X
1980	Small Consumer Products	Negative	Moderate	X	X	X		X
1981	Entertainment	N.A.	Moderate	X[b]		X		
1982	Medico	N.A.	Good	X	X	X		
1984	Laboratories	Negative	Moderate	X	X		X	
1985	Consumer Packaging	Negative	Moderate	X	X		X[c]	
1983	Container	N.A.	Moderate to Good	X	X	X		

[a]N.A. = not applicable as no turnaround occurred.
[b]Very little.
[c]Local.

Small Consumer Products, Inc.'s second MLBO, the unit management team were well acquainted with the investment banking and credit corporations.

With the exception of Small Consumer Products, Inc.'s second MLBO and the MLBO of Consumer Packaging, Inc., all the units experienced various degrees of difficulty in putting the financing package together. Finding financing was especially problematical for small companies with poor track records. I elaborate on the experiences of nine of the MLBOs, in order of decreasing difficulty of finding financing:

1. The most difficulty leads to the most creativity (Dancer).
2. Interference from inside corporate can almost lead to disaster (Small Consumer Products, Inc. the first time).
3. Declining corporate help can portend difficulty (Industrial Small Parts, Inc.).
4. Local banks cannot be relied on to identify a good deal (Medico, Inc.).
5. Finding financing takes several iterations (Entertainment Services, Inc.).
6. A change in the unit's performance leads to snags with the lenders (Laboratories, Inc.).
7. Getting outside investors on board is an option (Consumer Packaging, Inc.).
8. It helps when the investment banker comes calling (Container, Inc.).
9. The second time goes more smoothly (Small Consumer Products, Inc.).

The Most Difficulty Leads to the Most Creativity (Dancer): Dancer was the most extreme case in the set of MLBOs. The parent company, Consumer Products, Inc., went to considerable lengths to effect the MLBO. Indeed, the director of financial services later called the Kalo divestiture "the most creative, the one that required the most ingenuity."

The agreed-upon purchase price for Dancer was $2.8 million. The new corporation raised a down payment of $400,000, and the parent company financed the balance on a 12 percent note secured by all the assets of the new company. The equity funds came primarily from two sources: personal funds from the president, Tom Hanson, and most of the employees, and through the transfer of funds in a previously existing corporate profit-sharing trust to a new stock bonus plan established by Dancer. The parent company also permitted the following sources of funds to be converted to equity: severance pay, bonuses (including a special bonus designed to increase if the purchase price of the unit was over a certain limit), and the employees' accumulated vacation time. Thus Dancer became "a 100 percent employee-owned company."[89]

Interference from Inside Corporate Can Lead to Near-Disaster (Small Consumer Products, Inc. the First Time): In one other instance, the unit head had a difficult set of issues to work out in crafting the deal with corporate and in working out the financing. The parent company, Industrial Products, Inc., had decided to sell all of its consumer products companies. Ross Johnson, the head of Small Consumer Products Inc., originally found financing for the entire group of units that manufactured consumer products and made an offer of $450 million. In this deal, the investment banker offered the management team 12 1/2 percent of the equity. Industrial Products, however, broke up the group of consumer units and sold the units individually.

Ross was intent on buying SCPI but decided not to go back to the investment banker that had agreed to the $450 million package. Management control was the critical issue. Ross would not do business with a firm that would not give his management team controlling interest.

The management team approached several potential sources of financing. Two investment banking firms, B&B and C&C, evidenced considerable interest in the deal. C&C management had a strong relationship with a member of the board of SCP Inc.'s parent. At one point, SCP Inc. management found themselves pressured by the corporate chairman to work out the deal with C&C. C&C, however, offered management only 20 percent of the equity. Indeed C&C threatened to do the deal without management.

Direct inquiry to B&B indicated that it would not do the deal without management. Using the B&B commitment as leverage, the unit management team wrung a commitment of 75 percent of the equity for management from C&C, a wrenching process. (His description of the situation, along with comments from the unit CFO, appears in appendix 6A.)

Could the difficulty Small Consumer Products, Inc. had in negotiations with the investment bankers have been avoided? Perhaps if the management team had been willing to settle for a smaller piece of the ownership, negotiations might have been less onerous. Ross Johnson, the president of SCP, explained:

> It depends on what you're willing to settle for. If you are willing to settle for a small percentage of the company, then you can work with an investment bank and let them do that. It does mean financing for you, which means maybe you can get away without having a parent company carry back funds. But if you're trying to maintain control of the company, then it's paramount to have a good enough relationship with your parent company. It's a matter of control. If you're willing to accept 10 percent of the company as a management team, if that's what you're willing to live with, then it's a whole different scene that can be wrought. But if you're trying to maintain control as a management team, it's a different ball game. Of course, it's also riskier that way, too, from the standpoint of being able to pull it off because you don't have as much of a big name behind you that says, "The money is right here." . . . So it's a little riskier.[90]

Declining Corporate Help Can Portend Difficulty (Industrial Small Parts, Inc.): Industrial Small Parts was a unit of Major Food Conglomerate. The president of the unit declined help from the parent to find financing. He found trying to find financing independently difficult. His "search for money involved some scrounging and scratching but eventually paid off."

Do Not Count on Local Banks to Identify a Good Deal (Medico, Inc.): When working on an MLBO, the unit head has two simultaneous marketing tasks: to sell the deal with the parent company and to work out the financing package. The latter usually involves multiple sources. Bill Sheay, president of Medico Products, Inc., a former unit of Consumer Products, Inc., acknowledged that acquiring Medico from CPI was the biggest challenge, as well as the biggest thrill, of his career. The MLBO process brought its share of "headaches, big headaches," said Sheay as he pointed to two large volumes containing the memoranda that made up the deal. From the inception on January 4 until closing on November 26, Sheay was caught in a juggling act: trying to complete a financial package that met the terms mandated by corporate and those demanded by a lender. At the same time, Sheay wanted to remain in control with the majority interest.

Meeting all those demands is seldom easy. Sheay used an investment banker that sold stock to nineteen local investors, two of whom were also corporate officers. Sheay first canvassed local banks but failed to find financial support. He explained that they "looked at what we were asking, and they were neither creative nor progressive enough." Then he went to GE Credit Corporation's Acquisition Funding Corp. in New York: "They gave us everything we wanted. . . . Their decision was based on the company's past performance, our management team, and our future projections."

Finding Financing Takes Several Iterations (Entertainment Services, Inc.): Finding financing usually took several iterations. The head of Entertainment Services, Inc., a former unit of Conglomerate, Inc., described the difficulties he had in looking for financing:

> Well, the partner backed out [of the first deal], and I went to see my friend Stephen Newell of the Fourth National Bank in a town where we had some business locations. I said, "Here is a $25 million deal, and if I put in $4 million myself, would you put in the balance?" He said, "Yes. The only thing you have to tell me is what New York bank you want me to affiliate with because my lending limit is $12 million. I can go with Chase. I can go with Chemical. I can go with Manufacturers. . . ." I said, "I don't want you to go with Chase because that's Conglomerate's lead bank." Then my two sons said they didn't want me to put up that much money on my own for them.
>
> Then another fellow called me, and he said, "How would you like to have a financing partner?" I went to see him. He and his partners wanted badly to go in with me. But they sat down at the last minute and said, "We got a call from our partner in Los Angeles, and he says that your business is going to be nothing in six months. So he says for us not to put in a dime."

When asked whether he was seeing potential in a unit that a partner and the parent company were not optimistic about, he replied:

> Well, I know the business better than they do. I just thought we had a chance. A broker I met said he wanted me to meet Kenneth Kaufman. So I went up and met Kenneth Kaufman who is a broker who used to be with Forstmann Little. Ken is thirty-five. We started talking. After I met with him, I didn't think we had accomplished too much. Then someone sent him some material on the industry award I received in the mid-1970s. They sent him one of the brochures that was given to those who attended the award dinner in my honor. The brochure pointed out that I had been in a class with [some of the industry greats]. Finally Ken and his partners called me, and they said, "I think we can reconstruct this deal. How would you like to have half the company and not put up a penny?" I said, "That's very interesting. But we have to have complete management [control]." Then we worked it out eventually that I had 55 percent and they had 45 percent. I put up a total of $250,000 for the organization cost, which is a nice way to do the deal.

A Change in the Unit's Performance Leads to Snags with the Lenders (Laboratories, Inc.): Even when the process of finding financing is relatively smooth, a change in the performance of the unit can lead to some difficulties. Ed Versaw, the president of Laboratories, Inc., described the problem he ran into:

> After we signed the letter of intent, and I was lining up the financing, we happened to have a soft sales month. The banks began to get cold feet, and it looked like the deal was going to stall.
>
> I called the president of the bank and told him I had to meet with him to explain the situation. He said "My calendar is booked, but I'm going to a football game tonight. I've got an extra ticket. Why don't you come along?" So at half-time at a football game, I explained the situation, and the deal moved forward. There is only so much accountants and lawyers can do for you at times.

Getting Outside Investors on Board (Consumer Packaging, Inc.): The ease of finding financing appeared to be related to the institution's proximity to the unit and their resulting local knowledge of the unit or management's experience with the financing institutions. Peter Damary, president of Consumer Packaging, Inc., talked about how he found his financing:

> The way I did it, there's a bank here in town which has always been a major part of Conglomerate Inc.'s credit agreement. Conglomerate's lead bank was always either Chase or Chemical or another of the big guys, and then they picked up regional banks to participate. The banker here is Brad Benson, who has a long history with Conglomerate, and he has a long history with me. When I came to Consumer Packaging, Inc., Brad helped me with my home mortgage, and he was my local bank contact into the conglomerate system. Brad and I were friends. We went out socially together with our wives.

So I went down to talk to Brad and said, "Well, could we talk about what it would take for you to be interested in commencing this deal?" And he looked at the numbers. At that point it looked like maybe an $11 million deal—$11–$12 million cash at closing. And he said, "What I really need is about $3 million in equity." . . . So I said, "I might do that, but I can't do it comfortably." So we talked, and Brad had the idea. He said, "Well," he said to me, "If you could get Conglomerate to guarantee a Consumer Packaging note to our bank, it wouldn't be paper. It wouldn't be on Conglomerate's books. It would be somewhere out there in a footnote saying, 'The total of guaranteed obligations are . . .' And I would look at that as equity because it would be subordinated to everything."

So I went back to Conglomerate and said, "This is what I'd like to do. I'd like to come up with $1.5 million equity. If you would guarantee our $1.5 million note to the bank, the bank will put up the rest of it, and you'll have cash at closing. The deal would be based on book value of assets—not a dime more and not a dime less." I was dealing at Conglomerate with [two men he knew well]. And they said, "It sounds pretty good. We'll check with [Conglomerate's president]." And it was just really a few days later that he decided that's what we were going to do.

In the case of Consumer Packaging, Inc., the equity came from two primary sources, the executives and two outside investors. The president explained:

[The equity] entails ten people—the vice-presidents and some of the other key managers. Everybody I gave the opportunity to participate did participate. One share of stock was $5,000. So that was the minimum. We only had a couple in for the minimum. I went to key guys. The heads of marketing and finance are both in for over $100,000. I put in about $400,000. I have some friends in town. I've been very active with Young Presidents Organization. Some of those guys knew what I was doing, and they just simply said, "If you need any help, let us know." It was easy. I went to one of the guys and said, "I'm $400,000 short." He said, "Fine. Just tell me when you want it." The only other outside investor—a Far East agent—wanted to get involved in this. I saw this as an opportunity to tie him in. He's a very wealthy man. . . . So I made a three-day trip to the Far East. I mean three days from home back to home. . . . And the agent said, "How much can I come in for?" And I said, "$200,000." [He said], "Fine." So that's how I lined up the outside investors. . . .

[He said he had tried another bank, but they] . . . just couldn't really get organized on it, and Brad's bank was prepared to act quickly. . . .

This was our proposal, [but] the deal didn't follow exactly this way. For example, the loan proposal didn't end up quite the way I proposed. I ended up with just a straight revolving credit agreement and reducing revolving at 1 1/2 percent over prime. And the reducing part is the first year we got 90 percent of receivables. This year it decreased. So far we've been very comfortable. We haven't had a serious squeeze. . . . I'm basically a conservative fellow—I guess it's my accounting background. So I said, "Well what we got to do is make sure we don't do anything that would jeopardize the existence of the company." So I saw that role as just making darn sure that we stayed within the credit agreement with the bank. Our goal was very limited sales growth. I'm talking 5 percent per year. . . . We started off with $1.5 million equity and $7.5 million debt. And what I wanted to do was make the equity pile bigger and bigger and the debt pile smaller. And I saw that as my short-term objective: make the balance sheet stronger, make the bank comfortable with us, and just make sure that everything we do is profitable. . . . I would say in about one more year, our equity will be much more substantial than it is today. In the first year we added about $700,000 after-tax earnings to equity. We'll do the same this year. . . . We have every restriction you can think of with the bank. But they have not been important. They have not really cramped us in any way. . . . In fact, I set most of the restrictions. . . . For example, salary increases are limited to 10 percent per year. . . . They didn't want us to buy back any stock from stockholders . . . unless the bank approved what we want to do.

In this instance, the ease in finding financing related to the close relationships the president had developed with the banking community, as well as individuals with significant personal capital. In addition, the willingness of the parent to cooperate was a factor.[91]

It Helps When the Investment Banker Comes Calling (Container, Inc.): Petroleum Inc.'s 1983 MLBO of Container, Inc., was also a fairly easy financial transaction. In this case, the MLBO was initiated when the investment banker approached management. As the transaction unfolded, the investment banker encouraged a large local bank to make personal loans to various officers in the company so that they could purchase equity. The president of Container, Inc. explained:

I went to each one of the staff and told them what had been going on. I said, "If you want to become a part owner of our company, the investment banker will let you know how much stock you can buy. They will help you borrow money." So they borrowed the money from the fellows who underwrote our deal.

The investment bankers felt that helping management to have a piece of the action was important. The investment banker's initiation of the idea of the MLBO was an important factor in the smoothness with which this deal was consummated. Essentially the financing was in place before the president of Container, Inc. even went to the chairman of Petroleum, Inc.

The Second Time Around Can Be Easier (Small Consumer Products, Inc.): Ross Johnson and Allen Hope of Small Consumer Products, Inc. did their deal twice. The first buy-out was from Industrial Products, Inc. Two years later, they sold the company to MIC Inc., a larger company in a related industry. Several times after the transaction, Johnson asked the chairman of MIC Inc. to consider an MLBO if he decided to sell Small Consumer Products, Inc. Within three years, MIC Inc. sold itself to still another company. At that time, Johnson reminded MIC Inc.'s chairman of his promise, and ultimately the same management team repurchased its unit.

In this second MLBO for Small Consumer Products, Inc., finding financing was relatively easy. At least two factors seemed to be critical. One was the support of MIC Inc.'s chairman and CEO, who fulfilled his commitment to Johnson. The new parent company NAT Inc. thus carried some paper. In addition, this MLBO represented a third leveraged purchase of a company for Johnson. He knew the investment banking community and the credit corporations fairly well by this time:

> [Our financing] is basically the same way we had [it before]. In fact, it's almost identical. All we did was use the same basic deal that we did with Industrial Products, Inc. We changed it a little bit, but basically we have a subordinated note from [MIC Inc.'s new parent] for one-third of the purchase price. It's an eight-year loan at an under-market rate which acts as equity.
>
> We went to B&B, but they were not very cooperative. So we went back to [a major financing company]. The guy at [the major financing company] that I worked with on the leverage buy-out in 1970 is now a key guy at Westinghouse Electric. So, again, a relationship carried through. He had wanted to finance the first acquisition of Small Consumer Products, Inc. from Industrial Products, Inc. when he was at [the major financing company], but their top management was in a state of disarray, and they turned it down. And he was bitter about that . . . and I think there was an emotional incentive for him to want to do it. He was very fair. We negotiated with him personally. We borrowed $59 million from different pieces, but the total line is $59 million with the carry-back from [MIC Inc.'s new parent]. And that's it basically. We have very little in equity. . . . We own 100 percent of the equity other than 4 percent they have. That's part of the financing cost. MIC Inc.'s new parent has a 4 percent warrant that was part of the purchase price. Other than that, for all practical purposes we own 100 percent of the company.

Postdivestiture Strategic and Operational Actions

MLBOs are usually highly leveraged transactions. The companies in this study were no exception. In the postdivestiture period, the high leverage affected the companies in two ways: a careful focus on minimizing cash outflows and careful management of growth.

The pressure to minimize cash outflow comes primarily from the debt service, the interest charges and principal repayment. According to the president of Medico, "The only thing that changed was the ownership and how we managed cash—now we are borrowing money as opposed to being a cash rich company." While under CPI's ownership, cash flow had never been a problem.

In recent years the interest rate has not been a major issue. In the early part of the decade, however, it was sometimes critical, as the chairman of Entertainment explained:

> The first thing we wanted to do was to get the loan down to bite size, primarily because of the interest load. You know when we were talking about interest that was up to 18 percent, 17 percent. You figure out the interest on $25 million. That's a lot of money! Well, fortunately interest rates came down, but the first thing we wanted to do was clean that debt.

In order to minimize cash outflow, the firms in this research program undertook various actions, including:

- Maintain closer inventory control.
- Maintain closer accounts receivable control.
- Minimize capital expenditures by finding less expensive ways to build new sites, pressuring contractors by dropping older contractors who raise prices, and/or leasing in preference to purchasing assets.
- Offer severance incentives to more highly paid workers and replace with temporary help.
- Sell off assets.
- Keep growth at a minimal level.

Comments regarding each of these tactics appear in figure 6–5.

The situation is exacerbated if the company requires significant capital assets to bring it to a competitive state. One unit, Entertainment Services, Inc., was caught in such a bind, as its president explained:

> When we bought Entertainment, it was going like this [down]. It looked bad. And I want you to know that it looked pretty bad for us for a while. I mean it really did. For a while there we were asking ourselves, you know, "Why are we in this mess?" We bought the company for $25 million. I realized that we must spend somewhere in the neighborhood of $25 million more to make it new.

At the same time, the companies want to maintain their relationships with suppliers, as the CFO of Consumer Products, Inc. said:

> There was nobody [that] I wasn't able to make feel adequately comfortable. [We said,] it's business as usual. Yes, we are going to continue to pay our bills on time. We didn't start dragging payables for sixty days or anything like that. [We] wanted to keep a good supplier relationship so we could continue to pay on time. We took the risk of borrowing the money to do that.

- Closer inventory control and accounts receivable control:

    There was certainly more emphasis on cash. We've been watching receivables and watching inventory and had a pretty good track record in both those two areas. Also capital expenditures, we had those under control.

- Minimize capital expenditures by:
  Finding less expensive ways to build new sites:

    Before the divestiture, it was a different look. When you bought a site, you bought the building. You bought the land or you ground leased the land and built the building. Now I don't have that kind of money. I am still paying the original loan. So what I do is go into a marketplace and *lease* the site. I do a lease-back. [He explained that he had found ways to build at approximately two-thirds the going rate per square foot.]

    Pressuring contractors by dropping older contractors who raise prices: Entertainment Services, Inc. carefully hired their architectural firm and their general contractor. They also had a set of subcontractors whom they worked with. In at least one case, they changed to a new architectural firm when their former architects came in with a bid higher than they deemed reasonable. The president indicated that the former architectural firm was now doing business with several sister companies to whom he had recommended the firm. He was willing to train new firms in his cost-efficient methods even though he knew he would have to change firms every couple of years in order to keep his construction costs down as low as possible.

    Leasing assets in preference to outright purchase:

    My philosophy when we were on the LBO basis was, if it was nonproductive equipment, it made more sense to lease things as opposed buying in cash.

- Offer severance incentive to more highly paid workers and replace with temporary help: Another tactic (used only in one company) was to replace permanent with temporary employees. The president of Consumer Products explained that he gave the opportunity to one department of eleven people, thinking two or three would take the offer of severance pay of two weeks for every year they had been here. Ten took the offer. The department is now staffed primarily with temporary people. The Consumer Products president has found this work group to be stable and productive.

- Sell off assets:

    We had a few little things in the company that I had tagged for sale in the back of my mind, and we would pick up $200,000 here, $500,000 there, and $400,000 here. It would gut it some, but the assets we sold were not revenue producing too much. Then those new products hit the market early in the first year we owned Entertainment. Boy! We just came in and brought that debt down like that. When we brought the debt down substantially, then I reversed the field and said, "Okay let's make Entertainment really viable and then be aggressive."

A company under the kind of debt load that a leveraged buy-out has must move forward from where they are when they've purchased or they won't survive. The entrepreneur in a leveraged buy-out has to add either expertise or capital, or he has to be prepared to spin off assets to generate cash.

- Move to less expensive offices: Dancer withdrew from new plant facilities that had been purchased in an adjacent state and used instead an old plant several states away. In addition, the company located its central offices in less expensive quarters in the city where they had been housed with their corporate parent.
- Keep growth at a minimal level: Consumer Packaging, Inc. kept growth at 5 percent or less for the first two years of operations. The management team is now considering growth possibilities.

Figure 6–5. Tactical and Strategic Actions to Minimize Cash Outflow

In these companies, the CEOs were willing to undertake whatever efforts were needed to run operations effectively and efficiently. They were willing, if necessary, to sell assets. The effort does take its toll. The president of Laboratories, Inc. explained: "Finally I found out that I had to be prepared to work harder than I ever thought. That's not to say that I didn't work hard before this, but when you own your own business—particularly one that's leveraged—it stays with you around the clock.

Cashing Out

Were the results worth the effort? The oldest of the nine MLBOs is now seven years old. Two have gone public. One has been sold to another company (and then subsequently repurchased). Only one has run into severe difficulty. Thus eight are freestanding private companies run by essentially the same management team as existed at the time of the MLBO.

In all instances, there was concern about positioning the company to cash out. Cashing out took two forms among the firms in this study: going public and selling to another company. The process of cashing out requires attention, and it was clear that most MLBO management teams thought about this process from the begininng.

There are various options companies can follow to cash out. After the repurchase of Small Consumer Products Inc., its president enumerated the possible options:

> Right now we just want to stabilize things, be profitable, have modest growth, and get a better-looking balance sheet. If we can do that for a few years, then I think we have a lot of options [of] what to do with the company. I didn't get this going to be any family business or anything like that. My idea was to do something with the company where I could personally cash out, and

my top people feel the same way. . . . We could go with a key acquisition or two. We could go public with it. We could sell it as a unit. Once we get the balance sheet straightened out, the other management people could buy me out. . . . I've done a very good job. We've been into this thing nearly two years. We do not currently have a specific road map or a plan with a timetable that says that at the end of three years, this is what we want to do and five years is our strike date for either selling the company or going public. We haven't got any program like that going right now. We're simply trying to be profitable with every product line, with every customer, run things tightly and efficiently, and convert to equity. That's what we're doing. . . . I have a lot of friends who've gone public with over-the-counter companies, and I see what the advantages and disadvantages are. . . . So, I think I have a pretty clear vision of what the alternatives are and what the possibilities are. . . . We haven't chosen a path. We're still in the mode of being profitable, reducing debt, and creating a more attractive balance sheet. But we need to be getting some positive trends on income cycle too. And that's our intent this year.

Going public brings multiple return on the original investment. The father and son who invested $250,000 in Entertainment sold half of their equity in the secondary offering for about $8 million four years after they purchased the company. But another issue seemed to be paramount. For many, their personal situation was heavily at risk, as one executive put it: "In MLBOs there usually is someone who has his house, his wife, and even his dog on the line." The president of Small Consumer Products, Inc. talked about the situation in his unit after the first MLBO:

Things went well the three years when we were running. We continued to show improvement. It was a smooth three-year period. We thought about going public. The only objective in selling out was to take the money that we had made, the appreciation, and lock it into something that was less tenuous, rather than an ongoing business which is subject to the whims of the marketplace. That was our sole incentive for even thinking about selling out. . . . So we went and talked to several investment banks in New York with mixed results. It was not an overly enthusiastic reception at that point because the initial public offering market was a little flat, particularly for a company like us.

Emotionally we did not want to be part of another large company at all. We much preferred to make the acquisition of a couple of divisions that would fit in with us. But we simply could not make it happen. Anyway we met with MIC Inc. and we liked the chairman of the company. . . . He offered us substantially more than we thought we would get even by going public.

There are obviously qualitative payoffs also. Initially even the anticipation has its own exhilaration. A former executive of Consumer Products Inc. who became a stockholder and board member for Medico said, "I think the most excited I've ever seen him was when he had the opportunity to put together a group of private investors to purchase the company."

Even after several years of operating one's own company, the exhilaration does not necessarily die down. The president of Laboratories, Inc. explained:

> I can best describe it through an analogy. Working for a big corporation and being a big corporate manager is like driving a big truck down a highway—a very powerful vehicle moving at a very steady rate, not worrying about hitting anything as long as it doesn't hit anything too big. Being in business for myself in an entrepreneurial situation is more like driving a Ferrari on a country road. It's very, very fast! The scenary moves by quickly, and if you make a mistake and go off the road, it's very expensive, if not impossible, to fix. The feeling is exhilarating! There's nothing that really takes the place of it.

The CFO of Consumer Products, Inc. put it more simply: "The part that was the most pleasant was that we were running our own show."

Summary

This chapter has examined the recent experience of MLBOs in the United States and Europe. The evidence suggests that units that may be considered as MLBOs are not exciting opportunities from corporate management's perspective; sales growth is low to moderate, profitability at best moderate, and technology developments stable. The drop in interest rates since the early part of the decade and the bull market through most of 1987, however, offered unit management new opportunities. The experience with MLBOs to date suggests that the risks are modest for unit management and investors alike.

The general experience of MLBOs is reflected in those in this study. There has been increased interest on the part of corporate and unit management. Financing has become easier to obtain since the early 1980s. The experience of the MLBOs in this investigation add several dimensions to our understanding. First, unit management has eagerly initiated proposals regarding MLBOs. Circumstances under which unit management identifies the MLBOs opportunity are similar to the triggering events suggested in chapter 2. One in particular, however, appears to give unit management the impetus to approach corporate management: the observation that their unit no longer fits with the set of other companies in the corporate portfolio. From the perspective of corporate management, it appears that corporate executives are willing to consider MLBOs when unit management has been in place for a long period of time in a unit that has been at least moderately successful or unit management has successfully performed a turnaround of the unit in the recent past. In essence, unit management has augmented the value of the unit and then offered to purchase the value from corporate.

Recommendations for Corporate Management

MLBOs are a viable divestiture option in the current environment. Wherever the characteristics of the unit are comparable to those suggested in this chapter, the option should be considered. Indeed the evidence suggests that greater value might well be obtained through an MLBO than from outside buyers. Seeking outside buyers incurs marketing costs that will not be incurred with the unit management team. Among these costs are the risk of ending up with a shop-worn unit.

Recommendations for Unit Management

1. The time is riper for MLBOs than at any prior period.
2. The characteristics of the unit can be compared to the profile presented in this chapter.
3. Consideration should be given to how to approach corporate management. If a close relationship exists, testing the waters may be in order. If the relationship is distant, putting into place preliminary arrangements for a financial package may be advantageous in making the proposal.
4. It appears that unit management teams undertaking an MLBO will pay a premium for their unit. The lowest price that corporate management is likely to consider is its book value. Negotiations can focus on what assets are to transfer as part of the deal.
5. Local financing is more likely to be available than in the past. Banks, venture capital funds, local investment banking concerns, and private sources of capital are possibilities. Usually multiple sources will need to be approached. Management should have a carefully thought out presentation to make regarding their plan for purchasing, running, and providing for cashing out for investors. Investors must be able to earn a satisfactory return on their investment.
6. Under the leveraged situation, it is likely that plans for growth will have to be curtailed for two years or more. Careful attention should be given to asset management, especially accounts receivable and inventories. Plans for capital projects may have to be delayed, and consideration should be given to leasing arrangements. Suppliers should be paid promptly, and original financing arrangements should be made to continue strongly supplier relationships.

Recommendations for those Financing MLBOs

This chapter also has recommendations for individuals and companies that provide financing for MLBOs.

Do's

1. Have faith in management; they are the heart of a buy-out.

2. Make sure there is adequate interest cover and liquidity and that the costs will not undermine the prospects for success.

3. Make sure there is a second way out for the loans, such as the ability to sell off assets or a part of the business.

4. Structure the deal so that new money can come in without causing problems. If any influx of new money would wreck the balance of a transaction, be wary.

5. Focus on speed. The deal maker must be able to come to the table with the financing virtually in place to be successful in today's market.

6. Look beyond the debt-for-equity transactions at alternative sources of finance; equity-for-equity buy-outs, for example, look increasingly attractive as price-earnings multiples move higher and higher.

7. Arrange an appropriate balance between the three basic financing elements: the equity, the senior debt and the subordinated debt. This balance is the key to every successful buy-out.

Don'ts

1. Compromise sound lending principles to participate.

2. Put absolute faith in the projections; allow a margin for error.

3. Consider rejuggling a deal for a second or third time if it did not work the first time.

4. Make the deal too complicated. Intricate financing for its own sake blurs the essence of buy-out, which is profit maximization.

5. Consider buy-outs of businesses whose prices are set by government rather than the market (such as utilities) or that are already heavily leveraged (such as commercial banks).

6. Structure buy-outs where there may be a problem cashing out; cashing out is as important as cashing in.

Appendix 6A: Finding Financing: The Experience of Small Consumer Products, Inc.

Ross Johnson, president of Small Consumer Products, Inc.: A&A [a major investment banker] had agreed to finance the total consumer business at $450 million. When we got to Small Consumer Product's size, however, the size was smaller, and the purchase

---

The names of the three major investment bankers are disguised.

price obviously was a lot less. But it was small enough that we said to ourselves, "We didn't want to go back to [the original investment bankers] because we knew there we were only going to get 12 percent of the equity," which was small. We had a lot of shouting matches over that. The relationship was a brutal one. It was better than not doing it but not one that we particularly wanted to walk into.

So, we then said, "Okay, let's see if we can go in a different direction on this issue and get Industrial Products to carry some of the financing. So we went back and talked to some of the people I was familiar with. In the acquisition I made in the early 1970s before I came to Industrial Products, Inc., I had worked with a commercial credit finance company. We then replaced the commercial credit. As a result, I became familiar with the people at B&B [another major investment banker]. So we went back to B&B. We also went back to the banks. We went to Continental Bank, which was involved in financing [the previous acquisition]. In addition, we went out and talked to other banks. In essence, we were making cold calls. We spent a day in Dallas, for example.

We talked to several investment banks trying to see what kind of a deal we could structure, and we must have talked to six or seven. For example, we talked to Foresman Little. They're well known in leveraged buy-outs today. We talked to KKR. We made the rounds. Then we hit one door too many. We went to C&C [a major investment banker]. C&C was very interested in financing our deal, but, again, they wanted a big chunk of the equity. We thought we'd keep all of these doors open until we saw where we were going to get the money. C&C's management and Bill Apgar, a member of corporate parent's board, were very close friends. All of a sudden, we started to get a lot of pressure to go with C&C who originally offered us 20 percent or so, and they were going to keep 80 percent. And we got into a gnashing of teeth and a battle over that issue.

Allen Hope, CFO of Consumer Products, Inc.: Actually I think their first proposal was more like 10 percent [of the equity for management]. We balked enough the first time that it went to 20 percent fairly quickly. But that was all it went.

Ross: I think that's right. And the contract they sent us was onerous. It made us mad. It was selling your soul to the devil, and it made us mad. We said, "Okay, we're not going to work with C&C." We said, "Well, we have control of financing through B&B," and I said, "You don't have control of financing because I knew B&B before you even brought B&B up." They had brought B&B up in this meeting and said they knew the people at B&B. I said, 'Well, I know them, too." Anyway, they felt that they controlled B&B, and I felt that we controlled B&B. At, this point, Larry Thomas, the chairman of Industrial Products, Inc., said, "I want you to get this conflict worked out. Apgar [a member of Industrial Products' board] is uneasy, and Apgar thinks C&C should be involved. I want you to fly to New York and stop this." It was really bad because Larry Thomas was saying, "I want this settled, and I don't care what terms it's settled on." But if C&C has the deal and we said, "We're the management and without management the financing is not going to be there." But I wasn't sure whether that was true or not. So anyway, I went in to see one of B&B's people, and I told him what was going on. I said, "Ed, if the management pulls out, would you finance us?" Because C&C had said, "We don't need the management. We'll finance it anyway and bring management in." And we said, "We don't think you can do that." So anyway, we went to talk with B&B and said, "If we pull out, what happens to financing?" They said, "It goes." So then we knew that we had a fairly strong position. So then we went back to C&C

because we were afraid they could sue us to get an injunction claiming that they had lined up the financing, that they had found the deal. C&C could simply go in through Apgar with an offer and say to Industrial Products, Inc., "Here's the money with no carryback. We'll take you out right now. . . ." So we thought, "We'll make a compromise." So we went back to C&C and said, "We're going to fight you all the way, and we're going to pull the financing. You'll get nothing. Or, if you agree, we'll let you have 25 percent of the equity." They agreed.

Whether we ever had to give up that 25 percent, I don't know. But we ended up with 75 percent. They ended up with 25 percent. But it was a battle royal to get to that position and a lot of threats and gnashing of teeth. It was bloodied noses and very bitter feelings on both sides during that process. Anyway, we talked to Larry Thomas again. We needed Industrial Product's support. They agreed to carry much of the financing. I think they carried $16 million. We structured it ourselves. We didn't have an investment banker on how to put it together—the preferred stock, so much against fixed assets, and so much just a subordinated note. . . .

Allen: Actually $12 million of it was temporary until we could get our industrial development bonds.

Ross: We were fortunate that the business ran well during that time. We were at 21 percent prime when we closed, we were paying 4 or 5 [percent] over. . . . I know there were a lot of people that didn't think we'd make it. We had some doubts too on days.

B&B controlled it completely. In fact, their agreement basically said they had total control, and Industrial Products had to subordinate any of their demands to B&B. I mean it was a tough, one-sided agreement. In the negotiations, B&B said, "Look, you can talk about it all day, but this is the way it's going to be." We finally decided without legal counsel that there was little point in even trying to modify the agreement because it said, "If you want the money, you sign it the way it is." And that was it. Our lawyer pointed out that their financing was in the form of a demand note. Any one of several things can trigger a default. That's exactly what it was. But that's how we ended up.

It took us a year to negotiate back and forth with Industrial Products, Inc. It was on again, off again. Nothing went smoothly; everything was a battle. . . . Anyway, it was an agonizing year. It was not a smooth, pleasant negotiation, and it probably would not have gone through if Larry Thomas, the chairman, had not had some pretty good common sense and in some cases looked at the biger picture and said, "Look, in terms of what we're doing, we'll help them on this. We'll give them some support." So I think that without Larry, it would not have gone through. I think it would have been too difficult.

Now on the other hand, when he said, "Get to New York and make peace with C&C," that just about blew us out the other direction too. Fortunately, and again it's just a matter of circumstance, the guy at C&C couldn't see us. Because Larry had said, "You get on a plane tomorrow and make peace with this guy." Tomorrow was Saturday, and I said, "Why don't we wait until next week?" He said, "I want you on the plane tomorrow." So I called the guy at C&C, and fortunately he was going to be gone for three days, which meant I could get to B&B and find out whether we controlled it. I got to B&B and they said, "We'll back you—not C&C." So then I went back to Larry and I said, "Larry, he doesn't control that financing; we do." And then Larry backed off.

Notes

1. Charles Ruffell, "MBO: Funds Galore for LBO Prospects," *Euromoney: A Supplement to Euromoney and Corporate Finance* (December 1986): 2–4.

2. Terry Povey, "Floating Promise of Business: The Accountant's Role," *Financial Times,* October 10, 1986, p. 11.

3. William Dawkins, "Management Buy-outs: When Vendors Ask Too Much," *Financial Times,* July 3, 1986, p. 8.

4. Ruffell, "MBO."

5. "More Than They Want You to Know about Leveraged Buyouts," *Economist,* November 5, 1983, p. 83.

6. Nancy Dunne, "Scramble for Piece of the Pie," *Financial Times,* October 10, 1986, p. 14.

7. J.D. Culea, "The Entrepreneur and the Leveraged Buyout" (speech to University of Kansas, School of Business, February 1986. Culea is CEO of Northern Labs, Inc., previously a subsidiary of Johnson Wax.)

8. Dunne, "Scramble."

9. Stephen Quickel, "MBO: Warnings Fail to Dim LBO Dazzle," *Lucrative World of Management Buyouts, A Supplement to Euromoney and Corporate Finance* (December 1986): 20–29.

10. Source unidentified.

11. William Dawkins, "Buyout Survey Says Euphoria May Push Prices too High," *Financial Times,* September 10, 1986, p. 11.

12. Ruffell, "MBO."

13. "More Than They Want You to Know."

14. Ruffell, "MBO." Indeed, there have been very large sums of funding available for recent LBOs. If a company is facing a hostile bid, it can get fifty to one hundred calls from specialist investors wanting to help management buy the business. The biggest American buy-out to date is Beatrice Companies in 1985 at $6.3 million. "On a Slow Boat from America," *Economist,* January 3, 1987, p. 57–88.

15. Ruffell, "MBO."

16. "Management Buyouts: Leap out of Obscurity," *Financial Times,* October 10, 1986, C1.

17. Martin Dickson, "Finance Aplenty to Back Deals," *Financial Times,* December 8, 1986, p. 6.

18. "On a Slow Boat from America." Another alternative is a buy-in, which occurs when management comes from the outside.

19. "Management Buyouts."

20. Ibid.

21. Source unidentified.

22. "Boss-eyed about Bosses," *Economist,* July 11, 1987, pp. 70–71.

23. William Dawkins, "UK Buy-out Boom Threatened," *Financial Times,* September 10, 1986, p. 1.

24. Susan Lloyd, "Europe Is the Next Frontier," *The Lucrative World of Management Buyouts,* A Supplement to Euromoney and Corporate Finance (December 1986): 56. The information is drawn from *Review of UK Management Buy-outs* (Venture Economics and Center for Management Buy-out Research, University of Nottingham).

25. Ibid.

26. Ibid.

27. Liz Hecht, "Managers Who Succeed as Bosses," *The Lucrative World of Management Buyouts,* A Supplement to Euromoney and Corporate Finance (December 1986): 38–40.

28. Ian Hamilton Frazey, "The North: Erosion of London's Dominance," *Financial Times,* October 10, 1986, p. 4.

29. David S. Krause, "Leveraged Buyouts: An Opportunity for Entrepreneurs," *NBDC Report* (January 1987).

30. Frazey, "The North."

31. "On a Slow Boat from America," pp. 57–58.

32. Robin Reeves, "Waltes: Control Brought Closer Home," *Financial Times,* October 10, 1986, p. 4.

33. "On a Slow Boat from America."

34. Reeves, "Waltes."

35. There were cases pending in the mid-1980s that might require U.S. corporations to share overfunding of pension plans with participants.

36. Krause, "Leveraged Buyouts."

37. Quickel, "MBO."

38. "On a Slow Boat from America."

39. Frazey, "The North"; William Dawkins, "Latecomer Ships Its Reputation to Europe," *Financial Times,* October 10, 1986, p. 6; Quickel, "MBO."

40. Ruffell, "MBO"; Adam Seymour and James Maquire, "Leverage: The Opportunities for Industry," *Euromoney: A Supplement to Euromoney and Corporate Finance* (December 1986): 14–18; Frank Lipsius, "Muscling into the Top Tier: Profile: Drexel Burnham Lambert," *Financial Times,* October 10, 1986, p. 14.

41. Krause, "Leveraged Buyouts."

42. "Leveraged . . ." op. cit. "Buck Pass," *Economist,* September 16, 1981, pp. 57–58.

43. Hecht, "Managers Who Succeed."

44. Ibid; "More Than you Ever"; William Dawkins, "Funds Stretched to Find Deals," *Financial Times,* October 10, 1986, p. 2; "Boss-eyed about Bosses."

45. Frazey, "The North."

46. Quickel, "MBO,"*Euromoney: Supplement to Euromoney and Corporate Finance,* April 1988.

47. Ruffell, "MBO."

48. Ibid.

49. Source unidentified.

50. These amounts were often significant propositions of the managers' wealth base. In some instances, managers refinanced their homes or executed second mortgages and drew on family resources to come up with the capital.

51. Hecht, "Managers Who Succeed"; "On a Slow Boat from America."

52. William Dawkins, "Management Buyouts: Leap Out of Obscurity," *Financial Times,* October 10, 1986, pp. 1–2.

53. Hecht, "Managers Who Succeed."

54. Quickel, "MBO."

55. Hecht, "Managers Who Succeed."

56. Ibid.

57. However, asset collateral should be considered only as an insurance policy against failure. The strongest assets are not more important than a solid business plan.

58. Povey, "Floating Promise."

59. "Leveraged Buyouts: Too Good to be True?" *Euromoney* (April 1984): 20–23.

60. "More Than They Want You to Know."

61. Hecht, "Managers Who Succeed."

62. Ruffell, "MBO."

63. "Leveraged Buyouts."

64. "Management Buyouts."

65. Dawkins, "Funds Stretched"; William Dawkins, "New Generation of Giant Deals Hungry for Cash Flows," *Financial Times*, October 10, 1986, p. 3; William Dawkins, "U.K. Buy-out Boom Threatened," *Financial Times*, September 10, 1986, p. 1.

66. Liz Hecht, "Spawn of an Era: Specialist Firms," *The Lucrative World of Management Buyouts*, A Supplement to Euromoney And Corporate Finance (December 1986): 31–35.

67. "Leveraged Buyouts."

68. Martin Dickson, "Finance Aplenty to Back Deals," *Financial Times*, December 8, 1986, p. 6.

69. Ruffell, "MBO."

70. "Leveraged Buyouts."

71. Frazey, "The North."

72. Quickel, "MBO."

73. Anatole Kaletsky, "Predators High on Junk," *Financial Times*, January 13, 1987, p. 20.

74. Dawkins, "New Generation."

75. Mark Meredith, "Scotland: Anchor for the Economy and Boost to Morale," *Financial Times*, October 10, 1986, pp. 1–2.

76. "Leveraged Buyouts."

77. Ibid.

78. Dunne, "Scramble."

79. Source unidentified.

80. Dunne, "Scramble."

81. Source unidentified.

82. Actually there were ten since one, Small Consumer Products, Inc., was an MLBO from Industrial Conglomerate, Inc. About two years into the MLBO, the management group sold their company to MIC Inc., a company in a related industry. When the second parent sold out two years later to yet another company, the management group repurchased their unit. I have, however, counted this MLBO as one since there were no direct data from either the second or the third parent company.

83. Conglomerate Inc. undertook six other divestitures in 1985–1986. All but one were MLBOs. However, the data on each were fragmentary and therefore not included here. Conglomerate Inc.'s vice-president of business development explained that the company was willing to undertake MLBOs because there was a ready supply of financing available for such transactions; in looking for acquisitions, it found units overpriced and attributed the overpricing to the amount of financing available to fund MLBO transactions; and it therefore felt that Conglomerate could get the best value

through an MLBO without having to go to the effort of shopping the units. Conglomerate Inc.'s experience underscores the popularity of the MLBO movement in the mid-1980s.

84. The president of the Medico MLBO described his management team as a set of strong individuals and maintained that all were different: "There's not a single personality trait that runs through us all. So instead of six people saying 'Yes,' you have six people who each bring to the group a very strong will—no one is wishy-washy or goes along with the group for the sake of going along."

85. My notes contain the following notation: "Nonverbal behavior: shook himself as though he was trying to shake a bad memory."

86. Another father-son team was involved in one of the other divestitures by Conglomerate, Inc. in 1985–1986. Conglomerate corporate executives suggested an MBLO, but the father-son team could not find financing. Subsequently the vice-president of business development sold the firm to an East Coast investor who gave 20 percent of the equity to the father-son management team. The vice-president expressed his pleasure at having been able to execute a deal that provided equity for the team.

87. The experience of Entertainment Services is noteworthy here. The unit head had managed the unit for twenty years prior to its acquisition by Conglomerate, Inc. and then became president and subsequently vice-chairman of Conglomerate, Inc. When the decision was made to sell the unit, Conglomerate's chairman suggested that his vice-chairman consider buying the unit for his son. At that time the son had worked for more than a decade in the unit. The initiation in this case was by the chairman.

88. He cut the number of brand names, closed plants, cut inventory level, cut costs, and brought out new products.

89. I later asked CPI's director of financial services what he thought Tom Hanson would do strategically with Dancer. He said, "Milk it . . . probably for about ten years maybe. They don't have the capital to do R&D except on a very limited basis." In fact, Dancer was profitable and generated significant cash flow for several years. The company was able to pay back a considerable portion of the debt owed to the parent company. Hanson found another debt source, and Dancer began to acquire product lines and small companies. Recently, however, Dancer, which had been in operation as a freestanding company for somewhat less than six years, had filed for bankruptcy.

90. What is Ross Johnson's advice given his experience? "[But] try to do it yourself first. It's amazing how many doors you can open by just going in and knocking on the door without having an investment banker knocking on the door for you. In our experience, that's about all they've done for you—just knock on the door. They didn't even turn the knob. They just knocked on the door. I think it can be done without them."

91. The sales package is important for the parent company seeking a buyer. It can also be important for presenting the deal for an MLBO to potential investors of equity or debt. Allen Hope, the treasurer of Small Consumer Products, Inc., explained:

A key to getting it done if you're trying to do it youself without an investment banker is to put together a sales package to present to financial institutions that you're trying to get to finance the business. I don't mean a ten-color glossy kind of thing, but I mean a well-thought-out presentation covering who you are, what your experience is, what your business is, what your plans are, what your products are, and where do you think you're going. Put it in a real fancy, nice-looking binder and submit it to the banks or financial institutions or whatever it is, finance company, or whatever. And it makes a whole world of difference as to how you're perceived as being a professional manager. And it's amazing to me how much weight is placed on that, and it is a professional-looking presentation of what your business is, how you intend to buy it and where you see it going if you are successful. It's amazing how much weight that holds.

7

Negotiations: Who Gets the Better Deal

Once a potential buyer has been identified, the process of negotiations begins. Negotiation issues include choices made about the process itself and content issues that are covered in the course of negotiations. The process issues that must be decided by the firm include whether to use bidding or face-to-face negotiations, assessment of the possibility for smooth negotiations, price negotiation tactics, the size of the negotiation team, the role of experts (particularly the lawyer), the role of the board, and whether to use options. The content issues include potential deal-breaker issues, the use of an asset versus stock transaction, employee contracts, pension plans, and liability claims. Other issues that may be important in specific cases but do not usually become potential deal breakers are warranties, credit memos, confidentiality agreements, indemnity for financial statements and projections, and agreements not to compete. The relationships among these aspects of the process and content issues are depicted in figure 7–1.

The Process

Negotiation process issues focus on seven questions:

1. Why and under what circumstances is bidding used?
2. What differentiates smooth from difficult negotiations?
3. How should price be negotiated in face-to-face negotiations?
4. How big should the negotiating team be?
5. What role should a lawyer play in the negotiations?
6. What role does the board play?
7. When should options be used?

Circumstances for Bidding

Companies use bidding in order to obtain the highest price. The product manager of Leading Chemical Company, Inc. explained why and how his company had chosen to use the bidding process for a product line and its associated plant:

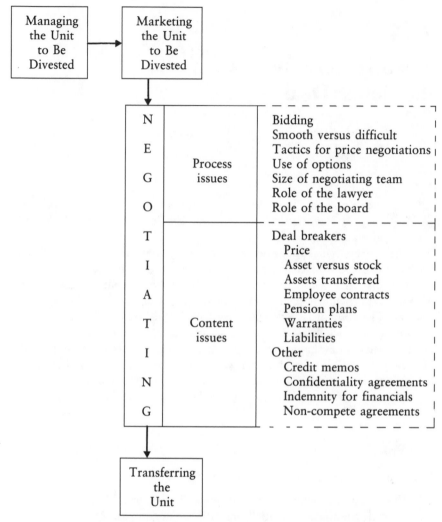

Figure 7–1. Process and Content Issues in Negotiations

Why? To get the highest price. How? I encouraged each of the potential buyers to come up with their own evaluation of the business and to let me know what it was worth to them. We set the price high enough so that I knew it was higher than we would realize. And then I encouraged them, if they didn't like that price, to come up with their own evaluation. I eliminated those that fell short of the mark. It was a cash transaction . . . a wire transfer.

The process for negotiating price ranges from the largely impersonal bidding process to face-to-face negotiations. Which process the firm will choose in order to maximize price will depend primarily on the expected number of buyers for a unit, although the visibility of the unit, determined largely by its size, is also a factor. However, executive preference for personal contact versus the more impersonal bidding process may lead to face-to-face negotiations. Figure 7–2 summarizes these characteristics.

In essence, then, bidding can be used where the company has a hot property that is highly visible. Moreover, it is very likely that bidding will be chosen in order to maximize price unless the firm's executives prefer the personal orientation of face-to-face negotiations.

A bidding process is usually carried out in three stages:

Stage 1: The first step is advertising. The call for bids is in the form of a public announcement, as in the *Wall Street Journal*, or through less public channels such as distribution of the announcement through the mail.

Stage 2: This stage takes about forty-five days. The target or minimum price is clearly stated, perhaps in a selling memorandum. A procedure is established so that during the time window, buyers can gather data. At the conclusion of this time period, the company may ask for an expression of price to weed out those who cannot meet at least a minimum price.

Stage 3: This stage takes thirty to forty days. The second stage has likely weeded the field down to two to three serious contenders. The seller may make known who these contestants are so that any company that cannot meet the minimum may opt out. The serious contenders are allowed to gather even more data. A senior executive described the process in this stage: "Then we will move into a second round with just those people who are interested in . . . staying in the process. You're probably down to two or three people. Then we move into another thirty to forty days' process where there is probably a hell of a lot more investigation that goes on, . . . a little bit of a feeding frenzy between two or three contenders.

Thus in a bidding situation, the following issues are out in the open: the minimum or target price (or something close), data regarding the unit to be sold,[1] and the other players.

Choice of Process	Bidding	Face-to-Face Negotiations
Characteristics of the unit		
Expected number of buyers	Many	Few
Size of unit	Large	Small
Preferred executive orientation	Impersonal	Personal

Figure 7–2. Factors Influencing Choice of Process

Bidding does not preclude face-to-face interaction. The final choice of buyer may be worked out by executives at the highest levels in the selling and buying organizations. In addition, the details of the contract must also be worked out. It may be very difficult to predict who will be a front-runner in the bidding process. A group president explained how he and the chairman were largely in the dark during most of the bidding process. He may have been surprised that the outcomes were so difficult to predict because he had a lot of industry contacts. After the preliminary bids were in, this group president and the chairman went to the top bidders:

> When I talk about selling . . . there had to have been 50 to 100 companies looking at the package. We didn't know who's fancy was tickled the most, that is, who was going to bid numbers at the end. When we got down to the last two to three weeks, [the CEO] and I knew. But until that critical time, we didn't have any idea. . . . We went to see the prime bidders in the last two or three weeks. They were told when the preliminary numbers came in. We then went to the to two bidders and sat down and talked to them. . . . Among some of the next highest bidders that lost there is a lot of bitterness.

After the final bidder is selected, the details of the contract need to be worked out. A member of the legal department for the above above unit at the time of divestiture described the process as he understood it:

> [The buying company] was the successful bidder for whatever reasons [the seller] determined to be relevant, and at that point it was a matter of hammering out the purchase contract. I don't know which side initially drafted the contract; eventually a fairly good draw-up became available, and our legal department was asked to review the draft and make any suggested changes that we thought were necessary. We reviewed the draft and had quite a number of changes. And that was the extent of our involvement before the transaction was consummated.

Smooth versus Difficult Negotiations

The four examples of relatively smooth negotiations in figure 7–3 illustrate the factors that facilitate negotiation. Several factors are significant in these examples. First, the selling parties wanted to sell the units. Second, the buying parties wanted to buy. Third, and perhaps even more critical, the parties understood each other. In the first example, the CEO of the selling company is known for his skill in adeptly developing an understanding of the buyer's interests. In the second example, the buying firm had been a customer of the selling firm for a number of years. In the third example, the parties had known each other for a number of years. In the fourth example (an MLBO), both parties had had the same training session that gave them a basis for common expectations about the rules of the process.

Sale of Unit A: The chairman of the selling company went to the potential buyer's home. The buyer asked him if he would like to go to a remote cabin. As the chairman described the negotiations, "I took a yellow pad, and before we came back we had hammered out a deal." The chairman then turned the notes over to his corporate legal counsel and accountants.

Sales of heavy equipment unit: "We were on the same wavelength," described the buyer. "We wanted the unit very much, and the seller wanted to sell." What the buyer did not emphasize here, although it was discussed later in the interview, was that the price was right. Indeed the buyer had tried to purchase essentially the same operations some years before at a much higher price. In the recently depressed market for the industry, however, the unit's price had fallen markedly. Its value to the buyer was significant because the unit manufacturered major components for one of the buyer's significant product lines.

Sale of fully integrated unit: This transaction was a sale among personal and professional friends who had known each other for many years. In addition, the executive in the buying company had once headed the unit he was buying.

The MLBO: The division president was the buyer. As he entered into negotiations, he said, "I was told, 'You are going to do your negotiation with George.' George and I had taken the same negotiation course! I said to George, 'We can start out high and see who is going to give in, [or] I will give you a number.' "

Figure 7–3. Four Examples of Smooth Negotiations

Differences in the level of experience of the negotiating parties can affect the level of trust. Where the seller's experience in negotiations is high, the advantage accrues to the seller. Where the buyer's experience with negotiation is high, the advantage accrues to the buyer. Where, as existed in two of the examples in figure 7–3, the knowledge about each other is about the same, the two parties can develop a high level of trust. Where the knowledge about each other is unequal, the degree of trust will depend on the integrity of both parties, but especially the one with the superior knowledge, and the willingness of the party with the superior knowledge to be open with the party with lesser knowledge.[2]

Negotiating Price in Face-to-Face Bargaining

The process of price negotiations is one of feeling the other party out, although some indication of where the other stands may be obtained earlier in the process, as the CFO of Consumer Products Inc. explained:

> People just love to look around. They make a whole career flying around and looking. . . . And it just eats you up. [But] say now there's one or two legitimate ones, [and] they want to know a price to go back to their board.

They say, "I want to remind them of my return." They're trying to get you up front. . . . "Give me a ballpark. . . ." So you hold up a little clue. "Between you and me . . ." Then the person comes and says, "Well, are you willing to take terms?" He doesn't think it's worth book, let alone net present value. "But will you take back some paper?" And you start getting this type of dialogue, which are kind of interesting, nonbinding negotiations, even on the front end.

Executives with experience in negotiations identified four tactics in price negotiations: giving a first price fairly close to target, giving the first price higher than the target price, having the buyer give the first price, and playing do-si-do. Each of these tactics has advantages and drawbacks and can be used in certain circumstances.

A Price Fairly Close to Target: The seller can start with a firm price if he or she knows the buyer and judges the buyer to be experienced, capable of making the decision, and having a reputation for integrity. The vice-president of corporate development for Medium Conglomerate, Inc. explained:

> In our case it really depends on who it is that we are dealing with, how well we know them, and what we believe to be the character of the people that we are dealing with. If we are dealing with very sophisticated people who buy and sell and are capable of making decisions, it's not going to go through a zillion committees. . . . We are dealing with principals who can basically make a decision. We'll say, "Here's the deal. Here's a fair price. You want to buy. We want to sell. Is this going to fly?" and we can get the thing done really fast.

If the buyer approaches the seller, it is clear that the seller has the advantage. Under these circumstances, the seller can generally set a price close to the target. The vice-president of corporate development for Conglomerate, Inc. said:

> It's a plain fact that if someone comes to us and says, "Would you please be willing to consider selling corporation X?" [that situation] gives us a leg up in terms of getting full value rather than saying to the world, "We want to sell Corporation X. Are there any buyers?" So there are times when a company's neither doing great nor poorly but it is a no-hassle deal.

The seller's leverage is generally raised where the buyer comes back a second time after the seller has broken off negotiations or where the buyer exhausts the patience of the seller. The following interchange illustrates:

> *Interviewer:* I had a case where the potential buyer came back a second time. The seller, in essence, said, "Well, if you want to open negotiations again, that's fine, but this is the price. You take it or leave.

Interviewee: Yes, that's right. That happens. . . . We have a client right now—it's not a big thing they are selling, but we set up a purchase all arranged, subject to the buyer's financing. The buyer's people just really haven't been very nice people. One of my partners and our client negotiated yesterday with them for six hours. Our team finally came to the conclusion that the negotiator on the other side—not the company but the chief executive—is not a nice person. So the buyer's negotiator left. Then, sort of in typical fashion, he called and said, "Well, I've changed my mind. Unless you give this much more and so forth, we won't buy it." We advised our client, "No matter what he [the buyer] does now, it's either this or forget about it." And if you have the attitude, truly that you're going to forget about it, then it works. Otherwise there's something in the vibrations if you don't say it strong enough.

First Price Higher Than the Target Price: The opposite circumstances suggest starting the price high. The senior vice-president of strategic planning for Diversified Food, Inc. explained:

If we get a sense that the folks we are dealing with are people who have to go back and report to committees and tell them what a great deal they got . . . and impress the boss and impress the board and so forth, we might start with a higher number and give them the opportunity to knock us down. So it really depends on who we are dealing with. If we don't know, we say, "We have got company X available for sale," and we'll start with a little higher number but not so high that it's going to seem outrageous and scare off two-thirds of the market but high enough because you never get more than you ask for on anything, and we would rather err on the high side than the low side, so we might mark it up anywhere from 10 to 20 percent more than what we expect to get.

If the unit is in a loss situation, negotiations tend to revolve around the book value. In these circumstances, there may be an advantage to starting high. The vice-president of business development for Paper Products, Inc. explained:

[If] it's not showing black ink, we don't have some of the traditional financial methods to help with the valuation. Then book value becomes a very critical variable for the selling entity. People don't want to take the book loss. But you don't say that in negotiations. You establish a price that's comfortably above book, and then you start negotiating down with the buyer.

On the other hand, not giving an indication of price can waste a lot of time for the seller and the buyer while they discover what range each has established. The CFO of Consumer Products Company, Inc. described his experience:

I guess we've had occasion to say, "This is a pretty fair price," and somehow let the guy know. Now if you do not want to state the number, you kind of say, "Gee, I'm really having a tough time convincing my board to take a book loss" and somehow send signals if you don't like this guy wasting a lot of time.

The Buyer Gives First Price: Another tactic is to insist that the buyer put forward the first indication of price. The senior vice-president of strategic planning for Diversified Food, Inc. discussed this tactic:

> I will almost never give a minimum price. I will almost never say anything. I would much rather somebody use, sort of a used car thing, "Tell me what your best deal is." I'd rather be responding to someone else's offer because the minute I expose myself in terms of any sort of price, that's pretty much what I'm going to get in those situations.

Playing Do-si-do: Another issue is whether the seller plays do-si-do. This occurs in situations where negotiations are suspended while the party receiving the last offer checks at the home office. The tactic is used if the lead negotiator does not have the authority to make the decision on the issue or wants to be able to come back and utilize greater leverage, usually by invoking an individual higher in the organization as the final authority. The division manager involved in an MLBO talked about the process that was used by the group executive in charge of negotiations:

> I remember thinking how we were going to put it together. I had to let the parent company out by the end of the fiscal year, and I had to have some in-season business to generate cash. . . . The group vice-president talked with me. He gave me a number which I thought was a little high. . . . [When the division manager counteroffered, the group executive responded,] "I don't know whether that is going to be enough, but I will take it to the chairman."

Price negotiations have a great deal of variation. The patterns to the choices were not fully clear in this project. The chairman of M&A Consulting Firm summarized the wisdom derived from his experiences in figure 7–4.

Negotiating Team Size

How large the negotiating team should be is a difficult question because the composition of the team responsible for the divestiture usually changes over time. Even the person responsible for coordinating the process may change from the postdecision stage to closure stage. Moreover, it is difficult to identify where the negotiation process actually starts. The analysis phase may involve a team, as the executive vice-president for Major Conglomerate, Inc. explained.

> We had a team: our group controller, one person from the controller's department because we have a small staff here, one person from the legal department, and the group vice-president. We went out and asked questions . . . you know, go through and what do you think we could sell it for and what would you do with the receivables and so on . . . and they gave us their opinion on such things as severance pay, pension obligations, warranty, and so on.

Chairman: In negotiations there's a lot of variation. You're finding that I'm saying constantly that there's a lot of variation, and it's difficult to put your finger on a negotiating process in that sense. We feel that the day of being cute about it is over, where if you meet in his office or your office or if you meet in a neutral place—all that kind of monkey business. It's much better if you're interested, you say you're interested instead of being coy about it.

Interviewer: So openness and being up front are important?

Chairman: Yes, I mean we feel that—not everybody does, and I must say in some instances where we've divested things, we ourselves played the game of saying, "We're not sure that our client would be interested in selling this divestiture. Our planning advisers think it's worth talking about. Maybe we can convince them to do it." So obviously you negotiated your posture, but to be superficial about it is a little passé. It used to be that, especially in a merger, but you had to be sure that he was coming to you, you know, because you can't show too much interest in the beginning because otherwise he thinks you are too anxious to sell. And if you are truly up front, you state exactly why you're selling it, etc. but you're firm on the fact that you have to get out of it or whatever.

Interviewer: If you were to think of a couple of things in general of how negotiations could be improved, what would they be?

Chairman: Well, I think in the first place, I think it's good to get professional advice and professional help in terms of structuring negotiations. It's hard for me to be objective about that because that's a big part of what we do. We think it's very important to look at the specific situation, understand the kind of person you're dealing with, and structure the negotiations accordingly. Some people are open, no nonsense [people]. Some people are very coy and less open. So then we have to structure it somehow. I mean, sometimes on the basis of the people in terms of structuring the negotiations. I think it's very important to really understand the values and to be prepared to present the values clearly. In other words, if you're divesting, have it so well worked out, have the answers to the questions that anybody would ask about it so well developed that you can give the rationalizations of the answers and demonstration of the values clearly.

Figure 7–4. Advice on Price Negotiations

It was really quite an undertaking we did in a very short time with a small number of people.

Two characteristics of the negotiation team are clear: the team should not be very large, and one member has to be clearly charged as a central figure in the group. How the group should be configured, however, depends partially on how the buyer's negotiating team is organized. The vice-president for business development for Conglomerate, Inc. explained:

Well, another thing, too, is that in the negotiations, you don't want a real large committee. You need to have a spokesman who is the principal spokesman.

Sometimes in our experience it's myself or one of the other business people, or it may be the lawyer, depending on what stage we are in or who's on the other side and how they're set up. It depends on a lot of things, but maximum three people, with one the principal spokesman looking for advice as needed.

There can be advantages to having only one person on the negotiation team. The vice-president of business development continued:

Some people much prefer to be basically by themselves when they negotiate. I don't do it this way myself, but other friends of mine do this sort of thing. They play the game as follows: If it's me against the four of you over there, I can be far more effective against the four of you than I can be one on one. 'Cause everybody's kinda looking for signals from each other as to what to do, and I'm reading that and I don't have anybody I have to give or receive signals from.

Who is involved also depends on the confidence level of the person charged with negotiations, as the following interchange between executives shows:

Executive 1: My own personal style is that I'd rather have an attorney with me at all stages . . . with the instructions to listen and interrupt and take me out of the room when he thinks it's important.

Executive 2: It depends on your degree of experience, and I'm not experienced in that enough to feel comfortable being by myself.

Executive 3: But rather than having the attorney doing the talking and the negotiating with the other side . . . I'd rather do the talking. And, as you say, let him pull me by the sleeve anytime.

On the other hand, some feel that the group should contain a broader set of individuals. The vice-president of Paper Products Inc. explained: "I think that you have to have everybody intimately involved in the negotiation. I agree that you wouldn't have the lawyer negotiating business aspects of the deal, but he might participate in that negotiation."

Role of the Lawyer

There is controversy over the role of the lawyer. Some believe he or she should be in charge of the negotiations, and some believe the involvement should be behind the scenes.[3] Whether legal counsel is directly and visibly involved depends on several factors. The executives interviewed generally agreed that:

1. When the negotiator lacks experience, legal counsel should be more intimately involved.

2. The preferred style of the negotiator affects legal involvement. If the negotiator experiences greater ease in solo negotiations, legal will be excluded from a direct and visible role.

3. Legal counsel may be the lead negotiator at appropriate points in negotiations.

Figure 7–5 examines this issue.

MLBO president: I did a couple of things right. I got a really good attorney. A contact who's got a big public company and does a lot of deals said, "[Lawyer's name] is without a doubt the best, the strongest negotiator, deal maker, low-key guy that I've ever dealt with. And he's the guy you want to do your job." Now [the lawyer] is sort of picky about whom he takes on as clients. . . . But I went down and talked to him and told him about the company and that I had a recommendation from this other guy. And he said, "Yes, I'll do it."

Interviewer: What difference did he make for you?

MLBO president: First, he's just an excellent attorney; he has some staff work to help him, too, but on the contracts, I mean, everything . . . in terms of who would absorb product liability and losses that come in the future and all that kind of stuff, he was really tough. He was tougher than I could have been. The two guys I was negotiating with were friends. In fact, I had hired both of them into the [selling] company. They were personally doing everything they could to make me be successful. But still there were things in the agreement I didn't think were right and the lawyer didn't think were right. So, the tough issues, he would handle them so I did not have to get in personal confrontation with them. . . . He was just a low-key guy. He would say, "Well, let's look at this one more time." He was the kind of guy you don't know he's beating you up until you get out of the meeting. After the one big session we had that lasted most of one day, he said, "Well, there were six important issues that we had, and we won all six of them." But [the selling company] didn't feel like they had lost all six.

In retrospect, the way the deal was written, I haven't gone back and said, "I wish we had done this differently." I have friends who went to lawyers who said, "Oh, yes, I can represent you on this." And my friends paid the price because the attorneys didn't do their homework. So I guess, when I think what I did right, the advice I would give somebody is, "Get the best, most expensive deal maker attorney." I would try to get somebody who's done it a lot of times before. Don't get the guy who helped you with your divorce or something. . . . Later on, the [selling company] people said, "You know, your attorney was about the best attorney we've dealt with in any of these negotiations." Things went smoother because they had a lot of confidence in him. . . . I saw some other people who did not do it right, and it cost them—it cost them a lot.

Figure 7–5. Using a Negotiating Lawyer

Role of the Board

Board members play various roles. Inside board members may be intimately involved with negotiations. Outside board members are likely to be involved in an indirect manner, such as acting as a third party to the transaction to interpret or influence.[4] Usually the board functions for approval or disapproval, as the following interchange illustrates:

Executive 1: Do you tell the board about that [that you were starting with a higher price but would move down to your target price in negotiations]?

Executive 2: Well, in our company, the board is a review process but not an active, integrated, involved-in-everything-that-goes-on type of thing. So the executive committee of the board is able to deal with these things, and we deal very closely with the executive committee of the board. So it's unlikely in my experience. We'll sort of agree with the executive committee that here is our range of what we expect to get and we are going to try for X but realistically we may end up with $X-20$ percent or $X-10$ percent and have approval.

Options

The use of options is not strictly part of the negotiation process, although it is used to weed the buyers down to those who are most interested in the unit and to protect the unit's propriety information from potential competitive abuse. During the time the option is in effect, the seller does not allow other potential buyers access to data on the unit. Using an option may lose time for the seller, and time is often important—even critical—in divestment transactions. However, an option, properly priced, weeds out all but the most serious of buyers, as the following illustrates:

Executive 1: I've used options once or twice of the kind that you're talking about, one with a very limited market and not a really exciting piece—an old piece of liver. I have done an option as you would a real estate [deal] and sold a thirty-day option to give them time to look at it. And I sell the option for a very small amount.

Executive 2: I think it's a very good technique. You often will get into these situations. It's not really a hot property at all. So you're not really running an auction. It has happened to me where someone says, "Look, I have a whole group of people looking at this thing. There are eighteen reasons why I don't want these other people around me." Some of them are quite reasonable, and you can always flush that one out really fast with that option, which is if they are really really serious then. . . . I've put a fairly fair price on the thing which is perhaps, say, $80,000.

Another situation where an option is a legitimate tool occurs when the potential buyer is concerned about losing the competitive advantage of what he or she is considering buying if others are allowed to look at it. The senior vice-president of Diversified Food, Inc. described an instance where the use of an option had been immensely useful to his firm and the ultimate buyer:

> I've got a slightly different example. The example I have in my mind is a situation where we had a technology. We had developed it in our laboratory. We did not have an ongoing business. It turned out it had no application in anything we were doing. [So] we went to a series of companies. It was a totally new way to produce [a common chemical] that would reduce the capital intensity by a factor of two. This was a divestiture of a technology, if you will, and in this case there were only going to be five or six people in the world producing that chemical. One of them, a very substantial company, came up very clearly and said, "The more you talk to all the other people who are producing [the chemical] about this process, the more concerned we are about this technology. You have a patent, but on the other hand, the more questions other companies ask, the more you're giving away in terms of that patent. I guarantee you we are very real buyers. The way you are running the process here is scaring the hell out of us. Can you take this off the market?" I said, "Well, there is one thing I can do very quickly. Put your money where your mouth is." They took the option. We literally took it off the market. They ended up buying the business, and everything was fine.

Thus the advantages associated with using an option include establishing that the other buyer is serious, protecting the competitive value of the unit, and motivating the buyer to get on with his evaluation more quickly.

The Negotiation Issues

The issues that firms deal with in negotiations clearly fall into two categories: those that were potential deal breakers and those that were seldom deal breakers. Deal breakers led to impasse in negotiations.

The foremost issue and most usual deal breaker, is price, although other issues clearly influence price. Whether the transaction is an asset or a stock sale is a major item in negotiation. Other major issues and potential deal breakers are the assets to be included in the transaction, employee contracts, pension plans, warranties, and responsibility for liabilities. Finally, there are four miscellaneous issues that some firms might confront: credit memos, confidentiality agreements, indemnity for financial statements and projections, and agreements not to compete.

Price

Price was overwhelmingly acknowledged by all selling companies as the paramount issue. Selling companies usually establish a minimum price, and they
usually have a target price. These two values thus establish an acceptance zone.
A division president who was actively involved in the divestiture process described this process of establishing the price range:

> The other key player in the [divestiture process] was the group controller. He
> ultimately died in an auto accident. He was instrumental in putting together
> the financials that said, if we keep the businesses running, this is what we
> can do, and here is the value of these businesses. We used his analysis as a
> guideline to determine how much money we were going to ask for the unit.
> Really, in the negotiations, we set a hurdle. We said if we keep these businesses
> going under this scenario, i.e., this strategic plan, we figure the businesses are
> worth in the neighborhood of $60 million to $70 million to us. That was the
> conservative estimate. [On] the high side they were worth $100 million. O.K.,
> so we had a bracket there of between $60 and $90 million which was the net
> value of those businesses over time to [the selling company].
>
> So we said to the buyer, "We want $100 million." I think that was the
> first [price]. They came back with $75 million as their first offer. So im-
> mediately we had bracketed the negotiations well within what we determined
> our true value to be, and it was positioned on the high side of the range. So
> from then on, it was let's just reach a number, and that number ultimately
> worked out to be roughly $86 million to $90 million, depending on how you
> count it. So the buyer acquired $100 million in value for about $90 million
> and that was on the high side of what it was worth to us, the seller, to keep
> the businesses. But conservatively, the unit was worth a little less than that.
> So the sale was a good deal from our point of view, plus it gave us dollars
> to reinvest in one of our growing businesses, an area we knew better.

The chairman of M&A consulting firm advises sellers to involve an ad-
viser in determining the value of the unit. He believes that sellers frequently
set their divestiture price too high.[5] In several instances, the decision to sell
was predicated on the price that could be obtained in the divestiture transaction. If the target price could not be obtained, the unit would be kept. In one
case, the company, much to its chagrin, did withdraw the unit from the market.
The vice-president of business development explained that they were in the
process of restructuring the unit and expected to keep it off the market for
several years. The situation was difficult because the unit executives were well
aware that they were slated for divestiture.[6]

There were certainly instances where the selling company did not get the
price targeted. In these cases, one of two outcomes occurred. In the first, the
selling executive indicated merely that they had not received the price and gave
very little additional information about the transaction. In the second, the

executive explained that there were other benefits from the sale, such as free-ing up management time. In one case, speaking two years after the divestiture, the executive explained that the price obtained for the MLBO transaction was $500,000 less than targeted. However, the resulting reinforcement of morale in the broader employee body of the parent corporation was worth more than the loss of the $500,000.[7]

Price can be modified by the timing of payments. Generally sellers preferred cash. The former vice-chairman of Conglomerate, Inc. put his advice regarding cash transactions succinctly: "So when you divest, always get as much down in cash as you can. There are always exceptions, but as a policy, I would rather have a little less money and have it all in cash than string it out over ten years."

The exceptions to total cash transactions occur in many circumstances. Commonly the unit was in a loss situation, and the selling firm wanted no less than book value. In these situations where the unit was probably not worth book value, the seller negotiated various terms. Thus the stated transaction price was at or near book, and the seller recognized neither gain nor loss. But the net present value of the cash flow from the transaction was below book value, a circumstance favorable to the buyer.

If the buyer really wanted the unit but was unable or unwilling to pay a greater amount of cash or incur a heavier load of debt, the seller sometimes offered creative arrangements, as the following example shows:

> We sold the unit to the fellow from whom we originally bought it. I felt badly when we sold it to him. I was in Europe on some sort of deal, and the general counsel called me and said, "He really wants to negotiate, and he's pretty close." I said, "Well, tell him this. Tell him for the difference in price between him and us, we'll take a $250 royalty on each [product unit] he sells for the next five years." Our general counsel called back and said, "He cashed in his child's trust and something else and bought the company back." We made more in royalties for the next five years than we ever did when we owned the company.

Sometimes the seller was willing to accommodate the buyer's preference regarding cash flow. In the following example, the seller wanted a positive, ongo-ing relationship with the buyer because some transactions would have to be resolved regarding the divested unit after the sale. The treasurer of Medical Supplies Company Inc. explained the arrangement:

> My involvement was really once we had identified [the buying company] as the most probable buyer. We were involved in discussions with them on essen-tially what the purchase arrangements would be, what the terms and condi-tions would be. One of the processes was done in two steps. They would give us a payment at the closing and then another payment at some future date. The future payment wasn't contingent on performance. It was just a method of helping them accommodate the transaction.

Assets or Stock?

Next to the issue of price, the issue of whether the transaction will be an asset-based transaction or a sale of stock is most critical to both parties. Sellers in the study usually preferred sale of stock if the unit was a legally constituted subsidiary or could be readily constituted as such.[8] In a stock sale, the unit's assets and liabilities transfer to the buyer. Thus issues such as pension plans configured for the subsidiary, warranty claims, and liability claims become the responsibility of the buying company. In contrast, an asset-based transaction transfers only the assets. The liabilities do not automatically transfer to the buyer.[9] Rather, the parties divide the liabilities by contract.[10] In an asset transaction, the seller remains in possession of the legal entity that sold its assets.[11]

Liability Claims

Next to price, pension funds and liability issues tended most frequently to become deal breakers in negotiations. An executive explained the critical nature of the issues:

> The other sticky issue that is, if anything even harder to wrestle with than pensions, is product liability. Of course, the [kind of] business is not one where you are apt to have a lot of product liability but take [another kind of] business, people do get injured or, it's sad to say, but there are quite a few deaths. The biggest problem is [he described typical situations], and it's not really the fault of the product if they are foolish enough to operate the product unsafely. But nevertheless, they always sue the manufacturer when a death or injury happens. Then sometimes there are things that go wrong with the equipment. But say we sold that business. Five years from now, we don't want to be handling a lawsuit, you know, because it's hard to defend yourself when you're no longer in the business and you've turned over the records to somebody else. On the other hand, the buyer may say, "Well, I'm willing to be responsible for things I make, but I don't want to take on the liability for something you made years before I bought it." This is something that there just isn't any good answer to. Every case you bicker and negotiate, and it depends on the personalities of the people as to how you come out. Generally we try to get out from the liability because the way the insurance operates, it's much more expensive to buy insurance for something when you're not in the business. I guess that's partly because it's harder to defend yourself. You don't have the experts on your payroll.

Resolution of the issue could be handled in several different ways. Generally the seller was responsible for liabilities arising from products produced prior to closing. The allocation of risk can be negotiated by contract. For example, the buyer can take all occurrences from closing time forward or all claims made from time of closing forward. In some instances, an escrow account is established, with an expiration date. Any balance in the escrow for product liability can be renegotiated in or out of court, split between buyer and seller, or returned to the buyer. In other instances, the seller's product liability insurance may provide continuing coverage for the products manufactured under the seller's ownership.[12]

One of the difficulties, especially in firms with low-value products, was ascertaining what products were produced (or sold, depending on how the contract was finalized) during what time period. The assistant general counsel of a major firm put forward one reason for the difficulty: "There is the problem of identifying who, in fact, did make the product. You know, many times the product that causes injuries is destroyed in whatever it is that causes someone to get hurt." The president of an MLBO explained how he stood staunch on the issue:

> The biggest, single issue was product liability. We didn't resolve that issue. We just flat won it. We said, "We will simply not take any exposure for any product that the company sold prior to the closing date." And the seller's answer was, "Well, that's just not practical. We can't identify products, so we'll just go three months out and settle any claim made by then." You know, we did the homework and satisfied everybody that we *could* identify when the product was sold that turned into a product liability suit. The seller ended up with the liability for everything sold prior to the closure date. We had the liability for everything sold after the closing date. So we were responsible for all inventory on hand. Then there were some questions on escrow accounts. They were related to product liability. The seller suggested some part should be withheld from the purchase price to cover the amount in escrow. We had quite a battle, but we ended up without those reserves coming out of the purchase price.

It was unusual for a buyer to take full responsibility for all liability claims, although a seller might start negotiations with this posture. Thus seldom was the expected value of liability claims included in the price. Usually the liability issue was a separately negotiated item based on the past experience of the selling company.

Employee Pension Plans

Employee pension plans varied on the basis of the organizational level at which the pension plan was administered, whether the plan was a defined contribution or defined benefit plan, and the degree of overfunding. Some plans were administered at the corporate level and extended to multiple units, including the employee body of the unit being divested; others were administered at the unit level and extended only to unit employees. The latter usually occurred when a legally configured wholly owned subsidiary was for sale. If the pension plan existed at the corporate level, a common resolution was to continue the employees of the divested unit in the corporate pension plan with no additional contributions. If an employee continued with the new owner until completion of the normal vesting time, upon retirement he or she would receive pension funds from both the selling company and the new parent. The executive vice-president of Major Conglomerate, Inc. talked about the approach:

> You know, if you're underfunded in your pension, the buyer certainly says, "I'm buying a problem, and you've got to pay me for that." If you're overfunded, he doesn't want to pay you for it 'cause he figures it's not real money. What we often do is say to the buyer, "You take it without any pension. You set up your own pension plan. If you're a big company, you've got a pension plan. You pull the people into it."
>
> And what we'll do is tell the employees that our plan requires ten years for vesting. So any employee with ten years or more, they're vested. When they retire, they'll get two pension checks. They'll get one from us for the years of service up to the sale, and they'll get one from the new employer for the years thereafter. For employees with less than ten years of service that aren't vested, we say that since they'll be under the new employer's plan from here on out, they won't earn any more years of credit under our plan. But if they stay with the new employer until they reach the ten-year mark or what would have been ten years, we'll pay them a pension for what they have. That is, if the person has five years of service, they're not vested. If after the sale they leave the new employer in less than five years, then they aren't vested and never would have been vested presumably, so they don't get anything from us. But if they stay with the new employer five years so that had we not sold they would have had ten years of service, we'll pay them a pension for the five years that they were with us.
>
> It saves us the negotiating with the buyers as to what our pension is worth. And from the buyer's point of view, if it's a large company particularly, it gives him the advantage of not having a different plan from these other employees. He just folds these people into his plan. If it's a better plan that the new employer has, the employee comes out ahead. If it's a poorer plan, they probably bargain or get something so that they get something comparable to ours. But it leaves the buyer to deal with his employees on his own basis instead of arguing about our pension plan. But pension plans are always a sticky issue.

Another approach was to liquidate the pension plan and make a distribution to the employees. The president of an MLBO explained how the situation was handled for his employees:

> [The former parent company] cashed out the pension plans, and everybody got a distribution. The plan was terminated. [The former parent] made some extra profit on it because they had funded liabilities that they got to turn into profit, and the deal was closed. But everybody who had anything accrued to his or her account got it. And there were some decent payments made. Everybody seemed pleased with it.

Of special concern were pension plans with excess funds[13] and unfunded pension plans. Both were negotiated carefully. Excess funded plans could be transferred intact if the buyer paid for the excess in the purchase price, or the excess funds could be retained by the seller and the obligation to the employees satisfied by purchase of an annuity contract (a common solution), annualized bond portfolio, or something similar. In negotiations, the selling firm's position was to reflect the amount of overfunding in the ultimate price for the unit being sold or to purchase annuities to meet the obligation and take the excess funding out of the unit. Unfunded pension liabilities were the hardest to negotiate.[14]

Employee Contracts

Executives concurred that price, asset versus stock-based transaction, liability claims, and pension plans were the most critical issues in negotiations. Other major issues were employee contracts, warranties, and assets to be included in the transaction. Several executives indicated that nonprice issues regarding employees were considered:

Will the buyer offer positions to the current employees?

How will the employees fit with the buyer's company?

Will there be continued career paths for current employees?[15]

Sellers indicated that they negotiated for the protection of employees. The vice-president of strategic planning for Technology Congomerate, Inc. said, "We insist on good benefits for the employees in a purchased company."

Issues regarding employees contracts ranged from union contracts to individual executive contracts. Union contracts went intact to the buyer in all instances. Under a stock sale—the incorporated company is being sold—employees contracts automatically go with the unit unless negotiated to the contrary. If the transaction is an asset sale, the employees are rehired by the buyer. Although under an asset sale, the buyer is not bound to the union contract,[16] in no instance in this study did the seller decide to terminate the union contract.

Mangement contracts were a frequent item of negotiation.[17] From the seller's point of view, the range went from corporate noninterest in the fate of management to seeking and negotiating with a buyer who would be interested in retaining the current management. The most extreme example of noninterest occurred when the unit had not done well and unit management had repeatedly ignored corporate advice, specifically advice from the chairman of the board and chief executive officer. In this case the COB-CEO did not concern himself regarding the fate of the employees. Indeed, the buying firm moved operations to their own headquarters three states away, and few employees went with operations. The unit head was not included in the move.

At the other end of this spectrum was the firm whose greatest satisfaction was the outcome of negotiations regarding management contracts. The buyer was the only foreign buyer represented in the group of companies and presumably had considerable dependence on the unit's U.S. management to continue the success of the firm. Indeed, general observations suggest that foreign buyers are likely to agree to good packages for the management of U.S. units. In this case, however, the victory over the management contracts was bittersweet since the price was not as high as the seller desired.

In another case, the selling firm was pleased about the deal offered to management. The buyer was a small New York investment firm that purchased companies but regularly offered management as much as 20 percent of the equity to continue in the management role. The seller expressed considerable satisfaction at the equity position for the management team, a father and son. The father, who was nearing retirement, had spent most of his career in the unit, and the son had been with the unit for more than a decade. The selling firm had offered the unit as a management buy-out, but the father-son team was unable to arrange financing. Under the circumstances, the selling firm was delighted that the buyer gave management an equity portion.

In sum, whether management contracts are an issue during negotiations related to at least three factors:

1. Performance of the unit: If the performance of the unit was poor, the selling firm did not have as much leverage unless the seller was willing to give a bargain price.

2. Relationship between corporate executives and the unit management: If it was positive and strong, selling corporate would strive hard for a good contract if management wanted to stay on.

3. Dependence of the buyer on the management skill of the unit it was buying: If buyer was a non-U.S. firm, there was likely to be high dependence. If the unit was in same industry and both parties were from the United States, there was less dependency, and the buyer had the greater leverage.

Warranties

The divested companies involved in the research program were primarily manufacturing entities. Among these firms, the issue of warranties ranged in terms of significance to the seller. Three issues were the subject of negotiation: the inventory for which the seller would continue to be liable, the amount of money that would be placed in escrow to handle claims, and who would handle claims processing. Warranty issues have aspects similar to liability claims, and the results of negotiation have similarities. However, warranty issues were typically easier to resolve than liability claims, which, although fewer in number, involve greater sums at risk.

Usually the buyer preferred the seller to be responsible for all inventory manufactured prior to the closing date. (The president of an MLBO pointed out that although insurance was available to cover the presale period, it was prohibitively expensive.) Especially when the unit's products were relatively small in value, it was sometimes difficult to determine whether a shipment consisted of units manufactured before or after the closing date.[18]

One resolution under these circumstances was for the seller to establish an escrow account based on the seller's experience with the product, with the account administered by the buyer for satisfying warranty claims. At the conclusion of the period, the excess was rebated to the seller or split between the seller and the buyer.[19] Underfunding would usually be the responsibility of the seller. Using such a resolution of the warranty issue left the seller with the complaint that the buyer, who typically administered the account, settled claims too readily and that the ease of settlement became even more evident as the end of the seller's warranty period came to a close.

Another alternative was for the buyer to service all warranties with the following provisions:

1. Up to a specified dollar limit, the warranty was honored by the buyer.
2. Up to a higher dollar limit, the buying firm must obtain consent from the selling firm in a telephone conversation.
3. Beyond a specified limit, permission to honor the warranty must be in writing.

Generally the buying firm charged the selling firm a service fee for each warranty claim submitted on products manufactured under the ownership of the selling firm, with the money, plus the warranty amounts, generally taken out of an escrow account. The vice-president of business development for Conglomerate, Inc. indicated how his firm usually resolved the issue:

> We have to consider the warranty issue when we are buying or selling. We usually specify the time period. For example, we negotiated an agreement that we would charge them $25 for each call we made [in response to a complaint] and time and parts for everything. We had up to a certain limit.

The situation became more complex when the products were of a capital expenditure nature, and it was exacerbated if the about-to-be-divested unit's products were component parts for the buyer's products. Under these circumstances, it was often difficult to determine what created the warranty claim; the component(s) from the unit being divested or component parts manufactured by the new parent. In such situations, each warranty claim would have to be negotiated, and a much closer tie between the old parent and the new parent would be necessary in the postsale period.

Assets Excluded from the Transaction

The assets that were excluded from some of the transactions were real estate and accounts receivable.[20] Real estate was usually excluded because the buyer wanted a lower transaction price. MLBOs were the most usual instances where real property was excluded. In at least one case, the buyer and seller agreed to remove the unit's manufacturing plant from the transaction, negotiating instead a long-term lease for the plant, which had been originally purchased for the unit's use.

Accounts receivable were excluded from the transaction in a few instances when the buying firm did not want to take the risk with the accounts receivable or wanted to decrease the initial purchase price. In one of the transactions where the seller kept the accounts receivable, the buyer took over the responsibility for collecting the accounts receivables. The treasurer of the buying firm explained the terms of the agreement:

> [For us] there never was a deal breaker. We were committed to buying it at that price. If they had had a liability suit or anything that the due diligence turned up that hadn't been disclosed to us or we hadn't covered ourselves in the purchase contract, then that could have broken the deal, but as it stood, there was no real deal breaker. It would have had to have been something undisclosed or unprotected.
>
> We, for instance, didn't buy any receivables. We left them with the seller, but we agreed to collect them for the buyer because they didn't have any people. So we're in the process of collecting, but the receivables are not ours, which is interesting. . . . But we set it up the easiest way we could [and still] not buy the receivables. . . .
>
> Well, [the charge for collecting] was more or less set in the original price to the extent that now we are charging them some fees since we are beyond the contract dates and they still want us to do special things on some credits that didn't get collected and things like that. We charged them a price, which was pretty much time and expense plus a little profit, to collect through the end of the year. And at the end of the year, it's open for negotiation again. If everything still hasn't been collected and they still want us to do it, well, we might do it again. It just depends.
>
> In fact, there was a question yesterday about a receivable. We've exercised all diligence to collect the thing, and our people would normally hire a collection agency and send all kinds of nasty letters or just forget it. . . . But to go to an outside lawyer or anybody, we have to have the seller's permission, or they do it themselves. Their assistant general counsel would be the one that would field whether they wanted to hire an outsider or just drop it. It turned out it was one of the items that they didn't care about or had already written off.

In this case, the buyer agreed to collect the accounts receivable for a period of time without a fee. After the specified six months, the buyer began to charge a fee for collections. The buyer had to resolve such issues as what to do with partial payments or refusals to pay during the postsale time period. Although relations between the two firms were amiable, the experience of these two firms underscores the rationale of one selling firm that selected the buyer partly because they felt comfortable dealing with the buyer in the postsale period.

In addition to what assets were to be part of the transaction, the parties to the transaction had to consider the value allocated to the various assets. The buyer prefers greater allocation to assets that can be depreciated most quickly (such as inventories). The seller prefers to take gains on items to which capital gains rates will be applied. The current changes in tax laws have altered the balance of these issues.

Miscellaneous Items

A number of miscellaneous issues affected only a few firms or were of little significance in most cases: credit memos, confidentiality agreements, indemnity for financial statements and projections, and non-compete agreements.

Credit Memos: The credit memo issue affected negotiations where the unit dealt with retail companies. The president of an MLBO explained the difficulty in his firm:

> A big issue was credit memos. We sell goods to K-Mart. Three or four months after the customer buys it and it doesn't work, he brings it back to the store. K-Mart takes credit against us. I mean, that's just the big part of our business unfortunately. My position was, anything sold before closing date that's going to produce a future credit should be an expense of the old company. The seller's position was, "Nonsense. Every month, as night follows day, you have sales, and you have credits. It's an ongoing thing—just goes on forever, and it's part of the expense of doing business." We basically won that. We pounded and hounded and finally set up a $400,000 reserve for future credits out of the old company. And we got the audit firm in our corner on that.

Credit memos were similar to the product warranty issue; however, they were negotiated as a separate item.

Confidentiality Agreements: When a potential buyer carries out an investigation of the unit to be divested, the potential for competitive abuse of the information is present. Confidentiality agreements are an attempt to protect the unit's value with regard to this issue.

Confidentiality agreements are intended to bind potential buyers from divulging proprietary information about the unit under consideration. During their investigation prior to purchase, potential buyers often do have access to information that they could use to enhance their competitive position. If properly drafted, confidentiality agreements are enforceable; however, proving damages when confidentiality agreements have been violated is often extremely difficult. Some firms in this study required formal written agreements as a matter of standard practice. Others preferred simply to accept an executive's word. The interchange between participants in the executive roundtable in figure 7–6 is illustrative.

Indemnity for Financial Statements and Projections: Most deals were consummated through asset transactions, and the issue of indemnifying financial statements was a moot issue in these circumstances. As one CFO put it, the seller during due diligence process has an opportunity to examine and evaluate assets (such as inventory). However, it is important to transfer to the buyer the tax statements because the Internal Revenue Service evaluates certain assets such as ending inventories, and the buyer needs to make sure that all tax claims have been accounted for.

Executive 1: If you have a number of prospective purchasers that want to take a look at all of your data, do you think it's a reasonable thing to let your legal department put out an agreement that says, "You can look at it, but by god, you can't tell anybody else. If you do, we'll sue you"?

Executive 2: How can you get them to comply with that? You can have the grestest letters and everybody signs them. . . . I'm sure they don't comply. I know where the pro stores 'em.

Executive 3: That's a little bit like selling a unit. They had the open room and every company in the industry in the United States went in and, you know, was pouring over records and details.

Executive 1: You raise a precise problem. A lot of senior management says, "Forget it. If their word isn't good, then nothing's good." But there are other people that say, "You really ought to have a formal agreement."

Executive 3: We have formal agreements. Most people do.

Executive 4: Whether or not it's enforceable, as a practical matter, it's sort of, a little bit besides the point, to the extent there's a psychological impact there that at least, I think, it slows down possible . . .

Executive 3: I think having the letter is a good idea.

Executive 5: Do you allocate any value to it for tax purposes?

Executive 1: No.

Figure 7–6. Confidentiality Agreements

The contrct between the parties can contain a clause indicating that the buying party relied on the selling party's projections on coming to a decision on price. One executive put the potential dilemma this way:

> Say you're really trying to sell a business, and you have some projections of where you think this business is gonna go, so you give that to the other side. They tuck it in their briefcase, and later you sign the contract. They come back later, about a year after the close, and say, "This business didn't do it." And you say, "Well, what are you talking about?" They say, "Well, you guaranteed that it would achieve a certain level of income," and you say, "We never guaranteed anything." They say, "Oh, yes you did. Here's this projection you gave us."

Generally reasonable business practice suggests that the selling parties put a disclaimer on all pro formas given to potential buyers. A general counsel explained that the issue could be significant: "There have been lawsuits based on the issue, and the plaintiffs have prevailed because the projections were relied upon and used in the decision-making process."

Non-compete Agreements: Non-compete agreements are generally written for three to five years and are enforceable in court, especially when substantial consideration is given. They were not a critical issue in buy-sell transactions between the companies in this investigation. They tend to be critical when an owner-founder is selling a firm. However, these agreements with executives in a divesting firm are generally not enforceable since the courts will not deprive an individual of his or her livelihood and executives in the selling firm do not usually receive consideration specific for agreeing not to compete.

Summary

Managing negotiations involved making choices regarding process and the resolution of various issues. Included among the process issues were the choice of bidding versus face-to-face negotiations, choices in the face-to-face negotiations, differences in the size of the negotiation team, variations in the role of a lawyer in negotiations, and the role of the board. Usually price was the most critical content issue in the negotiations. The two basic choices regarding price negotiation were bidding versus face-to-face negotiation. Several factors, including the expected market for the unit, the size or visibility of the unit, and the personal orientation of the executives involved, influenced the choice of bidding versus face-to-face negotiations.

Several factors differentiated between smooth and difficult negotiations: the desire of the buyer to buy and the seller to sell, the experience in negotiations on both sides, previous interaction, and the trust level between the parties.

The size of the negotiation team depended on the expertise of the individual charged with negotiations and how the seller's team was organized. Price negotiation tactics when dealing face to face varied between the seller giving the initial offer versus the buyer making the initial offer. If the seller made the initial offer, the choice was whether to set the initial offer high or offer the buyer a price close to the actual targeted price.

The issues in negotiations included those that were critical and could be deal breakers, major issues that seldom became deal breakers, and several issues of less significance. Price was, not unexpectedly, the most critical issue. Other major issues were asset or stock transaction, responsibility for liability claims, employee pension plans, employee contracts, warranties, and assets included in the transaction. The process results in various resolutions for each of these issues.

Other issues might also become the subject of negotiation. For example, companies selling foreign units enter into some delicate points regarding contractual obligations to employees given government requirements. However, the issues examined in this chapter—price, asset versus stock-based sale, employee contracts, pension liabilities, warranty claims, and liability suits—were the usual items of negotiation between sellers and buyers, both of whom were U.S. based in this research program. The resolution of the issues varied depending upon the degree to which the seller wanted to sell and the buyer wanted to buy.

Perhaps the best summary of the preferred style and outcome from the process of negotiations came from one of the executives who said:

> In my experience there is nothing that beats being straightforward and putting all of your cards on the table and dealing with integrity. I've run into people who are not that way. Buying and selling businesses is like working in the used car business. It can be a very tricky business. One of the keys, I think, in terms of actually being able to execute is to be able to isolate the two or three critical issues that matter and go forward on that basis. I think a lot of other people get bogged down in details that they are unable to come to a decision. So, one of the other keys is to have an entrepreneurial spirit, not only with the top guy but with the other people so that we are willing to make commitments based on our judgments of the facts as we see them, and not get frozen with indecision and a lot of handwringing. It's a risky business, when you're dealing with a lot of unknowns and dealing with very large numbers.

Recommendations for Corporate Executives

1. Price is the most critical issue in negotiations. However, the possible resolutions for issues beyond price have to be considered. I have suggested five critical issues that bear on the value derived from the unit: asset versus stock-based sale, employee contracts, pension liabilities, warranty claims, and liability suits. Each of these items must be considered in advance with regard to the position that the firm wants and their impact on price.

2. The range of resolutions represented among these firms was fairly broad. Since the buyer is likely to have some quite different ideas about how the issues should be resolved, various positions on the resolution continuum for each issue should be considered and their impact on the target price considered. These issues can sometimes be quantified and various negotiation positions fairly well substantiated. The issues should be examined qualitatively and the quantitative information readied for negotiations. For example, the past ten years of warranty claims is information that the buying firm will need. Such information must be available for the negotiation process.

3. The seller's desire to sell and the buyer's desire to buy must be assessed. The seller's primary objective is to maximize the value derived during the negotiation process. However, other issues affect that value and may be subject to negotiation. For example, how important is it to the selling firm that management is protected with strong contracts?

4. Divestitures are sufficiently traumatic that some concern should be evidenced regarding employee issues. Consideration has to be given to the employees with the unit. Benefits, pensions, union contracts, and other contractual agreements should be considered. Those who will not go with the unit and will need to be reassigned within the parent organization also need attention. Reassignment should take place as soon as possible. Decisions also will need to be made regarding those who will not have jobs. In addition, consideration should be given to the other employees in the parent company who will not be directly affected by the divestiture. How the divestiture is handled and the explanations given to all employees can make significant differences in morale among remaining employees and among employees of yet-to-be divested units.[21]

5. It is clear that whenever both parties "win," the value is enhanced. Achieving that final outcome requires the seller to consider his or her own position as well as that of the buyer and to be sensitive to the signals that are given about the possible positions the other party is willing to take. Moreover, the alternative positions that the seller is willing to take need to be reevaluated throughout the negotiations process. As one experienced negotiator put it: "I've worked on acquisitions before so I knew pretty well what the buyer concerns were. But it was a pretty smooth deal. . . . The people won. The buyer won. We won. So [it was] win, win, win. I guess if there's anything I can advise you, look for win-win situations in any negotiations."

Recommendations for Division Executives

Division executives are not usually involved directly in negotiations. Depending on the circumstances—which heavily relate to the degree of expertise residing

residing in unit personnel as contrasted to what resides in individuals at corporate—the expertise, counsel, and advice of division management, as well as other personnel, may be sought continually throughout the negotiation process. Where such expertise is embedded in the unit and less so at corporate, the division will usually have a fairly clear picture of the status of negotiations on a reasonably timely basis.

Where negotiations are carried on in the dark, the time period can be quite stressful, and the effect in both the workplace and personal life should be considered and prepared for. Suggestions might include seeking outside personal counsel and slimming one's outside responsibilities other than those that are strictly relaxing. In the worst case scenario, the outcome of one's career hangs in the balance. It is quite possible that division management is being sold out of a job. Contingency planning can help relieve some of the stress and tension that inevitably accompany this situation.

Notes

1. For example, in the 1980 divestiture of its petroleum subsidiary, Tri-Diversified Inc. set up locations where buyers could come to get additional data.

2. Or to negotiate so adeptly that the party with the lesser knowledge does not perceive that he or she has the lesser knowledge.

Executives indicated that the most difficult negotiations occurred with inexperienced sellers of companies. Usually these instances occurred when the seller was an owner-founder. Of special difficulty was the confounding of family and business financial affairs. In describing these negotiations, executives commented during the executive roundtable: "You got to educate the guy." "They're miserable." "Ask for his inventory record and he pulls it out of his pocket." and "I had a guy try to sell me his business by giving me the pro forma of what it would be if he didn't have all the wives and kids on the payroll . . . all this stuff there. I said, 'OK you got the tax liability for the stuff that comes back.' He said, 'No; you've got the tax liability.' I says, 'You mean to tell me you want me to buy your pro forma numbers while you're cheating the government and I'm gonna assume your liabilities for the tax?' He says, 'Sure, that's fair.' "

3. The legal staff is invariably involved with a divestiture. Among other issues, the legal staff will deal with the FTC. The legal staff generally handle the first Hart-Scott submission. If there is a second request, the business people get involved. From FTC's perspective, they find the business people may be over prepared by their legal staff.

4. In one MLBO, the outside board member was a conduit for the investment banker to bring pressure to bear on the division manager to accept the investment banker's financing deal.

5. On the other hand, at least one executive described—*accused* might not be too strong of a word—investment bankers as often deliberately setting the price low so that the transaction could be more readily consummated. The implication was that investment bankers wanted to be sure they could earn their fee.

6. I was unable to determine why this unit did not become an MLBO.

7. The $500,000 represented about 15 percent of the targeted purchase price and approximately $350 per employee in the total parent company at that time.

8. In contrast, in one MLBO the buyer and seller went to great lengths to structure the deal. In this instance, a shell corporation, jointly held by the buyer and seller, was created. The seller invested the unit in the shell; the buyer invested cash. The buyer then took out the subsidiary unit as a dividend. The seller took out cash. The shell was dissolved. The transaction is referred to as a *cash merger*. Under current tax laws, it is not tax free. The buyer, however, wanted the legal corporation because there were a number of leases associated with the unit. The buyer did not want to renegotiate those leases.

9. For example, one of the interviewees made a point of describing how his company purchased a string of acquisitions: "One strategy that we purchased was what we called bulk purchase acquisition. In that was the acquisition of a laboratory's assets. The bulk purchase laws of every state cover the sale of a business asset, and under bulk sales law, you acquire assets but you don't acquire liabilities. You don't acquire an ongoing business."

10. A general counsel involved in the study pointed out that the courts will not necessarily allow an asset sale to absolve the buyer from the liabilities. Indeed, if the buyer continues to operate the entity without change and then refuses to pay a claim based on the argument that the liabilities did not transfer, the court is likely to rule that the buyer is attempting to absolve himself of liability by disguising the purchase of the business as an asset transaction.

11. Most of the transactions in this research program were asset based.

12. The courts have not, however, gone back to the seller (often a large entity with "deep pockets") for products manufactured under the ownership of the buyer (often a smaller entity).

13. Another special set of circumstances comes up in employee buy-outs when the pension fund is used to purchase the company. Executive roundtable participants expressed concern because the employees' pension funds were at greater risk in the freestanding company. In addition, there is no requirement that the employees have a voice in this decision.

14. There are basically two kinds of pension funds: defined contribution and defined benefit. *Defined contribution plans* cannot be overfunded or underfunded since the employees are entitled to the ultimate market value of the contributions made over the time of employment. This end value of the contributions can swing widely, depending on the investment portfolio of the plan. *Defined benefit plans* can be overfunded or underfunded since the value contributed at any one point may or may not be sufficient to purchase the contractual obligation due at the time of the employee's retirement. Of the two alternatives, defined benefit plans are by far the more common. In the current market, pension plans tend to be more often overfunded than underfunded.

15. In this study, employee issues were more often a criterion for selecting a buyer and not an item for negotiation. Another observer has suggested that employee considerations are often sufficiently critical that the seller should ascertain, as nearly as possible, the buyer's intentions from the beginning. Under some conditions, it is probably better from the point of view of the entire company to cut negotiations short rather than have negative feelings spread throughout the selling parent company. See, for example, Peter N. Walmsley, *Handbook of Strategic Planning* (New York: Wiley, 1986), pp. 13.1–13.34.

16. One general counsel pointed out that he had had executives suggest to him that they would not honor the union contract. He pointed out that technically the executive could do so. However, he also pointed out that severe difficulties with the labor force could ensue, and he advised such executives that they decide ahead of time whether they wanted the work force.

17. In at least one instance, special arrangements were made to loan the seller's management team to the seller. One of the executives explained: "We lent [the buyer]—I guess you'd call it an indentured servant contract [for] the plant management for six months after the sale so they could train replacements."

18. One MLBO president persevered in negotiations, however, and demonstrated how the products produced before and after sale could be identified. The liability for products manufactured prior to the sale was retained by the seller.

19. Executives who negotiated splitting the remaining balance maintained that so doing provided incentive for the buyer to manage the escrow account judiciously.

20. Inventories could also be excluded; however, they are likely to go with the unit. No instance occurred in this study where inventories were withdrawn from the transaction at the initiation of the seller or the buyer.

21. One observer has described the situation well: "A divestiture is a traumatic event in varying degrees for all of the four groups described, engendering feelings of shock, concern, and insecurity. Management should be sensitive to this for both humanitarian and business reasons. . . . If they [unaffected employees] believe that the involved employees were not treated fairly, the company's image as a good employer will be tarnished, and employee relations will become more adversarial. . . . [Thus] when a business is identified as a potential divestiture candidate, it is well worth giving some consideration to how the business could be improved by eliminating excess staff or deleterious operations and product lines before offering it for sale. This way the seller has maximum control over the personnel questions and has a more profitable and attractive operation to present to the buyer." Walmsley, *Handbook,* pp. 13.14–13.34.

8

Ethical Issues, Future Research Suggestions, and Concluding Observations

T his chapter focuses on conflicts confronting decision makers and accompanying ethical issues—issues that arose during the process of this investigation. These issues were not necessarily referred to as ethical dilemmas. More typically, they were presented as conflicts in making choices. An executive would express chagrin at the negative outcomes from a decision in which he had participated.

This chapter also covers a number of possible future research focuses. A caveat needs to be made concerning this program of research. Although the project was broad in scope and encompassed the experience of firms, it was by no means complete. This book summarizes the analysis of the themes that arose from the research. It was not a definitive, full-scale empirical investigation. There are areas now ripe for more systematic, larger-scale investigations given the conceptualizations resulting from this analysis.

Ethical Issues

The evidence from this investigation suggests that the firms generally handled the process of divestiture in an ethical manner. There was only one instance in which an executive explicitly evidenced concern that some aspects of the transaction had violated ethical bounds: "[We] traveled around . . . and put potential buyers together and did things that the Lord didn't like us to do, but that was difficult too."

Certainly there may have been bias in firm participation in this study. We may reasonably argue only firms that had conducted the divestiture process ethically were willing to participate in a research program of this nature. But two aspects of the study suggest otherwise. First, I conducted most of the interviews in person. Only two individuals refused an interview. One of them talked extensively on the telephone, and the other has recently invited me to the site to write a case on the history of the unit during and after divestiture. The reason given at the time of first refusal—lack of time—has apparently been validated. Moreover, only a few executives refused a telephone interview. Generally they pleaded lack of time, although two were adamant that their firms did not discuss such matters with outside parties. In essence, then, there is little reason to suspect significant bias among the firms regarding ethical issues.

Second, I have developed a close acquaintance with several executives who participated in the study in the course of making multiple visits to the company site. In these conversations there has been little evidence of unethical behavior. Although, executives readily admit the process is sometimes poorly handled, the difficulties arise either from lack of skill and experience or the pressure of multiple factors fielded at one time—not from executive intent to win at all costs or deliberate intent to defraud.[1] There are, however, a number of points in the divestiture process where ethical issues are present, and these issues warrant attention.

Nearly every point in the divestiture process poses potential ethical conflicts or dilemmas. I define ethical behavior here as the fulfillment of implicit or explicit contracts. Thus, an issue has been handled ethically if the executive has fairly represented the areas over which he or she has control and has fulfilled implicit or explicit contracts. Ethical dilemmas put the individual in the position of having to make a decision that may benefit one participant at potential cost to another. Five sets of relationships were discussed in the course of this investigation that put participants in situations with potential ethical dilemmas: corporate versus stockholders; corporate versus potential buyers; corporate versus division management; corporate versus lower-level management; and division management versus rank and file.

Ethical dilemmas were not a focus of the study; rather, the issues arose during the analysis. Executives who participated in the research program did not invoke the notion of ethical concerns but instead evidenced concern about the inherent conflicts in the divestiture process. These dilemmas that confronted the executives are examined in response to the following questions:

1. How are contracts broken between corporate and division management and corporate-division management and other employees?

2. What compensation is made for broken contracts with unit personnel?

3. What ethical issues arise in dealing with buyers?

4. Do corporate executives recognize their responsibility to stockholders?

5. When do personal goals and relationships put the value for the organization in jeopardy?

6. How does one achieve ethical credibility, and what advantages accrue?

Breaking Contracts

In essence the trade-offs confronted by corporate executives in a divestiture may be viewed as follows:

Obligations To Shareholders	*Obligations to Employees*
Maintain value of unit Sell unit at as high a price as possible	Preserve career flow without interruption[2]

Usually when the decision is made to divest, the ultimate buyer is not known. Thus obligations to the employees are placed at risk.

There was discussion in the executive roundtable regarding unit management who know that the divestiture is to take place, contract to stay and help with the divestiture, and in the ensuing period necessarily bypass other attractive career opportunities. The consensus of the participants was that the manager understood the risk of undertaking the revised contract; there was no obligation on the part of the organization in these instances.

The dilemma comes when lower-level employees do not know about the impending divestiture. The purpose of withholding information from them is to avoid damaging the value of the unit by employees leaving for other opportunities. The trade-off is the enhancement of organizational value at the potential cost of individual value. The possibility is that individuals may bypass alternative career opportunities during this interim period.

What moral obligation does the organization have to these individuals? Although no firm answer came from this investigation, observations came from executives who were vocal about the results of being open or believed that the organization should be open with employees. One set of comments came from those who pointed out that their worst fears regarding employee desertion were not realized. Two instances are especially salient. The first concerns a former executive vice-president of administration:

> In my first experiences, the natural fear [was] that once everybody knew that this plant was for sale, everybody was going to quit. . . . I found quite the opposite. I recall going out and telling them about a week before Christmas that they were going, and in this instance many of them would be unemployed because in this particular instance the [new owners] weren't going to need as many people and, quite to the contrary, one individual who was physically a little limited and had the responsibility for cleaning floors and so on, came up, and said, "Mr. Conrad, I want you to know that when it goes, back there where I keep it, it will be clean." So all I found was that people rose to it, always.

The CFO of Consumer Products, Inc. told employees in Dancer about the impending divestiture shortly after the decision was made. He and other corporate executives fully expected that especially the sales representatives would leave. To their surprise, all but one of twelve representatives stayed throughout the period, which turned out to be far lengthier than originally envisioned.

The news of an impending divestiture is often a traumatic event for unit employees, primarily because their expectations may not be met. In essence, a contract—implicit or explicit—has been broken. The greatest difficulty appears to arise when the divestiture is of a major unit that is highly successful at the time of divestiture, and the unit is the firm's first divestiture. The comments of a COB-CEO and the head of a unit indicate the extent of the difficulty the COB-CEO had in convincing the unit head that divestiture was the appropriate move:

> *COB-CEO of Tri-Conglomerate:* It took time. I called [him] to come to [headquarters]. He said, "You're crazy." In essence, he was saying, "You don't sell your star pitcher." I said, "I think you are overestimating your pitching." It took time.

> *Unit executive of Tri-Conglomerate* [in a later interview]: You cannot really understand the trauma. Even after we sold the unit for significantly more than we thought we were going to get, the consensus was that it was a dumb deal. Corporate had made a dumb deal. They sold something that was really humming. You just don't sell things that are going good.

There is evidence, however, that no matter how many units the company has divested, the size, or the performance level, the trauma still occurs. The vice-president of strategic planning for a major conglomerate with considerable experience in divestiture put it this way:

> *Interviewer:* When did the top management division know they were going to be divested, and how were they informed?

> *Vice-president:* Well, they were just told that we were seeking to divest that business.

> *Interviewer:* That must have been pretty hard on them, considering they had been there twenty-five years.

> *Vice-president:* Well, I came from there too. Of course, it's an emotional thing. Anytime you divest anything, it's emotional.

The greatest difficulty may be with corporate and divisional management's relationship with rank and file. Part of the difficulty emanates from the fact that strong relationships more often exist between corporate executives and unit management. Moreover, corporate, more than unit management, has the power to effect the changes. Another part of the difficulty with rank and file is that in many instances corporate has allowed the unit to get fat. Thus the rank and file are at more risk in a divestiture. The divisional head of a major consulting firm explained the difficulty:

> You have not mentioned the rank and file. In many divestitures, the rank and file are decimated often because of realizing synergies or the division is just fat. Corporate management tends to worry about top management and not rank and file. Some managers, e.g., in Hewlett-Packard, worry about this issue, but other companies don't.

Compensation for Violated Contracts

Once the announcement of the divestiture is made, two aspects of violated contracts are critical. One, compensation for the value lost, was covered in chapter 4 and will not be reviewed here. The other is the renegotiation of the contract.[3]

In the case of Tri-Conglomerate, the personal relationship between the CEO-COB and the unit executive helped in mitigating the trauma, renegotiating the contract, and persuading the unit executive to come to personal reconciliation with the CEO's decision. The unit executive of Tri-Conglomerate explained the process of his personal reconciliation:

> Frank [COB-CEO] and I are close friends. We got away and talked privately about it. I could see he was extremely concerned about some of his other corporate problems. Also, as time went on, I could see he was dead serious about discussing the possibility of selling our unit. Even though I fundamentally felt that I'd rather be in [our] business than in the [remaining] business, it wasn't my draw to make. If he felt that was the best thing, and the directors felt that it was the best direction for the corporation and they wanted to get rid of our unit, that's what I'd do.

In the instance of Tri-Conglomerate, renegotiation of the contract between the COB-CEO and the unit executive was complete. Three aspects of the situation appeared to affect the outcome:

1. The close personal relationship afforded each man opportunity to understand the other's viewpoint.
2. The COB-CEO gave the unit executive time in which to reorient his expectations.
3. There was significant compensation for the unit executive.

The renegotiation of the contract was clearly mutually satisfactory. Three years after the divestiture took place, the unit executive talked about his ongoing relationship with the COB-CEO: "Friday, my wife and I are going up as his guest to the opening of [an exclusive social affair], a black tie affair, which will be a neat evening." This unit executive indicated that outsiders who knew both men were surprised that the relationship continued. The expectation was that divestiture meant rejection of the unit executive by the COB-CEO.

This example portrays the initial conflict in the interaction between the corporate executive and unit's senior executive. For these two men, the issues were resolved. But for the next level of unit management, the dilemma may be more difficult. For example, in Tri-Conglomerate, the COB-CEO worked closely with the unit's president. When the unit president went to his next layer of management with news of the divestiture, he was one person working with ten. The unit president had three months to reconcile himself to the decision, the next layer of management much less.[4]

The dilemma posed for corporate executives working with senior unit management and for unit management working with the next layer of management is violation of the implied or even explicit contracts. The expectation of all layers of management is often continuing encouragement of the growth.

The CFO of Consumer Products made this violation explicit when he talked about the difficulty that the unit executive of Dancer had accepting the news of the divestiture decision. Ernie, the unit president, had come into the position a short time before the decision to divest, and his decision to accept the position was predicated on the strategic plan for the unit, which anticipated significant growth. The issues echoed those confronted in Tri-Conglomerate.

Another area where potential dilemmas may be significant are sales of units where the work force is likely to be trimmed. The difficulties occur for the rank and file and for middle management. The dilemmas with the middle managers are twofold. One aspect is middle management's lack of opportunity for other employment. The second is that the process of informing them about the impending divestiture must elicit their cooperation. A unit executive explained:

> The one group that is the heartbreaking group is not the vice-presidents. It's the middle management. You've got a lot of Peter Principle. A lot of the middle managers are senior in age, and it's an extremely tough deal for them. They don't get any big incentive, and you're pushing them out there in a canoe. You know their days are numbered. Their odds of getting as good a job are nil. . . . [It's] too large of a group to make you feel very good. They are senior people who've been there for a long time. You know they're gonna be in trouble, O Lord, a heap of trouble.
>
> Fundamentally when it got down to the show and tells, all the vice-presidents and the two presidents handled the show and tells. That is the layer that has to be convinced that (a) you gotta just say this is the way it is, (b) why it does make some sense, and (c) you might have a better future where you're going. Don't assume negative. It's a bunch of hokey, but, you've got to say that.

Thus, we see the modification of contracts for employees in the divested unit may be conceptualized as follows:

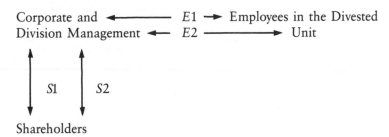

$S1$ and $E1$ are the initial contracts with shareholders and employees, respectively. $S2$ and $E2$ are the new contracts. The expectation is that $S2$ is greater than $S1$; but there is risk that $E2$ is less than $E1$. How can this dilemma be resolved? One necessary response appears to be personal support from one level of management to the next level. A second possible response is corporate's commitment to find a good buyer. As indicated by Tri-Conglomerate's experience, the personal presence and support of the next higher layer of management is critical. It is clear that managers understand that the most critical issue once a divestiture decision has been made is to keep the unit functioning. The next higher layer of management must be supportive of those reporting to them as the subordinates undertake the dual task of maintaining the unit and facilitating the divestiture. One executive when asked what the most critical issues were after the decision to divest had been made said:

> Keeping things running while people's minds were diverted. We get paid to be managers, and we have to continue to the best of our ability to manage what we're in charge of and at the same time know that you will have a new owner in six months. And, listen, we didn't know who'd buy our unit. It could have been a rich guy in Australia that wanted the whole thing, and he could have said, "Here's my money. I'm leaving everybody in place, your bonus plans, etc." My management team and I talked a long time about not presuming everything, taking each day as it came, don't try to guess who the buyer's going to be, and run your business as a professional man.

A second possible response is the commitment of corporate to find a buyer with whom the unit fits. One executive indicated that there was a basis for unit employees to have hope: "There are many situations in which the management of the division is much better off divested. For example, in LBOs, they can make a lot of money, and there are other companies that want them." Another cited his preference for persuading unit management:

Interviewer: Division managers do not necessarily react as you suggest.

Executive 2: Their initial reaction is still anxiety, and you have to work with getting them comfortable with the divestiture. You tell them we are not the best owner of this unit.

Executive 1: You tell them what our company direction is, . . . and your division doesn't fit. Your division fits better [with another company]. Why don't you work with us? There are companies that would like you as parents. Why don't you help the investment bankers? Where there are two bids within 5%, we are going to go with your preference. You can get a lot of enthusiasm going.

In essence, when corporate executives commit to finding a good buyer, they are saying, "Our firm wants to divest your unit. By doing so, we expect to enhance the value of our total firm. Also, we expect to find a buyer who will want you and a situation where you are more likely to have the contract carried out." The chairman of M&A Consulting firm expanded on aspects of a good buyer as he described the larger concept of a good divestiture:

> Now this may surprise you a little bit, but in the best divestiture, the buyer is just right for the acquisition. It fits good, and the people run it better. It does a lot for them, it solves the needs of the unit, and the seller got the right price. Now that may sound trite, but those are the kind that we consider good divestitures. . . . So it's very good for everyone. It sounds like too much of a cliché to say that what is good for everyone is the best, but those are the kinds that I consider the best divestitures.

Ethical Issues in Dealing with Buyers

Four issues arose regarding ethical issues in dealing with buyers: the degree of validity and reliability of the representation of the unit by the seller to the buyer, giving all participants in the bidding process equal information, cleaning up problems in a unit prior to sale, and unit management's dilemmas in dealing with buyers. The major issue in working with buyers is the degree of validity and reliability of the representation of the unit. The initial dilemma is that of corporate, but during the buyer's visits, division management also experiences the dilemma:

Obligations to Shareholders	Obligations to Buyers
1. Deliver maximum value for unit	Deliver value as represented
2. Long term value of firm depends on integrity of firm	

A prime obligation of managers to shareholders is to deliver maximum value. There is, therefore, a short-term temptation to puff the value of the unit. The trade-off is with the firm's long-term reputation and whether a reputation for integrity adds to value. The initial presentation package is a major issue in valid and reliable representation of the unit, as the chairman of M&A Consulting Firm suggested:

> The package is very important. It has to be orderly. It does not necessarily have to be humongous, but it has to be very orderly in terms of what a buyer wants to read. And that's a very important element of what we do for our clients. We do it more clinically than a client might do otherwise, because a client has a tendency to puff it—not intentionally sometimes, but if you're the seller, you can't say bad things about the unit for sale. We think it's important to be reasonably objective, and we think it's important to be very open.
>
> We did just that with a friend of ours recently. He had a good-sized, privately owned company. He'd gotten into legal problems around what he sells to the government, and, in effect, he had to sell because the government wasn't going to do business with his company. . . . I don't know the details too much. We made it very clear what the case was, what happened, because you know there's no point in not making it clear because it's a futile exercise. Particularly in our case. We don't need a futile exercise to go through the whole thing and not consummate the deal. We have enough experience to know that it's better to get the things out in the open that are going to be a problem two months from now in the negotiations when the lawyers get in or the accountants or whatever. It's better to get it all out and right down to hard, cold facts early in the game. So the presentation of the package is very important.

In addition, there are ethical dilemmas in the bidding process. In bidding, the rule of the game is that all players in the bidding process have access to the same information. One division president who assisted corporate activity in the bidding process for his unit and was also a very visible individual in a tightly knit industry talked about the dilemmas for him:

> *Executive:* It's almost like hawking stock. . . . We were all instructed to go through the investment banker and let the investment banker contact the person and give them the bidding procedures. This makes sure nobody can come back and say that they had more information or less than somebody else or were treated better or worse than somebody else.
>
> *Interviewer:* How did you handle meeting people in the industry during the time?
>
> *Executive:* (smiling) That's a very astute question. Practicalities of a guy like myself going through an investment banker—some of my closest friends would be insulted. You just tiptoe through the tulips. You explain your predicament. But that doesn't stop them from buying you a beer and saying, "Now, Jim . . . " All they wanted to make sure was that they had the same rights and privileges everybody else had. Other people were getting through the back door and

getting more information. . . . That's where they were trying to cover themselves with my friendship. . . . Once I said "No hankypanky. Everybody is
getting the same data." That was fine.

Another issue is whether the unit's problems should be untouched prior to
the sale of whether the buyer should make attempts to clean up the difficulties.
The chairman of M&A Consulting Firm indicated his preference with his clients:

> Management should look at the problems early in the game and get them
> taken care of before they get them out on the table if they possibly can. . . .
> There's a tendency to say, "Well, let's get the buyer, and then we'll see what
> the buyer wants to do. Maybe we can negotiate away the responsibility." It's
> almost better to face that because that's your problem anyway if you're a seller.
> If you keep the business, that's your problem. So, you know, you can't just
> sell it to somebody to get rid of it and have him accept your problem without
> compensation or something. Therefore you might as well face it.

In addition, the unit's management may run into difficulties in the on-site
visits. One executive explained the dilemmas of unit management:

> *Executive:* It is very hard to sell a division without management in the deal.
> You are more likely to get a higher price if they are on board. One issue occurs
> when the potential buyer does due diligence, and the unit management tells
> him what a wonderful unit this is and how much potential it has.
>
> *Interviewer:* What are the ethical dilemmas faced by the division managers?
>
> *Executive:* The most difficult position is that of the division manager dealing
> with a buyer. The buyer may become his owner, and so he would like to sell
> it for as low a price as possible so he can be a hero, and yet for his current
> owners he wants as high a price as possible. That is some of the roughest times.

The dilemma for corporate management is valid and reliable representation
of the unit. That dilemma exists also for unit management. The difficulty in
interacting with buyers is exacerbated when unit management hosts potential
buyers but knows there is a possibility of an MLBO. In one instance, said an
MLBO president, "We just had to bite our tongues many times."

Corporate Executives' Responsibility to Stockholders

Considerable discussion has gone on in our society generally regarding corporate executive concern for their fiduciary responsibility toward stockholders.
Executive participants in the roundtable discussed the issue of divestiture timing
and whether managers take action on the timing in a way that is best for shareholders. Participants suggested that managers who own significant stock relative to their personal wealth bases do take stockholder considerations into
account. The exchange appears in figure 8–1. Participants argued further that

Moderator: You mentioned on the timing aspect how sometimes you would like to offset a loss against the gain, or something like that. It seems to me that a number of times it could be inconsistent with what is best for the shareholders. The question I have is, Do you do things in the divestiture area that you perceive to be best for management, or where do the shareholders come in? It seems to me that you might time these things so it could be what is best for management and not necessarily best for the shareholders, particularly if you're trying to pigeon hole yourself in a particular quarter.

Executive 1: It's true in our company and may be the case for a lot of others here, but virtually, well, most of my net worth is in the stock of my company, and that's the case with my fellow officers as well. So we are shareholders, and largely we think of ourselves as the shareholders because we own so much of the stock and that stock means so much to our financial security, to tell you the truth. I had a couple of people ask me about this who were academics and not in business, as though there's management here and the shareholders are there. But I am going to tell you in our case, we are very much one and the same even though it's a publicly held stock.

Executive 2: I'm like [executive 1]. I like companies where management owns a lot of the rock. I think you err on the side of the shareholder when you own a lot of the stock yourself. Although there are people who say it doesn't make a difference, I don't believe it.

Executive 3: I don't either. I've worked in an environment where at least by background over many years, you were a wage earner, not a shareholder. I would say that that has influence. I don't mean to say that anybody actively does things for the management and not for the shareholder. I mean that the thought about the shareholders may not be primary in the minds of executives every step of the way. I would say that executives without stock are much more oriented toward operating profits by the month and things like that. They think about what's happening to the shares or earnings per share maybe once a quarter.

Executive 1: One other comment about quarterly earnings. One of the things that I sense is that in terms of stock market evaluation, what we are trying to do in large measure is to give a good return to the shareholders of which we are part and that return is in the form of dividends and capital appreciation. Capital appreciation, then, is, in part, a function of the stability of earnings and predictability of earnings so that you sometimes hear about companies shifting some income in one quarter versus another, and that's not for the convenience of the management. I don't know how much of that's really done, but, to the extent that it is done, it also has to do with evaluation of the stock but in the sense of having a relatively stable, steadily increasing stream of reported earnings. So it's not a management convenience thing. At least in the minds of those who do that, it has to do with evaluation of shares.

Moderator: Okay. So in general you don't view there's any kind of a conflict. That should be a fair summary.

Figure 8–1. Divestiture Timing: Stockholder Wealth or Management Convenience?

even where management wealth bases are not heavily in the stock of the company, management still concerns itself with the goals of the shareholders. For example, one vice-president of corporate planning stated, "I think it would be an unusual situation where the interests of the shareholders are not taken into account or are taken into account secondarily."

Jeopardizing the Organization: In several instances, there were strong prior relationships between participants in the buying-selling negotiations. In one, there was a particularly strong relationship, as well as other dimensions that appeared to affect the negotiations. The buyer's representative, Gordon Wright, had been in charge of the unit for the seller several years prior and, indeed, had been responsible for establishing the original vision for the unit. He had retained that vision as he took a senior position in a similar business activity at an interim company. Later, he moved to a corporate position with the present buyer. The ultimate price paid was close to the high side of the range established by the seller. Was the price paid too high, a reflection of Gordon's eagerness to purchase the unit he had once managed? Within eighteen months, the buyer became disenchanted with the unit and began carving it up for sale. The question is raised whether Gordon's relationship with the seller and his vision led to the buying firm's overpaying for the unit. Although the incident is not definitive, it raises the issue of personal goals and past relationships, affecting the price negotiation outcomes. The following exchange occurred between the interviewer and the head of the unit:

> *Interviewer:* I saw a situation where the players knew each other very well, and there was very high trust on both sides, and there was a premium paid for the business. Do you think that occurs frequently, I mean, when there's a premium paid? Is it because there is trust?
>
> *Division head:* I think trust facilitates. I mean, the buyer was so anxious to do the deal, and Gordon was anxious to do the deal. I think it facilitated the negotiation.

Achieving Ethical Credibility

Ethical credibility is acquired over a period of time. The executive vice-president of Major Conglomerate, Inc. talked about a buyer, a former executive of his firm. Not only did the individual's past reputation facilitate his obtaining a loan from a major bank, but the relationship clearly facilitated the buyer-seller negotiations. The vice-president described the situation when the former executive decided to buy a set of businesses. The price was $67 million, and the buyer put $1 million of equity into the deal.

> That was typical of Carl [the buyer]. The bank had so much faith in him. I won't bore you too much with these little side stories, but I think they're fun.

Carl is like our chairman. Our chairman has had a lot more publicity than Carl. But they're out of the same mold—extremely intelligent, extremely energetic, completely honest. They are like three brothers who had a little company down near Philadelphia. I did business with them some years ago. They were all Quakers, and I was going down to negotiate with them. A fellow I knew said, "Now, be careful. Those fellows are so honest that if they owed you a dime, they'd walk through snow five miles to pay the dime back. But when they got there, if they could negotiate you out of it, they would." And that's sort of Carl's approach. Everything's open and above board, but, you know, a hard, tough negotiator.

He formed a little company that was called XTech. He didn't even have time to think of a name for it. (*Laughing*) He went to a bank, but they didn't take the whole package. He cut [a large unit] out of the package. He couldn't get enough funding to swing the whole deal. But he took two large units.

At one point we were sitting at this table. I had the financial statements in front of me. As I was looking through, I said, "Well, you know, Carl, since you're taking all that [unit] business in [a particular geographical unit], we have another little company out there that you ought to take along with it." And he said, "What are their sales?" And I said, "$2 million." And he said, "What is their net worth?" And I said, "$1 million." And he said, "Did they make any money?" And I said, "They broke even last year." He said, "Okay, throw it in the package." We went on. Five or ten minutes later he said, "By the way, what does that company make?" And I said, "They make [a specialty health-related product]." And he said, "Oh, that's okay."

The question of whether personal relationships can put the buyer at a disadvantage is not answered definitively in this example from Major Conglomerate, Inc.

Future Research

The results of the investigation reported in this book have been fruitful, but the work cannot be considered definitive. The sample of firms, although broad for this kind of work (more clinical or qualitative) relative to what has been done before, is nonetheless small relative to the total population (all U.S. firms that have undertaken divestiture). Each of the stages of the process has aspects that warrant additional investigation. The following discussion is suggestive rather than exhaustive.

The experience of U.S. firms to date has been chronicled in chapter 1. I am indebted to two organizations (Mergers and Organizations and W.J. Grimms) for their activities in recording the aggregate phenomenon. Since the phenomenon changes over time, the aggregate experience requires periodic examination and contrast of the experience of the current period with prior ones. In addition, to date no investigation of the economic and social factors affecting the level of aggregate activity has been undertaken. Such factors as interest rates, level of stock market activity, tax provisions, and stage in the economic cycle certainly affect individual firm decisions. The links between these issues and the aggregate experience need to be examined.[5]

Chapter 2 reported on a more complete list of the conditions that trigger divestiture than has been reported before; however, our understanding is by no means exhausted. First, it is not clear which corporate-level factors are most influential in provoking divestiture and what the interaction between factors is. Second, although both this project and prior research have provided a foundation for understanding the unit-level factors that prompt divestiture, the factors merit additional attention. For example, it appears that when the CEO of a firm has spent a significant part of his or her career in a unit, that unit is less likely to be divested than others. Yet there are counterexamples. Don Kelly rose through the ranks at Swift, but in 1980, his leadership led to the divestiture of the original core of the business. Under what circumstances does the CEO release the "mother" of his or her career? What is the process by which such a decision is made? Such an investigation will need to track carefully the decision maker's career history, as well as the individual decision-making and issue-resolution processes. Further, capturing the dynamics of the relationships among the senior executives on a real-time basis during such a decision process would prove fascinating and fruitful. Do such decisions invariably leave the dominant coalition of the firm scarred from dissension? Under what conditions is there rapid and smooth consensus?

As reported in chapter 3, our understanding of the role of the division manager has been immensely enlarged from the work of Nees and this study. However, much of what we know comes from historical recollections two years or more distant from the actuality. The division manager is often an individual caught in the middle—required to understand and facilitate the corporate process of divestiture while maintaining or enhancing the performance of the unit. It is clear that the division managers personally resolve the dilemma. Further, it appears that modifying the available monetary rewards and providing interpersonal support between corporate executives and the unit executives helps to smooth the difficulties for the unit executives. Yet not all firms make changes in the compensation systems. And even when changes are made, the configuration varies across firms. These processes need more systematic investigation. Why do some firms make the adjustment in compensatory arrangements and the degree of interpersonal support provided and others do not? Specifically, we need to understand from a much larger set of firms the changes undertaken and their impact on the ability of the unit manager to undertake the dual-role challenge of facilitating divestiture while effectively and efficiently maneuvering the unit. Only then can we be more prescriptive about whether such changes have significant payoffs.

Our understanding of the factors affecting when the division manager is brought into the divestiture process has been significantly enhanced. The conceptualizations presented in chapters 3 and 4 form a basis for larger-scale

investigation. Included in such an investigation must be corporate-level factors (such as the expected time to divestiture) as well as individual-level factors (for example, what were the skills of the division manager, and what was the tenor of the relationship between the division manager and corporate executives?). Further, we need to understand more clearly the dilemmas of the unit executive on a real-time basis. We still know little, for example, about the effect of choices of messenger (CEO versus CFO), words, location, tone of voice, and professional provisions (compensation, role expected, personal support) when the division manager first learns his or her unit is slated for divestment. It is clear that there are situations where the decision and announcement are expected; there are others where the announcement is totally unexpected.

Another issue not fully understood is under what circumstances firms restructure to accommodate the divestiture. Some restructure so that the unit reports to a different executive than prior to the divestiture decision. What are the benefits and disadvantages of such restructuring?

The process of marketing reported in chapter 5 can undoubtedly be improved. What are the practices that are more effective? The current investigation suggests that preparing a book or selling packages, careful search for appropriate buyers, choice of process of approaching buyers (bidding versus multiple versus sequential approaches), and appropriate use of outside help can add to the ultimate value of the unit. The conceptualizations in chapter 5 provide the basis for larger-scale investigation so that more definitive prescriptions can be drawn.

Chapter 6 has enlarged our understanding of MLBOs in the United States, with some comparison to the European experience. The situation is ripe for more systematic investigation, especially given the British data base established by the University of Nottingham study. It appears that the American experience has been transported to Great Britain. Is it essentially the same, or do differences exist between the United States and Europe? What are they? Why do they exist?

There was a limited number of MLBOs involved in this study. Although the investigation enriched our understanding, questions remain. Chapter 6 suggested that where unit management has significantly increased value of the unit and the unit is at a low level of relative performance within the firm's portfolio, there is likely to be a basis for suggesting a buy-out. These relationships merit more systematic study. Further investigation closer to real-time is likely to yield fruitful observations about the resolution of dilemmas at the corporate and unit levels. What specific choices concerning timing, choice of arguments, and presentation of proposal on the part of unit management increase the likelihood of acceptance by corporate? How do corporate executives resolve the immediate conflict engendered by management-initiated suggestions for an MLBO?

A major issue that arises around MLBOs was addressed only peripherally in this investigation. When the firm receives an offer from a management group that wants to effect an MLBO, how can existing shareholders know whether they are being offered a fair price? The difficulty arises because the managers who are supposed to represent shareholder interests are doing the buying. This issue merits further investigation.[6]

Chapter 7 indicated that both the process of negotiation and the negotiation issues must be managed. There are many questions remaining. For example, what are the conditions under which bidding may yield a higher value for establishing price than private multiple solicitation of price or sequential face-to-face negotiation? The conditions that suggest face-to-face solo negotiation versus team negotiation have been suggested and are ripe for more thorough study. The conditions that affect the effectiveness of various tactics in face-to-face negotiations also warrant more in-depth investigation. For example, chapter 7 suggested that presentation of the first price offer close to target can be made when the seller knows and trusts the buyer and when the buyer has had greater experience in negotiation processes. Under what conditions are these factors violated?

Ethical dilemmas arose from the study, though they were not originally a focus of the investigation. Do the players confront these issues as ethical dilemmas? Or are they simply minor conflicts to be resolved as the divestiture process is played out? Much more needs to be done on this issue. In addition, there are differences in the trauma experienced between firms. For example, do companies experience higher trauma with their first divestiture experience? Evidence exists on both sides of the issue. A related question focuses on smaller companies, which presumably have less experience with divestiture and closer emotional ties with their units. Do smaller firms experience more trauma with the divestiture process?

Another avenue for investigation concerns the experience of lower-level employees during the divestiture process. What are their experiences, and what is the impact of divestiture on employees remaining in the selling corporation?

Throughout this book, I have presented the experience of both conglomerate firms (those that have pursued unrelated divestification) and firms that have pursued related diversification. Is there a different pattern of how divestitures are handled in these two types of organizations? Presumably firms pursuing related diversification would have more enlightened processes, but the results from this investigation are by no means clear. Indeed, we might wonder if the trauma is higher in firms that have pursued related diversification, even if their process was judged more enlightened. The satisfaction of participants in a conglomerate firm might be higher because expectations are lower with regard to how carefully the process will be managed.

The original purpose of this research program was descriptive in nature: to develop an enriched understanding of the process. That objective has been fulfilled. I have also developed an understanding of factors that contribute to effective divestiture. This study has suggested two kinds of components for evaluating the effectiveness of any particular divestiture. The quantitative component involves the price paid for the unit but also involves the relationship between the original targeted value and the value ultimately received. Further, there is a qualitative or interpersonal component that enters into at least some situations. In these situations, the divestiture may be judged successful if the relationships between corporate executives and the management of the divested unit remain positive. The current program provides a ripe base for more effectively investigating the criteria that form the effectiveness evaluation and the conditions that lead to effective divestiture.

Concluding Observations

The divestiture process is fascinating and multifaceted. The experiences of the firms represented in this book suggest that in the last two decades, firms have learned much about managing this process. However, many areas require greater understanding and improvement in practice. Any individual firm can learn from the experience of others. Indeed this transfer of process technology was a major purpose for undertaking this investigation.

No research program of this magnitude is undertaken without significant enlargement of the intellectual capital of those involved with the investigation. So it has been here. I remain grateful to the executives who have shared their expertise. I hope this book validly reflects the executives' experiences and can be used to improve divestment practices.

Perhaps the overall conclusion of the research was best summarized by the chairman of M&A Consulting Firm who was quoted earlier. An executive with more than two decades of experiences with divestitures, he said "nothing beats being straightforward and putting all of your cards on the table and dealing with integrity."

Notes

1. In addition, there were only two instances where executives described unacceptable behavior on the part of buyers. Both of these instances occurred during negotiations.

2. The individual has obligations to self (expectations) and others that cannot be met if career and income are disrupted.

3. Expressed in a different way, the individual must revamp his or her expectations of the situation. In some instances this comes close to a rationalization process.

4. In addition, their compensation is much less.

5. Indeed, the Field Studies Program at the University of Kansas did encourage a doctoral student to begin such a project. However, the project is "messy"; the data from Mergers and Organizations and Grimms can be sharply criticized, and the lead-lag relationships are not clear. The doctoral student turned his attention to other issues.

6. This issue has been raised by Bevis Longstreth, a member of the Securities and Exchange Commission, who has publicly aired his concern about the potential conflict of interests. One answer to the dilemma is that worried shareholders facing an unwelcome leveraged buy-out from their own managers can sue the directors for not representing their interests (they are entitled to an unbiased assessment of the offer price from an investment bank) or find a better bid. "More Than They Want You to Know about Leveraged Buyouts," *Economist,* November 5, 1983, p. 83.

Appendix A:
Selected Characteristics
of Companies Participating
in the Research Program

| | | Acquisitions (As) and Divestitures (Ds) | | | | | | | (000) | | |
		1980–1986	1975–1979	1970–1974	1965–1969	1960–1964	1959 and Before	Year	Sales	Profits	Description
A	As	3	2	1	0	0	0	1985	196,639	246,057	Involved, through subsidiary, in fabricated steel products such as industrial fasteners, structural steel members for bridges, etc. Also involved in title and trust operations through subsidiaries.
	Ds	2	0	1	0	0	0				
B	As	14	5	17	0	0	NA	1982	2,965,800	229.500	Multinational manufacturer and distributor of a wide range of products and services used and consumed primarily in the health-care field.
	Ds	1	1	0	0	0	NA				
C	As	5	0	0	0	0	0	1985	2,470,100	(59,900)	Primarily composed of four industry segments: the manufacture and sale of cosmetics, fragrances and toiletries; the manufacture and sale of fashion jewelry and accessories; the rental and sale of home health care equipment and medical supplies; and the sale of apparel.
	Ds	2	0	0	0	0	0				
D	As	7	0	5	0	1	0	1984	1,800,422	29,047	Engaged in the worldwide development, manufacturing, and sale of medical care products.
	Ds	3	3	0	0	0	0				
E	As	3	2	0	1	2	0	1985	13,363,000	566,000	One of the world's major aerospace firms. Principally operates in three industry segments: commercial transportation, military transportation, and missiles and space.
	Ds	3	1	0	0	1	0				
F	As	11	5	6	0	0	52	1985	4,716,172	193,804	Engaged primarily in the purchase, manufacture, processing, and distribution of food, dairy and chemical products.
	Ds	9	0	1	0	0	4				
G	As	1	0	0	0	0	0	1985	1,961,900	679,500	Company explores for, develops, and produces crude oil and natural gas.
	Ds	4	0	0	0	0	0				
H	As	8	4	0	0	0	0	1985	7,904,000	722,000	Largest manufacturer and distributor of soft drink concentrates and syrups. Diversified into foods and entertainment.
	Ds	7	0	0	0	0	0				

Co.								Year	Sales	No.	Description
I	As	11	0	0	0	0	0	1985	9,942,300	466,100	Manufactures and markets consumer products, chemicals, plastics, packaging, batteries, and cheese.
	Ds	11	0	0	0	0	0				
J	As	5	8	4	5	5	2	1985	4,101,800	604,700	Primary interests in energy, technology, and chemicals.
	Ds	6	0	1	2	0	0				
K	As	5	0	2	3	1	0	1985	11,537,000	58,000	Engages in extraction of chemicals and metals, production of plastics, and packaging and consumer products.
	Ds	6	2	2	1	0	0				
L	As	4	0	0	0	0	0	1985	4,111,200	196,400	Supplies products and services for industries involved in oil and natural gas, energy processing and conversion, and mining and construction.
	Ds	0	0	0	0	0	0				
M	As	38	5	2	1	1	0	1984	2,397,333	521,561	Primary line of business is publishing and marketing; new emphasis on business information services.
	Ds	5	0	0	0	0	0				
N	As	5	1	4	2	1	34	1985	29,483,000	1,118,000	Diversified company dealing in polymer products, agricultural and industrial chemicals, petroleum exploration, and production and coal.
	Ds	3	1	0	0	0	0				
O	As	5	10	1	0	0	NA	1982	3,303,220	107,566	Holding company with interests in four major operations: foods.
	Ds	5	4	0	0	0	NA				
P	As	2	5	5	4	3	21	1985	3,260,800	196,553	Company manufactures and sells a broad range of machinery and chemical products.
	Ds	8	5	0	0	0	0				
Q	As	3	0	3	2	1	2	1985	3,836,000	3,000	Principal product is rubber tires for autos but also produces natural rubber and latex, textiles, synthetics, and automotive parts and services.
	Ds	17	1	2	0	0	0				
R	As	7	3	0	0	0	16	1985	862,370	33,220	Diversified manufacturing, distribution, and service company with interests in lawn and garden, photo finishing, sporting goods, and seating.
	Ds	8	2	0	0	0	3				
S	As	8	0	4	12	5	4	1985	9,022,418	324,907	One of the world's leading processors and marketers of packaged grocery and meat products.
	Ds	2	6	1	0	0	4				

Appendix A continued

		Acquisitions (As) and Divestitures (Ds)						Year	Sales (000)	Profits	Description
		1980–1986	1975–1979	1970–1974	1965–1969	1960–1964	1959 and Before				
T	As	1	0	1	5	0	0	1985	74,003	2,756	Holding company engaged in the manufacture and sale of porcelain-enameled steel cookware, cast-iron and aluminum cookware, and kitchen furniture.
	Ds	2	1	0	0	0	0				
U	As	9	13	26	0	0	40	1985	4,285,200	(72,900)	Leading consumer goods company diversified in consumer foods, restaurants, and specialty retailing.
	Ds	10	3	0	0	0	0				
V	As	0	1	12	23	14	18	1985	538,486	(33,929)	Operates through its own retail stores and wholesale operations to penetrate the footwear and men's apparel industries.
	Ds	6	1	0	1	1	0				
W									Private	Private	
X	As	9	4	17	1	2	4	1985	2,400,000	159,900	Develops, manufactures, and sells a wide range of products for personal care. Major lines include blades and razors, toiletries, and cosmetics.
	Ds	1	0	0	0	0	0				
Y	As	40	30	34	38	11	1	1985	5,193,000	146,900	Principal lines of business are chemically based products, consumer operations, and natural resources.
	Ds	0	19	4	9	1	0				
Z	As	3	9	6	10	4	2	1985	2,561,663	120,088	Holding company with interests in five areas: transportation services and manufacturing, consumer products, and food, and financial services.
	Ds	6	2	4	0	0	0				
AA	As	4	8	10	45	47	6	1985	3,090,000	234,300	Diversified company with interests in manufacturing, apparel and home furnishings, consumer and agricultural products, natural resources, and financial services.
	Ds	15	3	2	0	0	0				

								Year	Revenue	Employees	Description
AB	As	3	2	0	1	2	0	1982	30,193,000	900,000	Integrated petroleum company with secondary operations in the chemicals, coal, and nuclear industries.
	Ds	5	0	0	0	0	0				
AC									Private	Private	Private
AD	As	31	4	1	3	0	8	1985	5,754,000	281,600	Engaged in the design, development, and production of guidance systems and controls for military and commercial aircraft and land vehicles, space vehicles, and missiles.
	Ds	1	0	0	0	0	0				
AE	As	1	0	2	1	2	1	1983	5,571,721	88,109	Diversified retailer engaged primarily in retail sale of food, drugs, and genral merchandise.
	Ds	1	2	0	1	0	0				
AF									Private	Private	Private
AG	As	6	1	0	0	5	3	1984	7,046,100	(378,200)	Diversified company operating in steel, energy products, and aerospace-defense.
	Ds	1	0	0	0	1	0				
AH	As	3	0	6	32	22	15	1985	4,590,649	251,800	Specializes in products in advanced electronics, industrial systems and services, marine engineering and production, and a variety of microwave products.
	Ds	9	0	7	0	0	0				
AI	As	2	0	6	1	0	0	1985	295,678	36,213	Principally engaged in the business of developing, manufacturing, and selling pharmaceutical products—both ethical and proprietary drugs.
	Ds		0	0	1	0	0				
AJ	As	2	2	0	5	0	4	1983	418,704	15,691	Develops, manufactures, and markets wood composite materials for construction, furniture, and interiors.
	Ds		0	0	0	0	0				
AK	As	5	4	11	8	1	7	1984	1,720,900	10,800	Manufactures and supplies electrical and mechanical products and related services for industrial applications.
	Ds	6	2	0	0	0	0				
AL	As	17	6	2	5	3	NA	1985	6,285,000	77,900	Principal segments of business are drug and health care, service merchandising, beverages, chemicals, and development.
	Ds	9	4	0	1	0	NA				

Appendix A continued

		Acquisitions (As) and Divestitures (Ds)							Sales (000)	Profits	Description
		1980–1986	1975–1979	1970–1974	1965–1969	1960–1964	1959 and Before	Year			
AM									Private	Private	Private
AN	As	2	0	5	2	6	10	1984	6,253,100	308,900	Major manufacturer, processor, and distributor of packaged foods and related products.
	Ds	4	0	1	1	0	0				
AO	As	18	5	15	2	1	0	1985	1,193,000	129,800	Engaged in the manufacture and sale of abrasives, petroleum and mining products, and engineering materials.
	Ds	3	1	4	0	0	0				
AP	As	1	0	6	7	1	0	1985	8,056,662	543,690	Engaged in foreign and domestic business in soft drinks, snack foods, and restaurants.
	Ds	2	0	1	0	3	2				
AQ	As	9	0	0	0	0	0	1985	15,636,000	418,000	Integrated petroleum producer, with interests in specialty chemicals.
	Ds	1	1	0	0	0	0				
AR	As	7	0	1	0	0	0	1985	13,552,000	635,000	Principal products are consumer goods including toiletries, food products, and household cleaners.
	Ds	2	0	0	0	0	0				
AS	As	0	0	2	0	0	1	1985	8,972,100	369,100	Manufacture, sale, distribution, lease, and servicing of electronic products.
	Ds	0	0	5	0	0	1				
AT									Private	Private	Private
AU	As	1	0	3	0	0	0	1985	11,337,600	595,300	Engages primarily in aerospace, electronics, and automotive products.
	Ds	9	7	0	0	0	0				
AV	As	2	6	12	19	0	0	1983	2,936,000	84,400	Diversified operation in aerospace and electronics, outdoor products, machine tools, engineering fasteners, industrial products, and venture capital and financing.
	Ds	2	9	11	11	0	0				

							Year	Revenue	Net Income	Description
AW	As	0	3	2	3	NA	1985	7,846,000	664,000	Manufactures and markets high-technology products based on precision coating and bonding and other capabilities.
	Ds	0	1	1	2	NA				
AX	As	0	1	1	0	1	1980	1,590,923	47,749	Exploration, production, refining, marketing, and transportation of oil and gas.
	Ds	0	0	0	0	0				
AY	As	4	0	0	0	0	1983	1,075,637	33,710	Diversified manufacturer principally in three areas: industrial products, building products, and consumer products.
	Ds	0	0	0	0	1				
AZ	As	4	13	4	3	0	1985	3,200,069	315,596	Manufactures and markets a wide line of health care products, as well as chewing gum.
	Ds	4	0	3	0	0				
BA	As	3	6	10	3	0	1985	10,700,200	605,300	Manufactures and sells equipment and components for the generation, transmission, distribution, and control of electricity.
	Ds	1	0	0	0	0				
BB	As	5	4	5	3	3	1984	1,905,738	(79,334)	Diversified manufacturer in three areas: products for the home, machinery and metal castings, and general industrial equipment.
	Ds	4	2	0	0	0				
BC	As	61	19	11	15	0	1985	1,054,338	38,802	Engaged primarily in retail sale of jewelry merchandise.
	Ds	1	0	0	0	0				

Appendix B:
Summary of Literature
on Divestment

Reference	Sample or Design	Findings and Conclusions
Lovejoy (1971)	Field research	Handbook on divestment. The primary factor in divestment decisions is the unfavorable performance of firms' units.
Hayes (1972)	Eighteen companies, part of a larger, ongoing project on divestiture	Predicted the 1970s as period when divestiture would be frequent and become more accepted as a valid element of corporate strategy. Argued divestitures are different from acquisitions in several critical ways: they are painful, they are permanent, and the risks and rewards are different. Identified characteristics of divestitures as in secretive manner, with little carried-out expertise and under time pressure.
Boddewyn and Torneden (1973)	425 large companies	About one-fourth of Fortune 500 have divested at least one foreign subsidiary. Concentration is high since 38 companies accounted for 54 percent of the total of the 424 divestitures identified. Only 11 percent of the divestitures were expropriations. The rest were voluntary sales (68 percent) or liquidations (29 percent).
Gilmour (1973)		Divestment decisions were preceded by replacement of top management personnel.
Torneden and Boddewyn (1974)	Fortune 500	The process of divestiture is not well managed and could be improved with resulting higher corporate profits. Book value is usually the target sales price. Limited use is made of net present value (NPV) analysis because corporate does not want the target unit price too high. The decision to divest is made at corporate among a small group of senior executives.
Torneden and Boddewyn (1974)	1967–1971: Fortune 500 companies with decisions to divest a foreign subsidiary. 204 made 561 divestments. Study incorporated 53 of the companies.	Divestment is serious and costly for most companies. It is necessary to break the stranglehold of a key manager who is in charge of the unit. There is a limited use of NPV techniques. Divestment decisions are usually preceded by significant organizational change. When the decision is made, the top unit manager is involved in implementation. The divestiture process is fairly haphazard.

Vignola (1974)	Unknown	The importance of unit interdependence may influence divestment, as may need for funds to avoid bankruptcy.
Chopra, Boddewyn, and Torneden (1975)	Update on 1973 and 1974 study	Identified over 1,000 divestitures, more than twice as many as in the prior period. Observed reasons for divestiture included: poor performance, adverse environmental conditions, bad acquisition, lack of strategic or managerial fit, insufficient resources, problems elsewhere in the firm, bad management, objectionable business practices, and prejudice against a given country. Firms tended to fall into one of three categories: the bloodletting was over, the bloodletting had barely begun, and acquisitions and divestitures were a normal part of the firm's evolution over time.
Torneden (1975)	Three phases: (1) Identification of companies undertaking foreign divestment (sample = Fortune 500); (2) interviews in 15 companies; (3) questionnaire to the 189 companies from step 1 with 20 percent response.	(1) Identification of 189 companies and analysis of some data, especially on kind of divestment. Found that nationalization accounted for only 4 percent of divestments (3) Findings revolved around factors leading to divestment (performance of parent company down; key management changes; poor acquisition analysis and subsequent operations) and characteristic of the process (initiation comes from president or head of international; few middle managers are involved; formal recommendation comes mostly from planning, finance, marketing, or legal; implementation contributions to implementation came from legal, finance, accounting, planning; few companies use outside consultants; mean length of time from first consideration through divestment substantially complete 25.5 months.

Appendix B (continued)

Reference	Sample or Design	Findings and Conclusions
Boddewyn (1976)	N = 32 multinational companies; interviews with key executives as well as brokers and bankers who participate in divestments frequently.	Close look at the divestment decision and its implication. Improvements to the process in the international setting may be: 1. The decision is triggered by multiple factors (similar to Duhaime and Narayanan/Taylor). Other alternatives to divestment are usually considered, and the time to finally decide to divest had M = 11 months with a range of 3 months to 2 years. 2. Implementation is a multiphase process that includes: setting up a divestment team, planning for the steps, setting up contingency plans, locating buyers, establishing a price, conducting negotiations, managing publicity, and (sometimes) using outside help. The author concludes that divestment is here to stay and that more and more firms are accepting it as a normal process of doing business. 3. Improving divestment is possible. A good divestment is, first, predicated by the financial outcomes. However, other considerations, such as whether the company's ability to do business in the country is unimpaired and whether the new owner takes a true business interest in the unit, also have an impact. More emphasis needs to be placed on preacquisition analysis as a deterrent to divestiture. However, the divestiture process itself can be improved by better planning, improved implementation, and helping executives and boards to lower the mental blocks against divestiture. As rapid depreciation as pssible and setting up reserves for divestment losses help to buffer.
Duhaime (1984)	Field research including semistructured interviews with executives in 40 com-	

Montgomery, Thomas, and Kamath (1984)

panies plus public documents. Focus was on divestments of whole business units or divisions.

Fortune 500 firms, as listed in *Wall Street Journal*, 1976–1979, announced 485 divestitures. Study used 78, which had available the information required for the study.

Market evaluations of the divesting companies over the ensuing 12 months as contrasted to the prior 12 months indicating varying returns associated with the reason for divestiture as follows: undertaken for strategic reasons had high returns (significant); because units were "undesired" (e.g., marginal or negative returns) negative (significant); in response to liquidity pressures positive (nonsignificant); forced divestitures were negative (nonsignificant).

Nees (1978–1979)

Case studies. $N = 3$ completed by researcher; $N = 14$ completed by others; analysis of videos of case study discussions in management development program used to validate findings

1. Six kinds of resistance to divestment: cultural, instrumental, psychological, organizational, economic, and financial.

2. Identifies three stages in the process: identification, development (decision), implementation.

3. Identification stage has four possible stances on part of executives to perceive the divestment as: an opportunity, a problem, or a crisis. Manager's attitudes correspond respectively: proactive; reactive, adaptive, or passive; and reactive.

4. Divestment is a decision of last resort.

5. Implementation has six subprocesses: negotiations with potential buyers, internal negotiations, internal communication, external communication, realization, and epilogue.

6. There are at least five kinds of actors in the process: the individual who assists in identification, the initiator, the coordinator, informants, and implementers.

Descriptive: focusing on length of process and its evolvement. Concerned even here about enlargement of the role of the division manager.

Appendix B (continued)

Reference	Sample or Design	Findings and Conclusions
Harrigan (1981)	61 firms in 8 declining industries. Used multigression analyses with seven different model specifications and reexamined where products had commodity-like traits *versus* not; where businesses were of high strategic importance *versus* not; and where economic barriers were high *versus* not.	Found that the following factors acted as exit barriers or deterrents to divestiture: an image of high product quality, the presence of a strong group of customers, facilities shared with other, apparently healthy businesses, good distribution channel relationships and strong product identification through previous expenditures for promotion and advertising, economic barriers related to manufacturing technology and its physical assets, a strong expectation that demand for this business unit's products will endure for a favorable period in the future.
Nees (1981)	See 1978–1979 entry.	1. There are five main functions for a division manager: information supplier; implementer of secondary decisions; protector of the division morale and productivity; host of potential acquirers while visiting the division; potential buyer. 2. The division manager's behavior is influenced by the behavior evidenced by the divestor-parent. If the parent withholds information, the division manager can be expected to be actively resistant; if parent is autocratic, division manager may be resistant or passively follow directions; where the parent invites the manager's participation, the divestor may expect active cooperation. Author argues for greater involvement of the division manager.
Caves and Porter (1976)	PIMS data excluding companies in introduction or start-up phase.	Exit barrier measures were important predictors of divestment of unprofitable businesses. Three broad classes of exit barriers were identified: structural, strategic, and managerial. Structural barriers included long-lasting assets that were specific to the

particular business. Strategic barriers included the relatedness of the companies' activities. Managerial barriers include lack of information and conflicting goals within the organization. Empirical investigation using specified measures confirmed existence of exit barriers. Recommended that exit barriers be more explicitly considered in augmenting the firm's asset base, sharing facilities, diagnosing competitors, and planning for organizational issues such as succession, characteristics of staff, reward mechanisms, and design of information systems.

Author/Year	Sample	Findings
Porter (1976)	Used 310 businesses from PIMS data base with ROI under 8 percent over prior 4 years	Found evidence suggesting presence of three classes of exit barriers: structural, corporate strategy, and managerial. Recommends that exit barriers be made explicit. All three kinds of barriers can be overcome largely by: Strategic decisions that strive for sound competitive situation yet prevent the company from getting into the strategic bind of unmanageable future exit barriers when time comes to exit. Organizational decisions that include top management's getting full and appropriate internal (e.g., market and competitive) information and making sure the top management team includes someone who will champion the exit decision.
Hamermesh (1977)	1,800 companies	Diversified companies need to identify divisions with profit problems and take steps to correct. There are barriers to timely identification, including layers between divisions and top managers, commitments made by various levels to levels below, the difficulties of admitting failure, and organizational and structural barriers. Suggests ways of reducing barriers to ready identification and approaches for remedying the difficulties.
Duhaime and Patton (1980)	Large industrial corporations	Discrepancies occur between the stated intentions of firms and the firm's reported actions. Barriers to action may include managerial attachment to units.

Bibliography

Alberts, William W., and James M. McTaggart. "The Divestiture Decision: An Introduction." *Mergers and Acquisitions* (Fall 1979): 18–30.

Allen, S.A. "Understanding Reorganization of Divisionalized Companies." *Academy
of Management Journal* 22, no. 4 (1979): 641–671.

Anderson, Douglas D. "Managing Disinvestment." Working Paper 1-785-059. Boston:
Harvard Business School.

Andrews, K. *The Concept of Corporate Strategy.* Homewood, Ill.: Dow Jones–Irwin,
1980.

"Asset Redeployment." *Business Week,* August 24, 1981, pp. 68–74.

Baker, George P., III. "Management Compensation and Divisional Leveraged Buyouts."
Ph.D. dissertation, Harvard University, 1986.

Becker, H.S. *Sociological Work: Methods and Substance.* Chicago: Aldine, 1970.

———. "Problems of Inference and Proof in Participant Observation." *American
Sociological Review* 23 (December 1958).

Berg, N.A. "Strategic Planning in Conglomerate Companies." *Harvard Business Review*
(May–June 1965): 79–92.

Bernstein, Peter W., "Who Buys Corporate Losers." *Fortune,* January 26, 1981, pp.
60–66.

Bing, Gordon. *Corporate Acquisitions.* Houston: Gulf Publishing Company, 1978.

———. *Corporate Divestment.* Houston: Gulf Publishing Company, 1978.

Boddewyn, J.J. *International Divestment: A Survey of Corporate Experience.* New
York: Business International, 1976.

———, and R. Torneden. "U.S. Foreign Divestment: A Preliminary Survey." *Columbia
Journal of World Business* (Summer 1973–Spring 1978): 25–29.

Boston Consulting Group. "Divestment and Growth." Boston: Boston Consulting
Group, 1972.

Boudreaux, K.J. "Divestiture and Share Price." *Journal of Financial and Quantitative
Analysis* (September 1975): 619–626.

Bower, J.L. *Managing the Resource Allocation Process.* Homewood, Ill.: Richard D.
Irwin, 1970.

Caves, R.E., and M.E. Porter. "Barriers to Exit." In R.T. Masson and P.D. Qualls,
eds., *Essays on Industrial Organization in Honor of Joe S. Bain,* pp. 39–70.
Cambridge, Mass.: Ballinger Publishing Company, 1976.

Chandler, Alfred D. *Strategy and Structure: Chapters in the History of the American Industrial Enterprise.* Cambridge: MIT Press, 1962.

———. *The Visible Hand.* Cambridge: Belknap Press of Harvard University Press, 1977.

Conway, Allen, and Norman Berg. "Textron in the Eighties." Boston: Harvard Business School Case Services, 1983.

Davis, James V. "The Strategic Divestment Decision." *Long-Range Planning* (February 1974): 15–18.

Dawkins, William. "Management Buy-outs: When Vendors Ask Too Much," *Financial Times,* July 3, 1986, p. 8.

Dickson, Martin. "Good Times for US Pillar of British Market," *Financial Times,* October 10, 1986, p. 10.

Duhaime, I.M. *The Divestment Behavior of Large Diversified Firms.* Oxford, Ohio: Planning Executives Institute, 1984.

———. "Influences on the Divestment Decision of Large Diversified Firms." Ph.D. dissertation, University of Pittsburgh, 1981.

———, and C.R. Schwenk. "Conjectures on Cognitive Simplification and Divestment Decision Making." *Academy of Management Review* 10, no. 2 (1985): 287–295.

———, and J.H. Grant. "Divestment Decisions Involving Interdependencies, Unit Strength and Managerial Attachment." In *Advances in Strategic Management,* 3: 302–322. Greenwich, Conn.: JAI Press, 1985.

———. "Factors Influencing Divestment Decision-Making: Evidence from a Field Study." *Strategic Management Journal* 5 (1984): 301–318.

———, and G.R. Patton. "Selling Off." *Wharton Magazine* (Winter 1980): 43–47.

Dundas, K.N.M., and P.R. Richardson. "Implementing the Unrelated Product Strategy." *Strategic Management Journal* 3 (1982): 287-301.

Dutton, Jane, Liam Fahey, and V.K. Narayanan. "Toward Understanding Strategic Issue Diagnosis." *Strategic Management Journal* 4, no. 1 (1983): 307–324.

Ellsworth, Richard. "A Note on the Decision to Divest." Boston, Mass.: Harvard Case Services, 1979.

Farrell, Kevin. "Yesterday's Managers, Today's Entrepreneurs." *Venture* (March 1982): 50–55.

"A Free Marketer Shows the Way." *Newsweek,* September 1983.

Fuller, Charles B. "Corporate and Industry Factors Influencing Closure Decisions." Paper presented to Academy of Management, August 1987.

Fuqua, J.B. "Size vs. Strength: The Making of Stockholder Wealth." *Directors and Boards* (Winter 1984): 10–14.

Galbraith, John Kenneth. *Economics and the Public Purpose.* Boston: Houghton Mifflin, 1973.

Gilmour, Stuart, C. "The Divestment Decision Process." Ph.D. dissertation, Harvard University, 1973.

Glaser, B.G., and A.L. Strauss. "Discovery of Substantive Theory: A Basic Strategy Underlying Qualitative Research." *American Behavioral Scientist* 8 (February 1965): 5–12.

––––. *The Discovery of Grounded Theory: Strategies for Qualitative Research.* Chicago: AVC, 1967.

Glueck, W.F., and R. Willis. "Documentary Sources and Strategic Management Research." *Academy of Management Review* 4 (1979): 95–102.

Gordon, Michael A. "Is Employee Ownership the Answer to Our Economic Woes?" *Management Review* (May 1982): 8–14.

Greiner, L.E. "Evolution and Revolution As Organizations Grow." *Harvard Business Review* (July–August 1972): 37.

Hall. "Reflections on Running a Diversified Company." *Harvard Business Review* (January–February 1987): 84–92.

Hammermesh, Richard G. *Making Strategy Work.* New York: Wiley, 1986.

––––. "Responding to Divisional Profit Crises." *Harvard Business Review* (March–April 1977): 124–130.

Harrigan, Kathryn R. "Deterrents to Divestiture." *Academy of Management Journal* 24, no. 2 (1981): 306–323.

––––. "Exit Decisions in Mature Industries." *Academy of Management Journal* 25 (December 1982): 707.

––––. *Strategic Flexibility.* Lexington, Mass.: Lexington Books, 1985.

––––. *Strategies for Declining Businesses.* Lexington, Mass.: Lexington Books, 1980.

Hayes, Robert H. "New Emphasis on Divestment Opportunities." *Harvard Business Review* (July–August 1972): 55.

Hearth, Douglas, and Janis K. Zaima. "Voluntary Corporate Divestitures and Value." *Financial Management* (Spring 1984): 10–16.

Hillman, Richard H. "How to Redeploy Assets." *Harvard Business Review* (November–December 1971): 11.

Hilton, Peter. "Divestiture: The Strategic Move on the Corporate Chessboard." *Management Review* 61 (March 1972): 16–19.

––––. *Planning Corporate Growth and Diversification.* New York: McGraw-Hill, 1970.

Holsti, O.R. *Content Analysis for the Social Sciences and Humanities.* Reading, Mass.: Addison-Wesley, 1969.

Kudla, Ronald J., and Thomas H. McInish. "The Microeconomic Consequences of an Involuntary Corporate Spinoff." *Sloan Management Review* (Summer 1981): 41–46.

Lamb, Robert Boyden, ed. *Competitive Strategic Management.* Englewood Cliffs, N.J.: Prentice-Hall, 1984.

Lasswell, H.D. "The Future of Comparative Method." *Comparative Politics* 1 (1968): 3–18.

Lewellen, W. *The Ownership Income of Management.* New York: Columbia University Press, 1971.

Lindgren, Ulf, and Kjell Spangberg. "Corporate Acquisitions and Divestments: The Strategic Decision-Making Process." *International Studies of Management and Organization.* 11, no. 2 (Summer 1981): 24–47.

Little, Royal. *How I Lost $100 Million and Other Useful Advice.* Boston: A.D. Little.

Long, Andrew. "Some Examples of Recent MBOs." *The Lucrative World of Management Buyouts,* A Supplement to Euromoney and Corporate Finance (December 1986): 47.

Lorsch, J.W., and G. Donaldson. *Decision Making at the Top.* New York: Basic Books, 1983.

Lovejoy, Frederick A. *Divestment for Profit.* New York: Financial Executives Research Foundation, 1971.

"The Lucrative World of Management Buyouts." *Euromoney: A Supplement to Euromoney and Corporate Finance* (December 1986).

"M & A for Richer, for Poorer," *Euromoney: A Supplement to Euromoney and Corporate Finance* (August 1987).

Mace, Myles, and George C. Montgomery. *Management Problems of Corporate Acquisitions.* Boston: Division of Research, Harvard Business School, 1962.

Marple, W. "Financial Aspects of Voluntary Divestitures in Large Industrial Companies." Ph.D. dissertation, Harvard University, 1967.

Marple, Wesley W., Jr. "Decision-Making for Divestment." In William S. Mishkin, ed., *Techniques in Corporate Reorganization: Selling, Divesting, and Shells, Multiple Corporations,* pp. 25–35. New York: Presidents Publishing House, 1972.

Merton, R. "Insiders and Outsiders: A Chapter in the Sociology of Knowledge." In Robert K. Merton, *Varieties of Political Expression in Sociology.* Chicago: University of Chicago Press, 1972.

Miles, J.A., and J.D. Rosenfeld. "An Empirical Analysis of the Effects of Spinoff Announcements on Common Stock Returns and Stockholder Wealth." *Journal of Finance* (December 1983): 1597–1606.

Mitroff, I. *The Subjective Side of Science.* Amsterdam: Elsevier, 1974.

Montgomery, Cynthia A., Ann L. Thomas, and Rajan Kamath. "Divestiture Market Valuation and Strategy." *Academy of Management Journal* 7, no. 4 (December 1984): 830–840.

Moore, Thomas. "Old-Line Industry Shapes Up." *Fortune,* April 27, 1987, pp. 23–32.

Morgan, G., and L. Smircich. "The Case for Qualitative Research." *Academy of Management Review* 5, no. 4 (1980): 491–500.

Narayanan, V.K., Marilyn Taylor, and D.G. Kinker. "Strategic Management of Divestment in the United States." Paper presented to the Strategic Management Society, Paris, 1983.

Nees, Danielle B. "The Divestment Decision Process in Large and Medium-Sized Diversified Companies: A Descriptive Model Based on Clinical Research." *International Studies of Management and Organization* 7, no. 4 (Winter 1978–79): 67–93.

———. "Increase Your Divestment Effectiveness." *Strategic Management Journal* 2, no. 2 (1981): 119–130.

Patton, G. Richard, and Irene M. Duhaime. "Divestment As a Strategic Option: An Empirical Study." Paper presented at the Academy of Management, San Francisco, August 1978.

———. "Selling Off." *Wharton Magazine* (Winter 1980): 43–47.

Patton, M.Q. *Qualitative Evaluation Methods.* Beverly Hills: Sage Publications, 1980.

Peters, T., and R.H. Waterman. *In Search of Excellence.* New York: Harper & Row, 1982.

Pinches, George E. *Essentials of Financial Management.* 2d ed. New York: Harper & Row, 1987.

Piore, M.J. "Qualitative Research Techniques in Economics." *Administrative Science Quarterly* 24 (December 1979).

Porter, Michael, E. "Please Note the Location of Your Nearest Exit: Exit Barriers and Planning." *California Management Review* (Winter 1976): 21–33.

Quickel, Stephen. "MBO: Warnings Fail to Dim LBO Dazzle," *The Lucrative World of Management Buyouts,* A Supplement to Euromoney and Corporate Finance (December 1986): 20–29.

Rankin, D. "Warm Welcome for Incentive Options." *New York Times,* June 13, 1982, p. F15.

Rappaport, Alfred. "Strategic Analysis for More Profitable Acquisition." *Harvard Business Review* (July–August 1979): 99–110.

———. "Do You Know the Value of Your Company?" *Mergers and Acquisitions* (Spring 1979): 12–17.

Reichardt, C.S., and T.D. Cook. *Qualitative and Quantitative Methods in Evaluation Research.* Beverly Hills: Sage Publication, 1979.

Riley, M. *Sociological Research.* New York: Harcourt Brace Jovanovich, 1963.

"Roundtable: Diversification and Divestiture." *Mergers and Acquisitions* (Winter 1983): 26–28.

Rumelt, Richard P. *Strategy, Structure, and Economic Performance.* Boston: Division of Research, Graduate School of Business Administration. Harvard University, 1974.

Salter, Malcolm S., and W. Weinhold. *Diversification through Acquisition.* New York: Free Press, 1979.

———, and Michael E. Porter. "Note on Diversification As a Strategy." Boston, Mass.: Harvard Case Services, 1982.

Saparito. "Unions Fight the Corporate Sell-Off." *Fortune,* July 11, 1983, pp. 145, 148, 152.

Schendell, Dan, G.T. Patton, and James Riggs. "Corporate Turnaround Strategies: A Study of Profit Decline and Recovery." *Journal of General Management* (Spring 1976): 4.

Shillinglaw, Gordon. "Profit Analysis for the Abandonment Decision." In Ezra Solomon, ed., *The Management of Corporate Capital,* pp. 269–281. New York: Free Press, 1959.

Stancil, J., "Search for a Leveraged Buyout." *Harvard Business Review* (July–August 1977): 3–4.

Steyer, Robert. "Leaning on the Levers." *Fortune,* July 11, 1983, p. 112.

Tavel, Charles. *The Third Industrial Age.* New York: Pergamon Press, 1980.

Taylor, Marilyn L., "Managing Divestiture Effectively." *Strategic Planning* Chicago: Communique, 1985.

———, in collaboration with V.K. Narayanan and Danny G. Kinker. "Factors Involved in Divestment Effectiveness." *Southern Management Proceedings* (November 1984).

———, in collaboration with V.K. Narayanan and Danny G. Kinker. "Management of Divestiture: Neglected Issues." Paper presented to Society for Strategic Management, Barcelona, October 1985.

———, in collaboration with V.K. Narayanan, John Garland, and Danny Kinker. "Managing the Divestment Process." Unpublished manuscript.

———, N.T. Taylor, and F.A. Hooper, "Corporate-Level Factors: Their Impact on Incidence of Divestiture." Strategic Management Society, 1987.

Taylor, Marilyn L., and V.K. Narayanan. "Summary of Issues: Executive Roundtable on Management Divestiture." Lawrence, Kans.: University of Kansas Field Studies Program. Privately distributed to Field Studies Program Associates.

Taylor, N.T. "Management Succession under Conditions of Deteriorating Strategic Performance: The Role of the Board of Directors." Ph.D dissertation, Harvard University, 1978.

——, F. Hooper, and Marilyn Taylor. "Why Diversified Firms Voluntarily Divest Ongoing Business Units." *Proceedings* of the Southern Management Association, 1987, pp. 208–210.

Thackray, John. "Disinvestment: How to Shrink and Profit." *European Business* (Spring 1971): 50–57.

Torneden, Roger L. *Foreign Divestment by U.S. Multinational Corporations.* New York: Praeger Publishers, 1975.

——, and J.J. Bodewyn. "Foreign Divestment: Too Many Mistakes." *Columbia Journal of World Business* (Fall 1974): 87–94.

Ulin, Peter A. "The Environment for Divestment." In William S. Mishkin, ed., *Techniques in Corporate Reorganization: Selling, Divesting, and Shells, Multiple Corporations,* pp. 25–35. New York: Presidents Publishing House, 1972.

Vignola, Leonard. *Strategic Divestment.* New York: American Management Association, 1974.

Webb., E., T. Donald, R. Campbell, I. Schwartz, and L. Sechrest. *Unobtrusive Measures: Nonreactive Research in the Social Sciences.* Chicago: Rand McNally, 1966.

Weiner, Daniel P. "Deals of the Year." *Fortune,* February 2, 1987, pp. 68–72, 74.

Welch, J.F., Jr., J.F. Burlingame, and E.W. Hood, Jr. "To Our Shareholders." General Electric Company Annual Report 1981. February 26, 1982.

——. "To Our Shareholders." General Electric Company Annual Report 1983. February 17, 1984.

Williamson, O.E. *Markets and Hierarchies: Analysis and Antitrust Implications.* New York: Free Press, 1975.

Yavitz, Boris, and William H. Newman. *Strategy in Action.* New York: Free Press, 1982.

Yin, R., and K. Herald. "Using the Case Survey Method to Analyze Policy Studies." *Administrative Science Quarterly* 20 (1975): 371–381.

Zelditch, Morris, Jr. "Some Methodological Problems of Field Studies." *Journal of Sociology* 67 (1962): 566–576.

Index

About the Author

Marilyn Taylor is associate professor of strategic management at the University of Kansas School of Business. Her areas of specialization include management of divestiture, family businesses, and managing significant careers. She received her D.B.A. and M.B.A. (with distinction) from Harvard University Graduate School of Business and her B.A. in Business Administration from the University of South Florida. She was founding director of the Small Business Development Center at the University of Kansas from 1982 to 1985 and director of the Small Business Institute from 1978 to 1985. She is cofounder and codirector of the University of Kansas School of Business Field Studies Program.

Dr. Taylor has authored *Business Policy: Strategic, Administrative, and Social Issues* (with Curtis E. Tate, Jr.) and will release *Divesting Business Units* in 1988. She has published articles in several journals including the *Journal of Case Research* in addition to many professional presentations and proceedings publications. She is author of numerous cases including "Marion Laboratories," which has been widely used in texts on Business Policy. She is active with several professional associations including Southern Management Association, North American Case Research Association, and MidWest Case Research Association.

She has consulted with a number of organizations on a variety of issues including strategic planning, business plans, women in management, and affirmative action. She participates frequently in management development seminars.

About the Author

Marilyn Taylor is associate professor of strategic management at the University of Kansas School of Business. Her areas of specialization include management of divestiture, family businesses, and managing significant careers. She received her D.B.A. and M.B.A. (with distinction) from Harvard University Graduate School of Business and her B.A. in Business Administration from the University of South Florida. She was founding director of the Small Business Development Center at the University of Kansas from 1982 to 1985 and director of the Small Business Institute from 1978 to 1985. She is cofounder and codirector of the University of Kansas School of Business Field Studies Program.

Dr. Taylor has authored *Business Policy: Strategic, Administrative, and Social Issues* (with Curtis E. Tate, Jr.) and will release *Divesting Business Units* in 1988. She has published articles in several journals including the *Journal of Case Research* in addition to many professional presentations and proceedings publications. She is author of numerous cases including "Marion Laboratories," which has been widely used in texts on Business Policy. She is active with several professional associations including Southern Management Association, North American Case Research Association, and MidWest Case Research Association.

She has consulted with a number of organizations on a variety of issues including strategic planning, business plans, women in management, and affirmative action. She participates frequently in management development seminars.